SACRED LATIN POETRY; CHIEFLY LYRICAL, SELECTED AND ARRANGED FOR USE

SACRED LATIN POETRY; CHIEFLY LYRICAL, SELECTED AND ARRANGED FOR USE

Richard Chenevix Trench

www.General-Books.net

Publication Data:

Title: Sacred Latin Poetry
Subtitle: Chiefly Lyrical, Selected and Arranged for Use
Author: Richard Chenevix Trench
General Books publication date: 2009
Original publication date: 1864
Original Publisher: Macmillan
Subjects: Hymns, Latin
Religious poetry, Latin
Latin poetry
History / General
Literary Criticism / Ancient Classical
Literary Criticism / Poetry
Music / Religious / Hymns
Music / Religious / Christian
Poetry / General
Poetry / English, Irish, Scottish, Welsh
Poetry / Ancient, Classical Medieval

CONTENTS

SECTION 1

PREFACE

THE FIRST EDITION.

fTlHE AIM tf'tue" present volume is to offer to members bf"our' English Church a collection of the best sacred Latin poetry, such as they shall be able entirely and heartily to accept and approve – a collection, that is, in which they shall not be evermore liable to be offended, and to have the current of their sympathies checked, by coming upon that, which, however beautiful as poetry, out of higher respects they must reject and condemn – in which, too, they shall not fear that snares are being laid for them, to entangle them unawares in admiration for ought which is inconsistent with their faith and fealty to their own spiritual mother. Such being the idea of the volume, 7V it is needless to say that all hymns which in any way k imply the Romish doctrine of transubstantiation are excluded. In like manner all are excluded, which s involve any creature-worship, or which speak of the j Mother of our Lord in any other language than that which Scripture has sanctioned, and our Church adopted. So too all asking of the suffrages of the saints, all addresses to the Cross calculated to encourage superstition, that is, in which any value is attributed to the material wood, in which it is used otherwise than in the Epistles of St Paul, namely, as a figure of speech by which we ever and only understand Him that hung upon it; all these have been equally refused a place.

Nor is it only poems containing positive error which I have counted inadmissible ; but I have not willingly given room to any which breathe a spirit foreign to that tone of piety which the English Church desires to cherish in her children; for I have always felt that compositions of this character may be far more hurtful, may do far more to rob her of the affections, and ultimately of the allegiance, of her children, than those in which error and opposition to her teaching take a more definite and tangible shape. Nor surely can there be a more serious mistake, than to suppose that we have really "adapted" such works to the use of her members, when we have lopped off here and there a few offensive excrescences, while that far more potent, because far subtler and more impalpable, element of a life which is not her life remains interfused through the whole.

Having thus in a manner become responsible for all which appears in this volume, I may be permitted toobserve, that I do not thereby imply that there may not be in it, here and there, though very rarely indeed, a phrase which will claim the interpretation of charity. The reader will in such a case remember how unfair it is to try the theological language of the middle ages by the greater strictness and accuracy which the struggles of the Reformation rendered necessary. Thus, for us at this day to talk of any " merits " save those of Christ, after all that the Reformation has won for us, would involve a conscious and a deliberate falling away from a sole and exclusive reliance upon his work. But it was a diiferent tlling once, and such language might quite be used by one who had *implicitly* an entire affiance on the work of Christ *for* him as the ultimate ground of his hope ; and who only waited to have the truth, which with some confusion he held and lived by, put before him in accurate form, to embrace it henceforth and for ever, not only with heart, as he had done already, but with the understanding as well.

Nor yet do I mean to affirm that there may not have found admission here one or two poems which some, whom I should greatly have desired altogether to have carried with me in my selection, may not wish had been away. It is indeed one of the mischiefs which Rome has entailed upon the whole Western Church, even upon those portions of it now deliveredfrom her tyranny, that she has rendered suspicious so much, which, but for her, none could have thought other than profitable and edifying. She has compelled those, who before everything else would be true to God's word, oftentimes to act in the spirit of Heze- kiah, when he said " Nehushtan " to the very " sign of salvation" – to the brazen serpent itself. Yet granting that the superstitious, and therefore profane, hands which she has laid on so much, must oftentimes make it our wisdom, and indeed our duty, that we abridge ourselves of our rightful liberty in many things which otherwise and but for her we might have freely and profitably used, there is still a limit to these self-denials : and unless we are determined to set such a limit, there *is* no point of bareness and nakedness in all of imaginative and symbolic in worship and service, which we might not reach; even as some Reformed Churches, which have not shewn the mingled moderation and firmness, that have in these matters so wonderfully characterized our own, have undoubtedly made themselves much poorer than was need.

Of course, those who consider that the whole medieval theology is to be ignored and placed under ban – that nothing is to be learned from it, or nothing but harm – those I must expect to disapprove, not merely

s, Wisd. xvi.

of a small matter or two in the volume, but of it altogether ; for the very idea of the book rests on the assumption that it *is* worth our while to know what the feelings of these ages were – what the Church was doing during a thousand years of her existence ; – on the assumption also that the voices in which men uttered then the deepest things of their hearts, will be voices in which we may also utter and embody the deepest things of our own. For myself, I cannot but feel that we are untrue to our position as a Church, that is, as an *historic* body, and above all to our position as members of a Protestant Church, when we thus wish to dissever, as far as we may, the links of our historic connexion with the past. We should better realize that position; if we looked at those Middle Ages with the expectation (which the facts would abundantly justify), of finding the two Churches, which at the Reformation disengaged themselves from one another, in the bosom of the Church which was then – if we looked at those ages, not seeking (as sometimes is done, I cannot but feel most unfairly, in regard to earlier times) to claim them as Protestant, but as little conceding that they were Romanist. It were truer to say that in Romanism we have the residuum of the middle age Church and theology, the lees, after all, or well nigh all, the wine was drained away. But in the medieval Church wehave the wine and the lees together – the truth and the error – the false observance, and yet at the same time the divine truth which should one day be fatal to it, side by side. Good were it for us to look at those ages, tracing gladly, as Luther so loved to do, the footsteps of the Reformers before the Reformation; and feeling that it is our duty, that it is the duty of each successive age of the Church, as not to accept the past in the gross, so neither in the gross to reject it; since rather by our position as the present representatives of that eternal body, we are bound to recognize ourselves as the rightful inheritors of all which is good and true that ever has been done or said within it. Nor is this all: but if our position mean anything, we are bound also to believe that to us, having the Word and the Spirit, the power has been given to distinguish things which differ, – that the sharp sword of judgment has been placed in our hands, whereby to sunder between the holy and profane, – that such a breath of the Almighty is now and evermore breathing over his Church, as shall enable it, boldly and with entire trust that He will winnow for it, to exclaim, " What is the chaff to the wheat ? " Surely it is our duty to believe that to us, that to each generation which humbly and earnestly seeks, will be given that enlightening Spirit, by whose aid it shall be enabled to read aright the pastrealizations of God's divine idea in the visible and historic Church of successive ages, and to distinguish the human imperfections, blemishes, and errors, from the divine truth which they obscured and overlaid, but which they could not destroy, being one day rather to be destroyed by it; and, distinguishing these, as in part to take warning from and to shun, so also in part to live upon and to love, that which in word and deed the Church of the past has bequeathed us.

In this sense, – namely, that there is here that which we may live on and love, as well as that which we must shun and leave, I have brought together the poems of this present volume, gathering out the tares, which yet I could recognize but as the *accident* of this goodly field, and seeking to present to my brethren that only which I had confidence would prove wholesome nutriment for souls. Undoubtedly there are tares enough in the field out of which these sheaves have been gathered, if a man will seek them, if he should believe that it is his occupation to do so ; which yet I have not believed to be mine. And I have published this volume, because, granting a collection made upon these principles to be desirable, it appears to me that it has not yet been made ; that those which we possess still leave room for such a one as the present. What need is there, for example, that the *Veni, RedemptorGentium,* or the *Dies Ira,* or any other of these immortal heritages of the universal Church, should be presented to us as part or parcel of the Roman or any other breviary ? They were not written for these ; their finding a place in these is their accident, and not their essence. Why then should they be offered, as coming through channels, and with associations linked to them, which can scarcely fail to make them distasteful to many ? Not to say that, while pieces of sacred Latin verse drawn from such obvious sources have been published again and again – and not only the good, but very often with it much also of very slightest worth, – other noblest compositions, whether contemplated as works of art, or from a more solemn point of view, have been left unregarded and apparently unknown. If I may conclude, in regard of others, from a few friends to whom I have submitted portions of this volume, as it was gotten together, most of my readers will acknowledge that they here have met something which was new to them, yet with which they were glad to be made acquainted.

And even were this not the case, the poems here offered in a collected form, are many of them only to be found, as a reader familiar with the subject will perfectly know, one here, one there, in costly editions of the Fathers or medieval writers, or in collections of very rarest occurrence. The extreme difficulty I have myself experienced in obtaining several of the books which I desired to use, and the necessity under which I have remained of altogether foregoing the use of many that I would most gladly have consulted, has sufficiently shewn me how little obvious they can be to most readers. Often too the poems one would care to possess are lost amid a quantity of verse of little or no value ; or mixed up with much which, at least for purposes such as those which the present volume is intended to serve, the reader would much prefer to have away. They are to be met too, for the most part, without those helps for their profitable study which they so greatly require – with no attempt to bring them into relation with the theology of their own or of an earlier day, which at once they illustrate, and from which alone many of their allusions can be explained.

In respect of the notes with which I have sought to supply this last deficiency, I will say at once that had I followed my own inclinations, I should much have preferred to give merely the text, without adding any of these. At the same time, the longer I was engaged with these poems, the more I was struck with the extent to which they swarmed with Scriptural and patristic allusions, yet such as oftentimes one might miss at a first or second perusal, or, unless they werepointed out, might overlook altogether. I felt how many passages there were, which, without some such helps, would remain obscure to many readers; or at any rate would fail to yield up to them all the riches of meaning which they contained ; and that an Editor had no right to presume that particular kind of knowledge upon their parts, which should render the explanation of these superfluous. Thus none, I trust, will take ill the space bestowed on the elucidation of these typical allusions with which many of these poems so much abound nor count that I have at too great a length explained these. Whatever the absolute worth of the medieval typology may be, its' relative worth is considerable, giving us such insight as it does into the habits . of men's thoughts in those ages, and the aspect under which they were wont to contemplate the Holy Scriptures and the facts of which Holy Scripture is the record. Nor may we forget that, however the Old Testament typology is now little better than a wreck, considered as a branch of scientific theology, – the capricious and oftentimes childish abuse which has been made of it having caused many to regard the whole matter with averseness and distaste, yet has it, as we are sure, a deep ground of truth ; one unaffected by the fact that we have been at so little pains accurately to determine its limits, or the laws which are toguide its application, and have thus left it open to such infinite abuse.

And yet, with the fullest sense of the necessity of giving some notes, I cannot hope that this volume has escaped that which, with only the difference of more or less, must be the lot of all annotated books. . Doubtless it has often a note where none was needed, and none where the reader might justly have looked for one. As in part an excuse for their inadequacy and imperfections, I must plead the very little that had hitherto been done in this regard; so that, although assistances from those who have gone before are not altogether wanting, yet these are only few and insufficient. Had my own notes been exclusively, or even mainly, critical, I should have felt myself bound to compose them in Latin, which has been so happily called " the algebraic notation of criticism ;" but being in the main theological, there would have been much loss with no compensating gain, in putting myself under the restraints of a language in which I certainly should not have moved as easily as in my own. At the same time I have endeavoured to avoid that which I have observed as the common evil of notes in English, namely, the " small talk" into which they are apt to degenerate.

In the arrangement of the different pieces which this
volume contains, two ways seemed open to me. I might either follow the chrono-logical order, which would have had a most real value of its own ; or else dispose, as I have done, the several poems according to an inner scheme, and thus combine them, as it were, anew into one great poem. To the choice of this last plan I was directed by the idea on which this volume is constructed. Had I desired first and mainly to illustrate the theology of successive epochs by the aid of their hymns, or to trace the rise and growth of Latin ecclesiastical poetry, the other or chronological would have been plainly the method to have adopted ; in the same way as, had I presented these poems as *documents,* I should not have felt myself at liberty to make the omissions which I have occasionally made in some, with no loss I believe to the reader, and without which their length, or even a more serious flaw, might have excluded them from the volume. But the personal and t the devotional being my primary objects, and all else merely secondary, it was plain that the order to be followed was that which should best assist and further the end I had specially in view.

That occasional liberty of omission which I have used – by which I mean, not so much presenting the fragments of a poem, as *thinning* it – is not, let meobserve, so periltms an interference with the unity, and thus the life, of medieval, as it would be of many other, compositions. *Form* these writers thought of but little; and were little careful to satisfy its requirements. Oftentimes indeed the instincts of Art effectually wrought in them, and what they gave forth is as perfect in form as it is in spirit. But oftentimes also the stanzas, or other component parts 6f some long poem, jostle, and impair the effect of, one another. It is evident that the writer had not learned the painful duty of sacrificing parts to the interests of the whole; perhaps it had never dawned on him that, in all higher art, there is such a duty, and one needing continually to be exercised. And when this is done *for* him, which he would not do for himself, the effect is like that of thinning some crowded and overgrown forest. There is gain in every respect; gam in what is taken away, gain for what remains: so at least it has seemed to me, when on more than one occasion I have used the knife, or even the axe, of excision.

Great as is the length to which these prefatory words have run, I cannot conclude them without giving utterance to this as my earnest desire and prayer, – that there may be nothing found in these pages to minister to error, or with which wise and understanding children a

PREFACE

THE SECOND EDITION.

FFHIS VOLUME Las been for several years out of .. print. Since the former edition was published, now some fifteen years ago, several collections of Sacred Latin Poetry have appeared. The most important of these are as follows: – Mone, *Lateinische Hymnen des Mittelalters,* 1853 ; in the second and third volumes, 1854, 1855, the title is changed to *Hymni Latini Medii JEvi.* Daniel has added two supplementary volumes (a fourth and fifth) to his *Thesaurus Hymno- logicus,* 1855, 1856. Dr. Neale has followed up his *Sequentia,* 1852, with a series of articles in the *Eccle- siologist;* while M. Gautier has given to the world *Les (Euvres Poetiques d'Adam de S. Victor,* 1858,1859. Mone's is on the whole a disappointing work. The notes seem at first sight full of promise ; but on closer inspection they prove rather appendages to the text, than elucidations of it; still, his illustrations of the Latin hymns from the Greek liturgies are often novel and interesting. Daniel by his later volumes has increased the obligation under which all lovers of the oldhymnology already lay to him; and for myself I must praise his magnanimity, that in reprinting a considerable body of my notes and prefaces, he has not excluded some in which I had spoken severely of certain small inaccuracies and errors in his earlier volumes. I rejoice to hear that a new edition of his *Thesaurus,* such as, it may be hoped, will fuse his five volumes into a harmonious whole, is preparing. Later in this volume I take occasion to speak of the happy discovery, by Gautier, of a large number of Adam of St Victor's hitherto unpublished hymns. The edition of Adam's poetical works, which in consequence of this discovery he has given to the world, is wanting in accurate scholarship, but has, notwithstanding, been gratefully welcomed by all to whom this poet is dear. The too favourable manner in which Dr. Neale has expressed himself in regard of any contributions of mine to the knowledge of the Latin hymnology makes it difficult for me to say merely the truth about his own. I will only, therefore, mention that by patient researches in almost all European lands, he has brought to light a multitude of hymns unknown before; in a treatise on *Sequences,* properly so called, has for the first time explained their essential character; while to him the English reader owes versions of some of the best hymns, such as often successfully overcome the almost insuperable difficulties which many among them present to the translator.

Maelay: *Aug.* 8, 1864.

INTRODUCTION.

CHAPTER I.

ON THE SUBSTITUTION OF ACCENT FOR QUANTITY IN LATIN VERSE.

THE Latin poetry of the Christian Church presents a subject which might well deserve a treatise of its own ; offering, as it does, so many sides upon which it is most worthy of regard. It is not, however, my intention to consider it except upon one side, or to prefix to this volume more than some necessary remarks on the relation in which *the forms* of that poetry stand to the *forms* of the classic poetry of Rome; tracing, if I may, the most characteristic differences between those of the earlier and heathen, and the later and Christian, Art. Yet shall I not herein be dealing so merely with externals, as might at first sight appear. For since the form of ought which has any real significance is indeed the manifestation and utterance of its innermost life – is the making visible, so far as that is possible, of its most essential spirit – I shall, if I rightly seize and explain the difference of the forms, be implicitly saying something, indeed much, concerning the differences between the spirit of this poetry, and that of the elder or classical poetry of Rome. A few considerations on this matter may help to B

remove offences which otherwise the reader, nourished exclusively upon classical lore, might easily take at many things which in this volume he will find; and may otherwise assist to put him in a fairer position for appreciating the compositions which it contains.

When, then, we attempt to trace the rise and growth of the Latin poetry of the Christian Church, and the manner in which, making use, in part and for a season, of what it found ready to its hand, it did yet detach itself more and more from the classical poetry of Rome, we take note of the going forward at the same time of two distinct processes. But these, distinct as they are, we observe also combining for the formation of the new, together giving to it its peculiar character, and constituting it something more than such a continuation of the old classical poetry, as should only differ from- it in the subjects which supplied to it its theme, while in all things else it remained unchanged. These processes, as I have said, are entirely distinct from one another, have no absolutely necessary connexion, closely related as undoubtedly they were; the first being the disintegration of the old prosodical system of Latin verse, under the gradual substitution of accent for quantity ; and the second, the employment of rhyme, within, or at the close of, the verse, as a means for marking rhythm, and a resource for the producing of melody. They have no absolutely necessary connexion. There might have been the first without the second – accent without rhyme – as in our own blank heroic verse, and occasional blank lyrics; nor are there wanting various and successful examples, in this very later Latin poetry, of the same kind. There was the second, rhyme without the displacing of quantity by accent, in the rhymed hexameters, pentameters, and sapphics wherein the monkish poets of the middle ages indulged, still preserving as far as they knew, and often altogether, the laws of metrical quantity, but adding rhyme as a further ornament to the verse.

Thus the results of the two processes, namely, an accentuated, and a rhymed, poetry, might have existed separately, as indeed occasionally they do ; and growing up independently of one another, they ought to be traced independently also. Yet still, since only in the union of the two could results have been produced so satisfying, so perfect in their kind, as those which the Latin sacred poetry offers to us; since they did in fact essentially promote and sustain one another; the manner in which they mutually re-acted one on the other, in which the one change rendered almost imperative the other, the common spirit out of which both the transformations proceeded, should not be allowed to pass unobserved – being rather a principal matter to which he who would explain and trace the change should direct his own and his reader's attention.

I propose to say something first on the substitution of accent for quantity, an accented for a prosodic verse; which, however, is a subject that will demand one or two preliminary remarks.

There is one very noticeable difference between the Christian literature of the Greek and Roman world on the one side, and all other and later Christian literatures on the other – namely, that those Greek and Latin are, so to speak, a new budding and blossoming out of an old stock; and this a stock which, when the Church was founded, had already put forth, or was in the act of putting forth, all that in the natural order of things, and but for the quickening breath of a new and unexpected life, it could ever have unfolded. They are as a second and a later spring, coming in the rear of the timelier and the first. For that task which the word of the Gospel had to accomplish in all other regions of man's life, it had also to accomplish in this. It was not granted to it at first entirely to make or mould a society of its own. A harder task was assigned it – being, as it was, superinduced on a society that had come into existence, and had gradually assumed the shape which now it wore, under very different conditions, and in obedience to very different influences from its own. Of this it had to make the best which it could ; only to reject and to put under ban that which was absolutely incurable therein, and directly contradicted its own fundamental idea; but of the rest to assimilate to itself what was capable of assimilation; to transmute what was willing to be transmuted; to consecrate what was prepared to receive from it a higher consecration; and altogether to adjust, not always with perfect success, but as best it might, and often at the cost of much forbearance and self-sacrifice, its relations to the old, that had grown up under heathen auspices, and was therefore very different from what it would have been, had the leaven of the word of life mingled with and wrought in it from the first, instead of coming in, a later addition to it, at the end of time. Thus was it in almost every sphere of man's life and of his moral and intellectual activity; yet we have here to speak only of one – that, namely, of literature and language. All the modern literatures and languages of Europe Christianity has mainly made what they are; to it they owe all that characterizes them the most strongly. For although, as it needs not to say, the languages themselves reach back in their elemental rudiments to a time far anterior to the earliest in which the Gospel came, or could have come, in contact with them, or indeed had been proclaimed at all; yet it did thus mingle with them early enough to find them still in that wondrous and mysterious process of their first evolution. They were yet plastic and fluent, as all languages are at a certain period of their existence, though a period generally just out of the ken of the history. And the languages rose to a level with the claims which the new religion of the Spirit made upon them. ' Formed and fashioned under its influence, they dilated till they were equal to its needs, and adequate exponents, as far as language ever can become so, of the deepest things which it possessed.

But it was otherwise in regard of the Latin language. That, when the Church arose, requiring of it to be the organ of her Divine Word, to tell out all the new, and as yet undreamt of, which was stirring in her bosom; demanding of it that it should reach her needs, needs which had hardly or not at all existed, while the language was in process of formation – that was already full formed; it had reached its climacteric, and was

See some beautiful remarks on the Christianizing of the German language in the *Thedl. Stud, und Krit.,* vol. xxii. p. 308, sqq.; and again in Rudolf von Raumer's *Eimvirkung d. Chris- tenthuma atifdie Althochdeutsche Sprache,* p. 168, sqq.

indeed verging, though as yet imperceptibly, toward decay, with all the stiffness of commencing age already upon it. Such the Church found it – something to which a new life might perhaps be imparted, but the first life of which it was well nigh overlived. She found it a garment narrower than she could wrap herself withal, and yet the only one within reach. But she did not forego the expectation of one day obtaining all which she wanted, nor even for the present did she sit down entirely contented with the inadequate and insufficient. Herself young and having the spirit of life, she knew that the future was her own – that she was set in the world for this very purpose of making all things new – that what she needed and did not find, there must lie in her the power of educing from herself – that, though it might not be all at once, yet little by little, she could weave whatever vestments were required by her for comeliness and beauty. And we do observe the language under the new influence, as at the breath ; of a second spring, putting itself forth anew, budding and blossoming afresh, the meaning of words enlarging and dilating, old words coming to be used in new and higher significations, obsolete words reviving, new words being coined – with much in all this to offend the classical taste, which yet, being inevitable, ought not to offend, and of which the gains far more than compensated the losses. There was a new thing, and that being so, it was of necessity that there should be a new utterance as well. To be offended with this is, in

SeeFunccius, *De Vegetd Latins Lingua Senectute,* p. 1139, seq.

truth, to be offended with Christianity, which made ' this to be inevitable.

We may make application of all which has been just said to the metrical forms of the classical poetry of Rome. These the Church found ready made to her hand, and in their kind having reached a very high perfection. A true instinct must have told her at once, or after a very few trials, that these were not the metrical forms which she required. Yet it was not to be supposed that she should have the courage immediately to cast them aside, and to begin the world, as it were, afresh ; or that she should have been enabled at once to foresee the more adequate forms to be one day developed out of her own bosom. But these which she thus inherited, while she was content of necessity to use, yet could not satisfy her. The Gospel had brought

Dans le monde grec d'abord, puis, dans le monde romain, les chrétiens éprouvèrent le besoin de se servir des formes de la poésie antique et de les appliquer aux idées nouvelles. Les IVt et Ve siecles virent naître un assez grand nombre d'efforts en ce genre, surtout en Italie et en Espagne. Evidemment, ces tentatives souvent renouvelées étaient sans portée, sans avenir; les sentiments chrétiens les traditions chrétiennes ne pouvaient s'accommoder des formes créées pour un autre emploi, vieillies au service d'une autre Muse ; évidemment, la littérature chrétienne devait produire sa propre forme, et c'est ce qu'elle a fait plus tard. . Ce n'est pas quand elle a cherché à traduire ses inspirations dans le langage de Virgile, qu'elle a enfanté des ouvrages de quelque valeur; c'est quand elle a inventé son épopée, avec Dante et Hilton, et Son drame dans les mystères du moyen âge, ou les actes saeramentaux de Calderon,' qui ne sont qu'une résurrection et un raffinement des mystères ; c'est quand elle a inspiré ces beaux chants qui, depuis Luther, n'ont cessé de retentir sous les voûtes des églises d'Allemagne. Alors la poésie chrétienne a fait son œuvre ; jusque là elle n'était qu'un calque pâle
,

into men's hearts longings after the infinite and the eternal, which were strange to it, at least in their present intensity, until now. Beauty of outline, beauty of form – and what a flood of light does that one word *forma,* as equivalent to beauty, pour on the difference
/between the heathen and the Christian ideal of beauty ! – this was all which the old poetry yearned after and strove to embody ; this was all which its metrical frameworks were perfectly fitted for embodying.

But now heaven had been opened, and henceforward the mystical element of modern poetry demanded its rights; vaguer but vaster thoughts were craving to find the harmonies to which they might be married for ever. The boundless could not be content to find its organ in that, of which the very perfection lay in its limitations and its bounds. The Christian poets were in holy earnest ; a versification therefore could no longer be endured, attached, as in their case at least it was, by no living bonds to the thoughts, in which sense and sound had no real correspondence with one another. The versification henceforth must have an intellectual value, which should associate it with the onward movement of the thoughts and feelings, whereof it professed to be, and thus indeed should be, the expression. A struggle therefore commenced from the first, between

efc un echo affaibli de la po&ie paienne (Ampere, *Hist. Liit. de la France,* vol. ii. p. 196). And again : Il fant qne le chant chr$- tien depouille entierement ces lambeaux de metrique aneienne, qu'il Sb fasse completement moderne par la rime comme par le sentiment; alors, on aura *cette prose rimee* empreinte d'uno sombre harmonie, qui par la tristesse des sons et des images et le retour menaant de la terminaison lugubre fait pressentir lo Dante, on aura le *Dies Ira* (vol. ii. p. 412).

the form and spirit, between the old heathen form and the new Christian spirit – the latter seeking to release itself from the shackles and restraints which the former imposed upon it; and which were to it, not a help and a support, as the form should be, but a hindrance and a weakness – not liberty, but now rather a most galling bondage. The new wine went on fermenting in the

We see already in Prudentius the process of emancipation effectually at work, the disintegration of the old prosodic system already beginning. He still affects to write, and in the main does write, prosodically; yet with largest licences. No one will suppose him more ignorant than most schoolboys of fourteen would be now, of the quantitative value which the old classical poets of Italy, with whose writings he was evidently familiar, had attributed to words; yet we continually find him attributing another value, postponing quantity to accent, or rather allowing accent to determine quantity, as in cyaneus, Sardinia, enigma, *As* his latest editor has observed: Metrum haud raro negligitur, quia poeta in arsi w. majorem vim accentui quam quantitati tri- buit *(Obbarii Prudentius,* p. 19). The whole scheme of Latin prosody must have greatly loosened its hold, before he could have. used the freedom which he does use, in the shifting and altering the value of syllables. We mark in him especially a determination not to be deprived altogether of serviceable words through a metrical notation excluding them *in toto* from a place in the hexameter. Thus he writes temulentus, delibutus, idololatrix, calceamentum, margaritum; though as regards this last word, in an iambic verse, where there was no motive, but the contrary, for producing the antepenultima, he restores to that syllable its true quantity, and writes margarita. In the same way not ignorance nor caprice, but the feeling that they must have tho word ecclesia at command, while yet, if they left it with the antepenultima long, it could never find place in the pentameter- and only in one of its cases in the hexameter, induced the almost universal shortening of that syllable among the metrical writers of the Church. Amid the many motives which prompted the

old bottles, till it burst them asunder, though not itself to be spilt and lost in the process, but so to be gathered into nobler chalices, vessels more fitted to contain it –

Christian poets to strive after emancipation from the classical rules of quantity, first to slight, and then to cast them off, this had its weight: true, the opposition to the metrical scheme lay deeper than this, which was but one moment of it: yet the fact,

' that the chief metres excluded a vast number of the noblest and even most necessary words, and though not absolutely excluding,

I rendered many more inadmissible in most of their inflexions, –

' this must have been peculiarly intolerable to them. Craving the whole domain of words for their own, finding it only too narrow for the uttering of all they were struggling to express, desiring, too, as must all whose thoughts and feelings are real, that their words should fit close to their sense, they could ill endure to be shut out from that which often was the best and fittest, by arbitrary, artificial, and to them unmeaning restrictions. Thus Augustine distinctly tells us that he composed his curious *Psalmus contra partem Donati* in the rhythm which he did, that so he might not be hampered or confined in his choice of words

- by the necessities of metre: Ideo autem non aliquo *carminis* genere id fieri volui, ne me necessitas metrica ad aliqua verba qsue vulgo minus sunt usitata compelleret. *Carmen* signifies here a poem composed after the old classical models ; his own, as being popularly and not metrically written, he counts only a *cnnticum.* The distinctive and statelier diction of the *carmen* is indicated by Terentianus Maurus, 298:

Verba si non obvia
Carminis servant honorem, non jacentis *cantici.*

One has but to turn to the lyrical poems of Horace, to become at once aware of the wealth of words, which for the writer of the hexameter and pentameter may be said not to exist. What a world, for example, of noble epithets – tumultuosus, luctuosus, formidolosus, fraudulentus, contumax, pervicax, in- solens, intaminatus, fastidiosus, periculosus – with many more among the most poetical words in the language, are under the ban of a perpetual exclusion.

new, even as that which was poured into them was new.

We can trace step by step the struggle between the two principles of heathen and Christian life, which were here opposed to one another. As the classical or old Roman element grew daily weaker in the new Christian world which now had been founded; as the novel element of Christian life strengthened and gained ground ; as poetry became popular again, not the cultivated entertainment of the polite and lettered few, a graceful amusement of the scholar and the gentleman, but that in which all men desired to express, or to find expressed for them, their hopes and fears, their joys and their sorrows, and all the immortal longings of their common humanity; – a confinement became less and less endurable within the old and stereotyped forms, which, having had for their own ends their fitness and beauty, were yet constituted for the expressing of far other thoughts, sentiments, and hopes than those which now stirred at far deeper depths the spirits and the hearts of men. The whole scheme on which the Latin prosodical poetry was formed, was felt to be capricious, imposed from without ; and the poetry which now arose demanded – not, indeed, to be without law; for, demanding this, it would have demanded its own destruction, and not to be poetry at all; but it demanded ; that its laws and restraints should be such as its own necessities, and not those of quite a different condition, required,

The *Instructiones* of Commodianus, a poem quite valueless in a literary point of view, is yet curious in this respect; and the more curious now that it is placed by scholars in the latter

It is something more than mere association, more than the fact that these metres, in all of most illustrious

half of the third century rather than in the fourth, where it used to be set. Very singular is it to find, more than a hundred years before the last notes of the classical muse had expired in Claudian, a poem of considerable length composed on the system of a total abandonment of quantity, and substitution of accent in its room – maintaining the apparent framework of the old classical hexameter, but filling it up on a principle entirely new. Nor can we suppose that a poem so long, and in its fashion so elaborate, is the first specimen of its kind, however it is the first which has come down to our days. It is of so little value as to be in few hands; three or four lines may therefore be quoted as a specimen. These are part of a remonstrance against the pomp of female dress, § 60 :

Obruitis collum monilibus, gemmis, et auro,
Neenon et inaifres gravissimo pondere pendent:
Quid memorem vestes et totam Zabuli pompam ?
Bespuitis legem, ctuu vultis mundo plscere.

Utterly prosaic if regarded aa poetry, this work still bears the marks of a strong moral earnestness, is the utterance of onewho had something to say to his brethren, and was longing to say it: and no doubt here lay that which tempted the writer to forsake a system of versification which had become intolerably artificial in his time and for him ; and to develop for himself, or finding developed to use, one in which he should in great part be released from its arbitrary obligations. In the following lines, forming part of a hymn first published by Niebuhr *(Rhein. Museum,* 1829, p. 7), lines plainly intended to consist of four dactyles each, dactyles, that is, in sound, which with a little favouring of one or two syllables, they may be made to appear, there is the same intention of satisfying the ear with accentuated and not prosodic feet. The lines relate to St Paul, and are themselves worthy to be quoted:

Factus ceconomus in domo regia,
Divini muneris appone fercula;
Ut quse repleverit te sapientia,
Ipsa nos repleat tua per dogmata.

This hymn also, though considerably later than the poem of
and most memorable which had been composed in them, had been either servants of the heathen worship, or at least appropriated to heathen themes, which induced the Church little by little to forsake them: which even at this day causes them at once to translate us into, and to make us feel that we are moving in, the element of heathen life. The bond is not thus merely historic and external, but spiritual and inward. And yet, at the same time, the influence of these associations must not be overlooked, when we are estimating the causes which wrought together to alienate the poets and hymnologists of the Christian Church ever more and more from the classical, and especially from the lyrical, metres of antiquity, and which urged them to seek more appropriate forms of their own. In those the heathen gods had been celebrated and sung, the whole impure mythology had been arrayed and tricked out. Were they not profaned for ever by these unholy uses to which they had been first turned ? How could the praises of the true and living God be fitly sung in the same? A like feeling to that which induced the abandonment of the heathen temples, and the seeking rather to develop the existing basilicas into Christian churches, or where new churches were built, to build them after the fashion of the civil, and not the religious, edifices already existing, must have been here also at work. The faithful would have often shrunk from the involuntary associations which these metres suggested, as we should shrink from hearing a psalm or spiritual

Commodianus, is certainly of a very early date. Niebuhr thinks he finds evidence in the MS. from which it is taken, that it cannot be later than the seventh century.

jng fitted to some tune which had been desecrated to lowd or otherwise profane abuse. And truly there is, und we find it even now, a clinging atmosphere of heathen life shed round many of these metres, which it is almost impossible to dissipate; so that, reading some sacred thoughts which have arrayed themselves in sapphics, or alcaics, or hendecasyllables, we are more or less conscious of a certain contradiction between the form and the subject, as though they were awkwardly and unfitly matched, and one or other ought to have been different from what it is.

The wonderful and abiding success of the hymns of St Ambrose, and of those so-called Ambrosian which were formed upon the model of his, lay doubtless in great part in the wise instinct of choice, which led him to select a metre by far the least markedly metrical, and the most nearly rhythmical, of all the ancient metres out of which it was free to him to choose; – I mean the iambic dimeter. The time was not yet come when it was possible altogether to substitute rhythm for metre: the old had. still too much vitality to be cast aside, the new had not yet clearly shaped itself forth; but choosing thus, he escaped (as far as it was possible, using these forms at all, to escape,) the disturbing reminiscences and associations of heathen art. f While in a later day hardly anything so strongly

Take, for instance, this from a sapphic ode in honour of the Baptist:

Oh nimis fclix, meritique celsl,
Nescius labem nivei pudoris,
Prsepotens martyr, eremique cultor
Maximo viitum.

t See Bahr, *Die Christl. DichterRoms,* p. 7.

revealed the extent to which Roman Catholic Italy had fallen back under pagan influences, was penetrated through and through at the revival of learning with the spirit of heathen, and not of Christian, life, as the offence which was then everywhere taken by Italian churchmen, Leo the Tenth at their head, at the un- metrical hymns of the Church, and the determination manifested to reduce them by force, and at the cost of any wrong to their beauty and perfection, to metre ; – their very exemption from which was their glory, and that which made them to be Christian hymns in the highest sense.

This movement, then, which began early to manifest itself, for an enfranchisement from the old classical forms, this impatience of their restraints, was essentially a Christian one. Still we cannot doubt that it was

The history of the successive revisions which the non- metrical hymns sustained, is given by Arevalus, an enthusiastic admirer of the process, in his *Hymnodia Hispanica,* Romse, 1786, pp. 121 – 144, with this ominous heading: Romanorum Pontificum in reformandd Hymnodia Diligentia. Daniel (*Thesaurus Hymnologicus,* Hulls, 1841; Lipsise, 1844 – 6) has frequently given in parallel columns the hymn as it existed in earlier times, probably as it came from the author, and as it was recast in the Boman breviary. The comparison is very instructive, as shewing how well-nigh the whole grace and beauty, and even vigour, of the composition had disappeared in the process. With Scripture upon our side, it would not much trouble us, if Rome had for the present that aBsthetical superiority, that keener sense of artistic beauty, which she claims: this would not trouble us, since, ultimately, where truth is, there highest beauty must be as well. But such facts as these, or as the hideous Italian Churches of the last three hundred years, need to be explained and accounted for, before she can make good her claim.

assisted and made easier by the fact that the metrical system, against which the Church protested, and from which it sought to be delivered, had been itself brought in from without. Itself of foreign growth, it could oppose no such stubborn resistance as it would have done, had it been native to the soil, had its roots been entwined strongly with the deepest foundations of the Latin tongue. But this they were not. It is abundantly known to all who take any interest in the early poetry of Rome, that it was composed on principles of versification altogether different from those which were introduced with the introduction of the Greek models in the sixth century of the City – that Latin hexameters, or ' long' verses, were in all probability first composed by Ennius, while the chief lyric metres belong to a much later day, having been introduced, some of the simpler kinds, as the sapphic by Catullus, and the more elaborate not till the time, and only through the successful example, of Horace. f It is known too that while the hexameter took comparatively a firm root in the soil, and on the whole could not be said to be alien to the genius of the Latin tongue, the lyric metres remained exotics to the end, were never truly acclimated, – nothing worth reading or being preserved having been produced in them, except by those who first transplanted them from Greek to Italian ground. J It was not that the Latin language should

Cicero, *De Legg.* ii. 27.

t Horace, *Epistt.* i. 19, 21 – 34.

) Quintilian's judgment of his countrymen's achievements in lyric poetry is familiar to most *(Instit. Orat.* x. 1, 96): Lyrieo- rum Horatius fere solus legi dignus.

be without its great lyric utterances, and such as should be truly its own ; but it was first to find these in the Christian hymns of the middle ages.

The poetry of home growth, – the old Italian poetry which was thrust out by this new, – was composed, as we learn from the fragments which survive, and from notices lying up and down, on altogether a different basis of versification. There is no reason to believe that quantity, except as represented by and identical with accent, was recognized in it at all. For while accent belongs to every language and to every age of the language, – that is, in pronouncing any word longer than a monosyllable, an *ictus* or stress must fall on one syllable more than on others, – quantity is an invention more or less arbitrary. At how late a period, and how arbitrarily, and as from without, it was imposed on the LatinJ the innumerable anomalies, inconsistencies, and contradictions in the prosodical system of the language sufficiently testify.

I know, indeed, that some have denied the early Latin verse to have rested on a merely accentual foundation. I certainly would not have gone out of my way to meddle with a controversy upon which such high names are ranged upon either side. But lying as it does so directly in my path as not to be avoided, I cannot forbear saying, that, having read and sought to make myself master of what has come within my reach upon the question, and judging by the analogy of all other popular poetry, I am convinced that Ferdinand Wolf. Ea'hr f,

Ueber die Lais, p. 159.

t *Gesch. d. Romischer Litteratur,* vol. i. p. 89; Edelestand du Meril, *Poieies populaires Latines,* Paris, 1843, p. 45. C

and those others are in the right, who, admitting indeed the existence of Saturnian, that is old Italian, verses, deny that there was properly any such thing as a Saturnian metre – that is, any fixed scheme or frame-work of long and short feet, after the Greek fashion, according to which these verses were composed ; these consisting rather, as all ballad-poetry does, of a Iposely denned number of syllables, not metrically disposed, but with places sufficiently marked, upon which a stress of the voice fell, to vindicate for them the character of verse. Into what these numbers would have unfolded themselves, as the nation advanced in culture, and as the ear, gradually growing nicer and more exacting in its requirements, claimed a finer melody, it is not easy to say; but Latin poetry at all events, as it would have had a character, so would it have rested on a basis of versification, which was its own. And knowing this, we can scarcely sympathize without reserve in the satisfaction which Horace expresses at the change which presently came over it; however we may admit that, with the exception of his one greater predecessor, he accomplished more than any other, to excuse and justify, and even to reconcile us to, the change. That change came, as is familiar to all, when, instead of being allowed such a process of natural developement from

It is characteristic of this, that *numeri* should be the proper Latin word for verses rather than any word which should correspond to the Greek *metre*. The Romans, in fact, counted their syllables and did not measure them, a certain *number* of these constituting a rhythm. *Numeri* is only abusively applied to verses which rest on music and time, and not on the number of the syllables (Niebuhr, *Lectures on Early Roman History*, p. 11).

within, it was drawn out of its own orbit by the too prevailing attractions of the Greek literature, within the sphere and full influence of which the conquests of the sixth century brought it, – though indeed, that influence had commenced nearly a century before. ' It is, indeed, a perilous moment for a youthful literature, – so youthful as not yet to have acquired confidence in itself, – aild, though full of latent possibilities of greatness, having hitherto actually accomplished little, – to be brought within the sphere of an elder, which is now ending a glorious course, and which offers to the younger for its imitation finished forms of highest beauty and perfection. Most perilous of all is it, if these forms are not so strange, but that with some little skill they may be transplanted to the fresher soil, with a fair promise of growing and flourishing there. For the younger to adhere to its own forms and fashions, rude and rugged, and as yet only most imperfectly worked out – to believe that in them, and in cleaving to them, its true future is laid up, and not in appropriating the more elaborate models which are now offered ready to its hands – for it thus to refuse to be dazzled by the prospect of immediate results, and of overleaping a stage or two of slow and painful progress, this is indeed most hard; the temptation has proved oftentimes too strong to be resisted.

It was so in the case which we are considering now. The Roman spirit could not, of. course, utterly disappear, or be entirely supprest. Quite sufficient of that

See the limitations upon Horace's well-known words, Grsecia *capta* ferum vietorem cepit *(Epp.* ii. 1, 156), which Orelli (in loc.) puts, and in like manner Niebuhr.

spirit has remained to vindicate for Roman literature an independent character, and to free it from the charge of being merely the echo and imitation of something else; but the Roman forms did nearly altogether disappear, and even the Roman spirit was very considerably depressed and affected by the alien influence to which it was submitted.

The process, in truth, was wonderfully like that which found place, when, in the first half of the sixteenth century, the national poetry of Spain yielded to the influence of Italian models, and Castillejo was obliged to give place to Boscan and Garcilasso. The points of resemblance in these parallel cases are many. Thus in either case, the conquered, and at that time, morally, and so far as strength went, intellectually, far inferior people, – the people, therefore, with much less of latent productivity for the future, whatever may have been the marvels it had accomplished in the past, – imposed its literary yoke on the conquering and the nobler nation; caused it in a measure to be ashamed of that which hitherto it had effected, or of all which, continuing in its own line, it was likely to bring to pass. Nor was this the only point in which the processes were similar. There were other points of resemblance – as this, that it is impossible to deny but that here, as there, poetry of a very high order was composed upon the new models. Great results came of the change, and of the new direction in which the national taste was turned. Every thing, in short, came of it but the one thing, for the absence of which all else is but an insufficient compensation ; namely, a thoroughly popular literature, which should truly smack of the soil from which itsprung, which should be the utterance of a nation's own life; and not merely accents, which, however sweet or musical, were yet caught from the lips of another, and only artificially fitted to its own.

But with the fading and growing weak of every thing else in the classical literature of Rome, this foreign usurpation faded and grew weak also. It is more than possible, for indeed we have satisfactory evidence to the fact, that traditions of the old rhythms were preserved in the popular poetry throughout the whole period during which the metrical forms borrowed from the Greek were alone in vogue at the capital, and among those who laid claim to a learned education, that Saturnian or old Italian verses lived upon. the lips of the people during all this interval. We have continual allusion to such rustic melodies : and even were we

' Huratori *(Antiqq. Hal. Diss.* 40): Itaque duplex Poeseos genus olim exsurrexit, alterum antiquius, sed ignobile ac ple- beium ; alterum nobile et a doctis tantum- modo viris excultum. Illud *rhythmicum,* illud *metricum* appellatum est. Sed qnod po- tissimum est auimadvertendum,, quamquam Metrica Poe'sis primas arripuerit, omniumque meliorum suffragio et usu probata lau- dibus ubique ornaretur: all amen Rhythmica Poesis non prop- terea defecit apud Grsecos atque Latinos. Quum enim vulgus in- doctum et rustica gens Poe'tam interdum agere vellet, nec legibus metri addiscendis par erat; quales poterat, versus efformare per- rexit: hoc est, Rhythmo contenta, Metrum contemsit: Metrum, iu- quam, hoc est, rigidas prosodise leges, quas perfectaPoesis sequitur. So Santen, in his *Notes on Terentianus Maurus,* p. 177 : Nee tamen post Grsecise numeros, ab Andronico agresti Latio introduc- tos, vetus Saturniorum modorum rustieitas cessavit, immo vero non solum ejus vestigia, sed ipsa etiam res in omne sevum superstes mansit. Yet he has certainly committed an oversight in adducing among his proofs the well-known lines of Horace, *Epp.* ii. 1.156 –

without any such, we might confidently affirm that a people could never have been without a poetry, which existed under circumstances so favourable for its production as the Italian peasantry; and, if possessing a poetry, that it would be such as should find its expression in the old Italian numbers, and not in the Greek exotic metres. It is true that verses composed in these old and native numbers, on rhythmic, and not on metrical, principles, do not openly re-appear, that is, with any claims to be considered as literature, until the foreign domination began to relax its hold ; but that no sooner was this the case, than at once they witness for their presence, putting themselves forth anew.

160, in which, having spoken of the ruder verses of an earlier day he goes on to say:

. . . sed in longum tamen sevum Honserunt, hodieque manent vestigia runs.

All that he is here affirming is, that there were yet marks of rusticity (vestigia ruris) which had not been quite got rid of, cleaving to the cultivated poetry of his country, to that which in the main was formed upon Greek models. Muratori falls into the same error, who explains the words of Horace in this way: Hoc est, quamvis a Grsecis didicerimus metri regulas, et pro rudibus rus- ticorum rhythmis castigatos nunc politosque versus conficiamus, attamen rhythmica poe'sis perduravit semper et adhuc apud vul- gus viget.

There is much instructive on this subject in a little article by Niebuhr, in the *Rhein. Museum,* 1829, p. 1 – 8. On the reappearance of the supprest popular poetry of Italy, he says: Es ist auch wohl sehr begreiflich wie damals, als das eigentliche Latein, und die Formen der Litteratur nur muhselig durch die Schulen erhalten wurden, manches, volksmiissige sich frey machte, wieder empor kam, und einen Platz unter dem einnahm, was die verblodete Schule seit Jahrhuuderten geweiht hatte. Der neu-griechische politische Vers, welcher dem Tact des Tanzes eut-

As something of an analogous case, we know that many words which Attius and Nsevius used, and which during the Augustan period seemed to have been entirely lost, do begin to emerge and present themselves afresh in Appuleius, Prudentius, and Tertullian. The number of words which are thus not Augustan, and yet are at once *ante-* and posi-Augustan, must have struck every attentive observer of the growth and progress of the Latin tongue. The reappearance of these in writers of the silver age, is often explained as an affected seek. ing of archaisms on their parts ; yet much more probably, the words were under literary ban for a time, but had lived on in popular speech, and when that ban was removed, or was unable any more to give effect to its decrees, shewed themselves anew in books, as they had always continued alive in the common language of the people.

By thus going back toward the origins of the Latin literature, we can better. understand how it came to pass, that when there arose up in the Christian Church a desire to escape from the confinement of the classical metres, and to exchange metrical for rhythmical laws, the genius of the language lent, instead of opposing, itself to the change. It was instinctively conscious, that this new which was aimed at was also the old, indeed,. the oldest of all ; the recovering of a natural position from an unnatural and strained one: – to which therefore it reverted the more easily.

spricht, ist ja der namliche wonach Konig Philippus siegstrunken tanzte:
nur dass Accent, nicht Sylbenmaass, dabey beachtet wird.

And other motives, – having their origin no less in the same fact, that quantity was not indigenous to the Latin soil, and therefore had struck no deep root, and obtained no wide recognition, in the universal sense of the people, – were not wanting to induce the poet of these later times to abandon the ancient metres, and expatiate in the freer region of accented verse. Such a consummation was helped on and hastened by that gradual ignorance of the quantity of words, which, with the waning and fading away of classical learning under the barbarian invasions, became every day wider spread. Even where the poet himself was sufficiently acquainted with the quantitative value of words, the number of readers or hearers who still kept this knowledge was every day growing less in the Roman world; the majority being incapable of appreciating his skill, or finding any satisfying melody in his versification, the principles of which they did not understand; while the accentual value of words, as something self-evident, would be recognized by every ear.

And this fact that it was so, wrought effectually in another way. For perhaps the most important step of all, for the freeing of verse from the fetters of prosody, and that which was most fatal to the maintenance of the old metrical system, was the introduction of liturgic chanting into the services of the Church – although this indeed was only the working out, in a particular direction, of that new spirit which was animating it in every part. The Christian hymns were composed to be sung, and to be sung at first by the whole congregation of the faithful, who were only little by little thrust out from their share in this part of the service. But theclassical or prosodical valuation of words would have been clearly inappreciable by the greater number of those whom it was desired thus to draw in to take part in the worship. If the voices of the assembled multitudes were indeed claimed for this, it could only be upon some scheme which should commend itself to all by its simplicity – which should appeal to some principle intelligible to every man, whether he had received an education of the schools, or not. Quantity, with its values so often merely fictitious, and so often inconsistent one with another, could no longer be maintained as the basis of harmony. The Church naturally fell back on accent, which is essentially popular, appealing to the common sense of every ear, and in its broader features, in its simple rise and fall, appreciable by all; – which had also in its union with music this advantage, that it allowed to those, who were much more concerned about what they said, than how they said it, and could ill brook to be crossed and turned out of their way by rules and restraints, the necessity ot which they did not acknowledge, far greater liberty than quantity would have allowed them; inasmuch as the music, in its choral harmonies, was ever ready to throw its broad mantle over the verse, to conceal its weakness, and, where needful, to cover its multitude of sins.

See F. Wolf, *Ueber die Lais,* p. 82 – 84.

CHAPTER II.

ON RHYME IN LATIN VERSE.

' much on the substitution of accent for quantity. J- But hand in hand with the process of exchanging metre for a merely accentuated rhythm went another movement, I mean the tendency to rhyme. Of this it might doubtless be affirmed no less than of the other, that it was only a recovery of the lost; having its first origin, or at all events its very clear anticipation, in the early national poetry of Rome. This too, except for that event which gave to the Latin language a second lease of life, and evoked from it capacities which had been dormant in it hitherto, might not and probably would not now have ever unfolded itself there, the first and apparently more natural opportunity having long since past away. Such an opportunity it had once enjoyed. There is quite enough in the remains of early Latin poetry which we possess, to shew that rhyme was not a new element, altogether alien to the language, which was forced upon it by the

Christian poets in the days of its decline. There were early preludings of that which should indeed only fully and systematically unfold itself at the last. The tendencies of the Saturnian, and of such other fragments of ancient Latin verse as have reached us, to terminations of a like sound, have been often noticed, as this from the *Andromache* of Ennius:

Lange however goes much too far, when he affirms (see Jahn, *Jahrbnch der Philologie,* 1830, p. 256) that it systema-

Hsec omnia vidi inflammari,
Priamo vi vitam evitari,
Jovis aram sanguine turpari.

The following, of more uncertain authorship, is quoted by Cicero *(Tusc.* 1, 28):

Coelum nitescere, arbores frondescerp,
Vites Isetifiese pampinis pubescere,
Rami bacarum ubertate incurvescere.

Of that poetry rhyme may be considered a legitimate ornament. And even after a system had been introduced resting on altogether different principles of versification, that, I mean, of the Greek metres, yet was it so inborn in the language and inherent to it, that it continually made its appearance ; being no doubt only with difficulty avoided by those writers, whose stricter sense of beauty taught them not to catch at ornaments which were not properly theirs ; and easily attained by those, who with a more questionable taste were well pleased to sew it as a purple patch on a garment of altogether a different material. Thus we cannot doubt

tically found place in the old popular poetry of Rome; which was Casaubon's opinion as well *(ad Pers. Sat. i.* 93, 94). Nake *(Rhein. Museum,* 1829, p. 388-392) takes a more reasonable view.

See Bahr, *Gesch. d. Rom. Literatur,* vol. ii. p. 681. It is evident that the Latin prose writers, even the best, and the comic writers whose verse was so like to prose, were quite willing sometimes to avail themselves of the satisfaction which the near recurrence of words of a similar sound affords to the ear. Thus Cicero himself *(Brut.* 87): Volvendi sunt libri Catonis: intelliges nihil illius lineamentis, nisi eorum pigmeutorum, quse inventa nondum erant, *florcm* et *colorem* dofuisse. So Pliny the younger: Illam *veram* et *ineram* Greeciam. And Plautus *(Cistell.* i. 1, 70): Amor et *melle* et *felle* est fecundissimus. And Caracalla of thuthat these coincidences of sound were sedulously avoided by so great a master of the proprieties as Virgil – in whose works therefore rhyming verses rarely appear : while it is difficult not to suspect that they were sometimes sought, or, if not sought, yet not diligently shunned, but rather welcomed when they offered themselves, by Ovid, in whom they occur far more frequently, and whose less severe taste might not have been unwilling to appropriate this as well as the more legitimate adornments which belonged to the verse that he was using.

They occur indeed, verses with middle and with final rhymes, in every one of the Latin poets. Thus, as examples of the middle rhyme, we have in Ennius: Non cauponantes bellum, sed belligerantes ;

and in Virgil:

Limus ut hie durescit, et hsec ut cera liquescit; so too in Ovid :

Quem mare carpentem, substrictaque crura gerentem;

brother whom he murdered : Sit licet *divm,* dummodo non *vivus.* In the Christian prose-writers they are more frequent still, especially in Augustine. All readers of his will remember how often such chimes as this (having reference to Stephen's sharp chiding of the Jews) recur: Lingua *clamat,* cor *amat;* or this, on the two Testaments: In Novo *patent.* quse in Vetere *latent;* or, on the Christian's ' hope of glory': Preecedat *spes,* ut sequatur *res ;* or, on faith : Quid est enim *fides,* nisi credere quod non *vides ?* or. interpreting John xxi. 9 : Piscis *assus,* Christus est *passus* - or, on obedience and reward: Hoc agamus *b"nc,* ut illud habeamus *plene;* or, once more, of the Heavenly City : Ibi nullus *oritur,* quia nullus *moritur.* Kake *(Rhein. Museum,* 1829, pp. 392-401) has accumulated examples in like kind from almost all the Latin prose writers.

and again:

Quot coelum Stellas, tot habet tua Roma puellas ; and in a pentameter :

Quserebant flavos per nemus omne favos ; and in Martial:

Sic leve flavorum valeat genus Usipioram ;

thus also in Claudian :

Flava cruentarum prsetenditur umbra jubarum.

These examples might easily be multiplied. As we descend lower, leonine verses become still more frequent. They abound in the *Mosella* of Ausonius.

Nor less have we final rhymes even in Virgil, as the following :

Nee non Tarquinium ejeetum Porsena jubebat

Accipere, ingentique urbem obsidione premebat.

and again :

omnis campis diffugit arator, Omnis et agricola, et tuta latet arce viator.

and in Horace, as in his well-known precept:

Non satis est pulcra esse poemata; dulcia sunto,

Et quocumque volent, animum auditoris agunto.

once more:

Multa recedentes adimunt. Ne forte seniles

Mandentur juveni partes, pueroque viriles.

As we reach the silver age, they are more frequent: they abound in Lucan, though one example may suffice:

Crimen erit Superis et me fecisse nocentem,

Sidera quis mundumque velit spectare eadentem ? f

Other examples of this in Virgil, *Mn.* i. 319, 320; iii. 656, 657; iv. 256, 257 (where see Forbiger); v. 385, 386 ; viii. 620, 621.

t I have not seen any collection of i; uoior&eura out of Greek

When therefore at a later day rhyme began to enter as a permanent element into poetical composition, and to be accounted almost its necessary condition, this was not the coming in of something wholly strange or new. Rhyme, though new to Latin verse in the extent to which it was now adopted, yet had already made itself an occasional place even in the later or prosodic poetry of Rome ; as no doubt it was, and would have continued to . be, of far more frequent recurrence in that earlier national poetry, which, as we have seen, was supprest without having ever reached its full and natural development.

This much may be said in proof that the germs, so to speak, of rhyme were laid in the versification already existing, that it had that ' early anticipation' which one has urged as among the sure marks of a true development. Here indeed it would be a serious mistake, and one which all the documents that have reached us would refute, to regard the hexameter or pentameter as the earliest sphere in which rhyme displayed itself, the attempt having been first made to reconcile the old and the new, and to preserve the advantages of both ; while

poetry, in which, indeed, they would be scarcely of so frequent occurrence as in Latin. The author of the treatise *De Vita et Poesi Homeri,* sometimes ascribed to Plutarch, adduces (c. 35) the *ilwiorfatirrov* as one among the *exfiiwera* of the Homeric poetry, and very distinctly recognizes the charm which rhyme has for the ear ; for, having instanced as an example,

Il'r,,,; c *sK* yAacf, vprjc *a. el vc* he goes on to say : Ti *Si* t'(/jur' ra *na Ra* roiaOra

only at a later day it was discovered that the two were incompatible, and that nothing of abiding value could result from this attempt to superinduce rhyme upon a system of versification resting wholly on a different basis, and to which it served but as a new patch upon an old garment. The regular addition of rhyme to the old Greek and Latin metres, with all the artificial and laborious refinements into which this ran, was of much later date than the birth of rhyme itself in the Latin poetry of the Church, the first leonine verses, or hexameters with internal rhyme, not certainly dating higher than the sixth, and, any large employment of them than the eighth or ninth, centuries; other more elaborate arrangements of rhyme being later still. Rhyme itself, on the contrary, belongs to the third and fourth centuries : and that poetry in which it first appears was far too genial and true a birth of something altogether different from literary idleness, to have fallen into any tricks or merely artificial devices, such as were afterwards abundantly born of the combined indolence and ingenuity of the cloister. Rather it displayed itself first in lines, which, having a little relaxed the strict-

See the wonderfully curious and complex rules about rhyme, and directions for an infinite variety of its possible arrangements, in Eberhard's *Labyrinthus,* a sort of *Ars Poetica* of the middle ages, published in Leyser's *Hist. I'oett. Mid. Mci,* p. 832-837. Something may be fitly said here on the leonine, and other kinds of verses, more or less nearly related to the leonine, which figure so prominently in the literary productions of those ages. The name leonine, which is sometimes, although wrongly, extended to lines with final as well as with sectional or internal rhymes, has been variously derived from various persons of the name of

ness of metrical observance, sought to find a compensation for this in similar closes to the verse – being at

Leo, who were presumed first to have written them. Thus Eberhard:

Sunt inventoris de nomine dicta Leonis.

Oftener still they have been derived Wom one Leonius or Leo- ninus, a canon of Notre Dame and Latin versifier of the twelfth century. We have a curious example here of the manner in which literary opinions once started are repeated again and again, no one taking the trouble to enquire into their truth. Eor, in the first place, it is certain that leonine verses existed long before his time. Muratori *(Antt. Ital. Diss.* 40) has abundantly proved this, adducing perfect leonine verses which belong to the eighth, ninth, and tenth centuries; as the following, which do not date later than the ninth ;

Arbor sacra Crucis fit mundo semita lucis ;
Quam qui portavit, nos Christus in astra levavit.

And thus too J. Grimm *(Latein. Ged. d.* x. *u.* xi. *JH.* p. xxiv): In Deutschland erscheinen leoninische Verse gleich mil dem Beginn der lateinischen Dichtkunst, und sind die Lieblings- form der Monehe vom neunten bis zum funfzehnten Jahrhundert. Some, still wishing to trace up the leonines to this Leonius, have urged, that though not the first to compose, he was the first to bring these verses to any perfection *(Muratori,* vol. iii. p. 687). But this is only propping up error with error; for Edelestand du Meril asserts *(Poesies populaires Latines,* p. 78) from actual inspection, that in his poetry, which is considerable in bulk, there does not occur a single leonine verse (except, I suppose, such accidental ones as will escape from almost every metrical writer in Latin). His chief poem, on the history of the Old Testament, is in the ordinary heroic metre. There is indeed one epistle written with final or tail rhymes, but no other portion of his poetry with rhyme at all. Du Meril himself falls in with the other derivation, namely, that this metre was so called, because as the lion is king of beasts, so is this the king of metres ; or as one has said: Leonini dicuntur a leone, quia sicut inter alias feras majus habet dominium, ita hsec speciesthis time very far from that elaborate and perfect instrument which it afterwards became. We may trace

versuum. Slow as one may be to admit this kingly superiority of the leonine verse, it must be acknowledged that sometimes it is no infelicitous form for an epigram or a maxim, uttering it both with point and conciseness. We may take the following in proof:

Permutant mores homines, cum dantur honores:
Corde stat inflate pauper honore dato.

Or this, expressing an important truth in the spiritual life :

Cum bene pugnabis, cum cuncta subacta putabis,
Queg mox infestat, vincenda superbia restat.

or this, on the different ways in which wise and foolish accept reproof:

Argue consultum, te diliget; argue stultum,
Avertet vultum, nee te dimittet inultum.

or on hid talents:

In mundo duo sunt, quse nil, abscondita, prosunt;
Fossus humi census, latitans in pectore sensus.

or this, on the permanence of early impressions :

Quse nova testa capit, inveterata sapit, or this, on the venality of Rome:
Curia Romana non quserit ovem sine lana ;
Dantes exaudit, non dantibus ostia claudit.

or once more, on the need of elementary teaching:

Parvis imbutus, tentabis grandia tutus.

Not a few proverbs clothe themselves in this form ; as the following:

Est avis in dextra melior quam quattuor extra.
Non habet anguillam, per caudam qui tenet illam.

Sepes calcatur qua pronior esse putatur.
Amphora sub veste raro portatur honeste.
Qno minime reris de gurgite pisce frueris. And here is a brief epigram in praise of Clairvaux

Clara vale Vallis, plus claris clara metallis ;
Tu, nisi me Jallis, es rectns ad sethera callis.

They were sometimes used in more festive verse, which also they did not misbecome:

Cervisise sperno potum, prsesente Falerno,
Sed tamen hanc qusero, deficiente mere.

it step by step from its rude, timid, and uncertain beginnings, till, in the later hymnologists' of the twelfth

Est pluria bellus sonipes quam parvua asellus,
Hoc equitabo pecua, si mihi desit equus.

And here is a bitter epigram on the *villein* of the middle ages, one of the many sayings which bridge over the space between the word's original and present meaning:

Qnando mulcetur villanus, pejor habetur :
Ungentem pungit, pungentem rusticus ungit.

And the writer of this one expresses without reserve his opinion of lawyers:

Dirne Juristas, Deus, ut Satana? citharistaa ;
O Deus, extingues hos pingues atque bilingues.

So too the story of Boniface the Eighth's pontificate is summed up in another couplet:

Vulpes intravit, tanquam leo pontificavit;
Exiit utque canie, de divite factus inanis.

Easily recollected, they were much in use to assist keeping in remembrance the arrangement of the Church Calendar, and the order of the Festivals. Durandus in his *Rationale* often quotes them. Jacob Grimm observes well: In ihnen ergeht sich die Kloster-poesie am behaglichsten, und ihre Feierlichheit fordert sie: daher Inscriften fur Graber und Glocken, kleinere Spruche und Memorabilien fast nur in ihnen verfasst wurden : sie tonen auch nicht selten klangvoll und prachtig. Thus on the fillet of a church-bell it was common to have these lines:

Festa sonana mando, cum funere pnelia pando;
Meque fugit quando resono cum fulmine grando.

The Frankish monarchs, as claiming to be Roman emperors, had a leonine verse on their seals:

KoTaa caput mundi regit orbis frama rotundi.

In most of these lines there is a certain strength and energy. Here is a somewhat longer specimen, drawn from a poem by Reginald, an English Benedictine monk, cotemporary and friend of Anselm and Hildebert:

Ssepe jacet ventua. dormit sopita juventus :
Aura vehit lenie, natat undis cymba serenis;

and thirteenth century, an Aquinas, or an Adam of St Victor, it displayed all its latent capabilities, and

2Equore sed multo Nereus, custode sepulto,

Torquet et invertit navem dum navita stertit:
Mergitur et navis, quamvis vehat aura suiivis:
Res tandem blandse sunt mortis causa nefandse.

A brief analysis of this poem, and further quotations not without an elegance of their own, may be found in Sir A. Crooke's *Essay on the History of Rhyming Latin Verse,* pp. 63-75. These too of Hildebert on the Crucifixion are good:

Vita subit letn. m, dulcedo potat acetum :
Non homo sed vermis, armatum vincit inermis,
Agnus prsedonem, vitulus moriendo leonem.

It is curious to observe how, during the middle ages, rhyme sought to penetrate and make a place for itself everywhere. Thus we have leonine sapphics as well as leonine hexameters and pentameters. The following may belong to the twelfth or thirteenth century (Hommey, *Supplementum Patrum, p.* 179), and, like the poem of Commodianus, see p. 11, must be scanned by accent only, and not by prosody:

Virtutum chori, summo qui Rectori
Semper astatis atque jubilatis,
Ovis remote memores estote,
Kosque juvate.
Felices estis, patrisg ccelestis
Cives, cunctorum nescii malorum,
Qua nos infestant, miseramque prastant
Undique vitam.

Hexameters and pentameters with final rhymes, and these following close upon one another, as in our heroic verse, not artificially interlaced *(interlaqueati),* as in our sonnet or Spenserian stanza, were called *caudati,* as having tails *(caudas).* They were not, I think, quite as much cultivated as the leonine, although of them also immense numbers were written; nor do they very often reach the strength and precision which the leonine sometimes attain ; yet they too are capable of a certain terseness and even elegance, of the same character as we have seen the leonine verses to display. Thus Hildebert describes attained its final glory and perfection, satiating the ear with a richness of melody scarcely anywhere to be sur-

how the legal shadows are outlines of the truth, which as such disappear and flee away, Christ the substance being come :

Agnus enim legis carnales diluit actus,
Agnum prsesignans, qui nos lavat hostia factus :
Quis locus aurorse, postquam sol venit ad ortum ?
Quisve locus votis, teneat quum navita portmn ?

He sums up in two lines the moral of Luke xiv. 16-24:

Villa, boves, uxor, coanam clausere vocatis :
Mundus, cura, caro, ccelum clausere renatis.

A passing and repassingfrom one of these arrangements of rhyme to the other is not uncommon. Thus to quote Hildebert again *(Opp.* p. 1260), and here, as everywhere, I seek to make citations which, besides illustrating the matter directly in hand, have more or less an independent merit of their own:

Crux non clara parum spoliis spoliavit avarum ;

Crux *setse* sortis victi tenet atria fortis;
Crux indulcavit laticem, potumque paravit;
Crux silicon fregit, et aquas exire coegit.
Crux per serpentem Crucifix! signa gerentem
Lsesos sanavit- lsedentes mortificavit;
Crux crucisopprobrium, Crux ligni crimen ademit;
Crux de peccato, Crux nos de morte redemit;
Crux miseros homines in ccelica jura reduxit;
Omne bonum nobis cum sanguine de Cruce fluxit.

Or take another example from the *Carmen Parteneticum* ascribed tojSt Bernard *(Opp.,* vol. ii. p. 909):

Amplius in rebus noli sperare caducis,
Sed tua mens cupiat seternse gaudia lucis :
Fallitur insipiens vitse prsesentis amore,
Sed sapiens noscit quanto sit plena dolore.
Quidquid formosum mundus gerit et pretiosum
Floris habet morem, cui dat natura colored
Mox ut Biccatur, totus color annihilatur ;
Postea neo fiorem monstrat, neo spirat odorem.

He presently passes back from the leonine to the tail rhymes, intermingling besides with those a third form, springing from a combination of the two. The *caudati tripertiti* are divided, as their name indicates, into three sections, each containing twopassed. At first the rhymes were often merely vowel or assonant ones, the consonants not being required to agree ; or the rhyme was adhered to, when this was convenient, but disregarded, when the needful word was not readily at hand; or the stress of the rhyme was suffered to fall on an unaccented syllable, thus scarcely striking the ear ; or it was limited to the similar termination of a single letter; while sometimes, on the strength of this like ending, as sufficiently sustaining the melody, the whole other construction of the verse, and arrangement of the syllables, was neglected.

feet; the first and second sections in every line rhyme with one another, and so far they resemble the leonine; but they are also *tailed,* in that the close of one line rhymes with the close of the succeeding. I know none of this kind which are not almost too bad to quote. Here however is a specimen:

Est data ssevam causa per Evam perditionis,
Bum meliores sperat honores voce draconis.

They are curious, however, inasmuch as in these triparted distichs we trace the rudiments, as F. Wolf has clearly shown *(Ueber die Lais,* p. 200), of that much employed six-line strophe of our modern poetry, in which the rhymes are disposed thus, *a a b o c b,* the stanza which has attained its final glory in Wordsworth's *Ruth;* each of the Latin lines falling into three sections, and thus the couplet expanding into the strophe of six lines. Besides Wolfs admirable treatise just referred to, there are two treatises on the rhymed poetry of the middle ages in *Gebaveri Anthologia Dissertationum,* Lips., 1733; one, p. 265, *Pro Rhythmis, sen Onwioteleutis Poeticis;* another by Elias Major, p. 299, *De Versibus Leoninis.* Sir A. Crooke, in his *Essay on Rhyming Latin Verse,* has drawn freely on these, but has also information of his own.

It may be that they who first used it, were oftentimes scarcely or not at all conscious of what they were doing. Thus

The first in whose hymns there are distinct traces of the adoption of rhyme is Hilary, who died bishop of Poitiers in 368. His hymn on the Epiphany,

Jesus refulsit omnium

Pius redemptor gentium,

consists of eight quatrains, the four lines composing each of which have a like termination, while otherwise they observe the ordinary laws of the iambic dimeter. In the hymn of Pope Damasus (who died a very few years later) on St Agatha, the four lines of the quatrain do not rhyme all together, but two and two; and the verses consist, or are intended to consist, of three dactyls with a terminal rhyming syllable, as thus :

Stirpe decens, elegans specie,

Sed magis actibus atque fide,

Terrea prospera nil reputans,

Jussa Dei sibi corde ligans.

It is true that earlier than either of these is the poem of Commodianus, referred to already, and that in cue section all the words end in *o*. This could not be accidental; yet at the same time, as nothing similar occurs in other parts of the poem, it must be counted,

Ampere says very beautifully upon the hymns of St Ambrose, in which he traces such unconscious preludings to the later rhymed poetry of Christendom: Ces hymnes sont versifies d'apres la regle de la metrique ancienne, mais il est curieux de voir une tendance a la rime se produire evidemment dans ces strophes analogues a celles d'Horace. Ce qui sera le fondement de la prosodie des temps modernes, la rime, n'est pas encore une loi de la versification, et deja un besoin mysterieux de l'oreille l'introduit dans les vers pour ainsi dire a l'insu de l'oreille clle meme *(Hist. Litt. de la France,* vol. i. p. 411).

where it does appear, rather as an arbitrary ornament than an essential element, of the rhythm.

Seeing, then, that it thus lies in our power to trace distinctly, and as it were step by step, the rise and growth of the Latin rhymed poetry, to preside at its very birth and cradle, – one cannot but wonder at a very common assertion, namely, that it borrowed rhyme from languages, which assuredly do not now preserve any examples in this kind that are not of far later origin than much which we possess in the Latin tongue. " I know of no poem," says Dr. Guest, " written in a Qothic dialect with final rhyme, before Otfrid's Evangely. This was written in Prankish, about the year 870." He, it is true, supposes the Latin rhymers to have gotten rhyme from the Celtic races, – among some of whom undoubtedly it existed very early, as among the Welch in the sixth century – and then in their turn to have imparted it to the Gothic nations. But a necessity for this unlikely hypothesis rests only on the assumption, that " the Romans were confessedly ignorant of rhyme." Certainly, if we found it in the Latin poetry suddenly starting up in its final perfection, complete and lacking nothing, – as we do find some of the Greek lyric metres, the complex alcaic, for example, in the pages of Horace, – we could then hardly come to any other conclusion, but that it had been imported *ab extra,* even though we might not be able to say with certainty from what quarter it had been obtained. But everything about its introduction serves rather to mark it as autochthonic. j

History of English Rhythms, vol. i. p. 119. t Ampere has expressed the same conviction. Of the Latin poetry of the eleventh century he says: La tendance a la rime,

We see it in its weak and indistinct beginnings, not yet knowing itself or its own importance; we mark its irregular application at first; the lack of skill in its use, the poor assonances instead of the full consonances; with an only gradual discovery of all which it would effect; – the chimes having been at first, probably, but happy chances, found, like the pointed arch, without having been sought; but which yet, being once lighted on, the instinct of genius did not let go, but adopted and improved, as that very thing which it needed, and unconsciously had been feeling after; and now at length had attained.

But when we thus refuse to admit that the Latin rhyming poetry borrowed its rhyme from the Romance or Gothic languages, we are not therefore obliged to accept the converse, and with Tyrwhitt and others to assume that *they* obtained it from the Latin, however that might be of the two the more tolerable supposition. For, after the investigations of later years, no one ought any longer to affirm rhyme to have been the exclusive invention of any one people, and from them to have past over into other languages and literatures; which Warton and Sismondi have done, who derive it originally from the Arabs. Rhyme can as little be considered the exclusive discovery of any one people as of any

qui nous avait deja frappes chez Saint Ambroise, a toujours $te. de siecle en siecle, s'accusantplus nettement. Au temps tm nous sommes parvenus, elle a fini par triompher. Ce qui n'etait d'abord qu'une fantaisie de l'oreille a fini par devenir un besoin imprieux et par se transformer en loi. Il n'est done pas necessaire de chercher d'autre origine a la rime; elle est nee du sein de la poesie latine degeneree. *Essay on the Language and Versification of Chaucer,* p. 51.

single age. It is rather, like poetry, like music, like dramatic representation, the natural result of a deep craving of the human mind ; as it is the well-nigh inevitable adjunct of a poetry not quantitative, being almost certain to make a home for itself therein. This last point has been well expressed, and the causes of it rightly stated by a writer already quoted, and whose words must always carry weight: "When the same modification of sound recurs at definite intervals, the coincidence very readily strikes the ear, and when it is found in accented syllables, such syllables fix the attention more strongly than if they merely received the accent. Hence we may perceive the importance of rhyme in accentual verse. It is not, as it is sometimes asserted, a mere ornament: it marks and defines the accent, and thereby strengthens and supports the rhythm. Its advantages have been felt so strongly, that no people have ever adopted an accentual rhythm, without also adopting rhyme."

In this the universality of rhyme, as in the further fact that it is peculiar neither to the rudeness of an early and barbarous age, nor to the over-refined ingenuity of a late and artificial one, but runs through whole literatures from their beginning to their end, we find its best defence; – or, more accurately, that which exempts it from needing any defence against charges like that brought by Milton against it f; for there is

Guest, *History of English Rhythms,* vol. i. p. 116.

t It will be remembered what he calls it in the few words which he has prefixed to *Paradise Lost* – "the invention of a barbarous age, to set off wretched matter and lame metre; . . . a thing of itself to all judicious ears trivial and of no true musical delight" – with much more in the same strain. here the evidence that it lies deep in our human nature, and satisfies an universal need, since otherwise so many people would not have lighted upon it, or having lighted, so inflexibly maintained it. For we do encounter it everywhere – in the extreme West, in the earliest Celtic poems, Welsh and Irish – in the further East, among the Chinese, in the Sanscrit, – and no less in the Persian and Arabic poetry, – in the Gothic and Scandinavian ; – no formal discovery, as no borrowed skill, in any case; but in all the well-nigh instinctive result of that craving after periodic recurrence, proportion, limitation, – of that sense out of which all rhythm and all metre springs, namely, that the streams of passion must have banks within which to flow, if they are not to waste and lose themselves altogether, – with the desire to mark and to make distinctly noticeable to the ear these limits and restraints, which the verse, for its own ultimate good, imposes upon itself. We may

Over against this we might set what I much esteem the wiser words of Daniel in his *Defence of Rhyme,* or indeed more honourably confute him out of his own mouth, and by the fact that the noblest lyrics which English literature possesses, being his own, are rhymed.

Ewald (0! *the Poetic Books of the Old Testament,* vol. i. p. 57) has expressed himself very profoundly on this matter: " A stream of words and images, an overflowing and impetuous diction, a movement which in its first violence seems to know no bounds nor control – such is the earliest manifestation of poetic diction '. But a diction which should only continue in this its earliest movement, and hurry onward, without bounds and without measure, would soon destroy its own beauty, even its very life. Yea rather, the more living and overflowing this onward movement is, by so much the more needful the restraint and the limitation, the counteraction and tranquillization, of this becomes. observe that the prosodic poetry of Greece and Rome was equally obliged to mark this, though it did it in another way. Thus, had dactyles and spondees been allowed to be promiscuously used throughout the hexameter line, no satisfying token would have reached the ear to indicate the close of the verse; and if the hearer had once missed the termination of the line, it would have been almost impossible for him to recover it. But the fixed dactyle and spondee at the end of the line answer the same purpose of strongly marking the close, as does the rhyme in the accentuated verse: and in other metres, in like manner, licenses permitted in the beginning of the line are excluded at its close, the motives for this greater strictness being the same.

The non-recognition of this, man's craving after, and deep delight in, the rhythmic and periodic – a craving which nature everywhere meets and gratifies, and which all truest art seeks to gratify as well, – a seeing nothing in all this but a trick and artifice applied from without, – lies at the root of that singular theory concerning the unfitness of poetry to be the vehicle for our highest addresses to God and most reverent utterances about Him, which the accomplished author of the *Day in the Sanctuary* has put forth in the preface to that volume. Any one who, with at all the skill in versification and command over language which he himself has manifested elsewhere, undertakes to comply with the requirements

This mighty inspiration and exspiration ; this rise with its commensurate fall; this advance in symmetrical diction, which shall combine rest and motion with one another, and mutually reconcile them; this is rhythm, or regulated beautiful movement."

which verse imposes, knows that the obligations which he thus assumes are very far from being felt as a bondage, but rather that here, as everywhere else, to move according to law is felt to be the freest movement of all. Every one, too, who without this peculiar experience has watched the effect on his own mind of the orderly marching of a regiment, or of the successive breaking of waves upon the shore, or of ought else which is thus *rhythmic and periodic,* knows that in this, inspiring as it does the sense of order, and proportion, and purpose, there is ever an elevating and solemnizing power – a truth to which language, the best, because the most unconscious, witness, sets its seal, having in the Latin but one and the same word, for the solemn and the recurring.

I have said above, that we are not bound to assume that the poetries of modern Europe derived rhyme from the Latin ; because we reject the converse proposition, that the Latin derived it from them. At the same time the medieval Latin poetry, without standing in so close a technical relation as this to the modern poetry of Europe, without having been thus the source from which the latter obtained its most characteristic ornament, does yet stand in most true and living relation to it; has exerted upon it an influence which probably

Goethe's noble words, uttered with a larger intention, have yet their application here:

Vergebens werden ungebundne Geister
Nach der Vollendung reiner Höhe streben:
In der Bsschrankung zeigt sich erst dsr Meister,
Und das Gesetz nur kann uiis Freilieit geben.

has been scarcely estimated as highly as it deserves. To how great an extent must it have acted as a conductor of the thoughts and images of the old world to the new, making the stores of that old world to be again the heritage of the popular mind – stores which would else have been locked up till the more formal revival of learning, then perhaps to become not the possession of the many, but only of the few. How important was the part which it played, filling up spaces that were in a great measure unoccupied by any other works of imagination at all; lending to men an organ and instrument by which to utter their thoughts, when as yet the modern languages of Europe were in the first process of their formation, and quite unfit to be the adequate clothing for these. '

Thus the earliest form in which the *Reineke Fuchs,* the great fable-epic of the middle ages, appeared, – the significance of which in European literature, no one capable of forming a judgment on the matter will lightly esteem, – is now acknowledged to have been Latin. A poem in four books, in elegiac metre, whose author is unknown, supplied mediately or immediately the ground-plan to all the subsequent dispositions of the matter. Of course it is not meant hereby to deny the essentially popular character of the poem, or to affirm that the Latin poet invented that, which, no doubt, already lived upon the lips of the people ; but only that in this Latin the fable-lore of the German world first took shape, and found a distinct utterance for itself.

The existence of such an original was long unsuspected, even after an earnest interest had been awakened in the *Beimke*And thus, too, out of that dreariest tenth century, that wastest place, as it is rightly esteemed, of European literature and of the human mind, James Grimm has published a brief Latin epic of very high merit; while Fulbert, bishop of Chartres, who died early in the eleventh (1027), could celebrate the song of the nightingale in strains such as these :

Cum telluris, vere novo, producuntur germina,
Nemorosa cireumcirca frondeseunt et brachia;
Fragrat odor cum suavis florida per gramina,
Hilarescit Philomela, dulcis sonus t conscia,
Et extendens modulando gutturis spiramina,
Reddit veris et sestivi temporis prseconia.
Instat nocti et diei voce sub dulcisona,
Soporatis dans quietem cantus per discrimina,
Necnon pulcra viatori laboris solatia.
Vocis ejus pulcritudo clarior quam cithara;
Vincitur omnis cantando volucrum catervula;
Implet sylvas atque cuncta modulis artmstula,
Gloriosa valde facta veris prse Isetitia.
Volitando scaudit alta arborum cacumina,
Ac festiva satis gliscit sibilare carmina.
Cedit auceps ad frondosa resonans umbracula,
Cedit olor et suavis ipsius melodia;
Cedit tibi tympanistra et sonora tibia;
Quamvis enim videaris corpore permodica,
Tamen cuncti capiuntur hac tua melodia:

Fuchs itself. It was first published by Mone, *Reinhardus Vidpes,* Stuttgart, 1832.

Waltharius. It had been published indeed before ; and has since been so by Du Meril, *Poesies popul. Lat.* 1843, p. 313- 377.

t *Somis* re-appears here as of the fourth declension (see Freund's *Lat. Wiirterbuch,* s. v.).

Nemo dedit voci tuse hsec dulcia carmina,
Nisi solus Rex coelestis qui gubernat omnia.

Surely with all its rudeness and deficiencies this poem has the true passion of nature, and contains in it the prophecy and pledge of much more than it actually accomplishes. In that

Gloriosa valde facta vens prse lsetitia,

we have no weak prelude of that rapturous enthusiasm and inspiration, which at a later day have given us such immortal hymns as the *Ode to the Skylark,* by Shelley. Or consider these lines of Marbod, bishop of Rheims in the twelfth century ; which, stiffly and awkwardly versified as they may be, have yet a deep interest, as touching on those *healing* influences of nature, the sense of which is almost, if not entirely, confined to modern, that is to Christian, art. They belong to a poem on the coming of the spring; and, as the reader will observe, are in leonine hexameters:

Moribus esse feris prohibet me gratia veris,

Et formam mentis mihi mutuor ex elementis.
Ipsi naturse congratulor, ut puto, jure:
Distinguunt flores diversi mille colores,
Gramineum vellus superinduxit sibi tellus,
Fronde virere nemus et fructificare videmus:
Egrediente rosa viridaria sunt epeciosa.
Qui tot pulcra videt, nisi flectitur et nisi ridet,
Intractabilis est, et in ejus pectore lis est;
Qui speciem terrse non vult cum laude referre,
Invidet Auctori, eujus subservit honori
Bruma rigens, sestas, auctumnus, veris honestas.

D. FiUberti Opera Varia, Paris, 1608, p. 181. I believe we owe to Dr. Neale the following very graceful translation : " When the earth, with spring returning, vests herself in fresher sheen. And the glades and leafy thickets are arrayed in living green ; When a sweeter fragrance breatheth flowery fields and vales along, Then, triumphant in her gladness, Philomel begins her song : And with thick delicious warble far and wide her notes she flings, Telling of the happy spring tide and the joys that summer brings. In the pauses of men's slumber deep and full she pours her voice, In the labour of his travel bids the wayfarer rejoice. Night and day, from bush and greenwood, sweeter than an earthly lyre. She, unwearied songstress, carols, distancing the feathered choir, Fills the hillside, fills the valley, bids the groves and thickets ring, Made indeed exceeding glorious through the joyousness of spring. None could teach such heavenly music, none implant such tuneful skill. Save the King of realms celestial, who doth all things as He will."

May we not say that the old monkish poet is anticipating h'ere – and however faintly, yet distinctly – such strains as the great poets of nature in our own day have made to be heard – the conversion of the witch Mai- muna in Thalaba, Peter Bell, or those loveliest lines in Coleridge's *Remorse ?*

With other ministrations thou, 0 Nature,
Healest thy wandering and distempered child ;
Thou pourest on him thy soft influences,
Thy sunny hues, fair forms, and breathing sweets,
Thy melodies of woods, and winds, and waters!
Till he relent, and can no more endure
To be a jarring and a dissonant thing
Amid this general dance and minstrelsy;
But bursting into tears wins back his way,
His angry spirit healed and harmonized
By the benignant touch of love and beauty.

Hard measure is for the most part dealt to this poetry. f

Hildeberti et Marbodi Opera, ed. Beaugendre, Paris, 1708, p. 1617.

t Few are so just to it as Bahr (*Die Christl. Dichter Rom's,* p. 10): Wenn wir daher auch nieht unbedingt die Ansicht derje- nigen theilen konnen, welche die Einfuhrung dieser Christlichen Dichter statt der heidnischen in Schulen zum Zwecke des Sprach- unterrichts wie zur Bildung eines acht christlichen Gemiiths vorschlagen, aus Griinden, die zu offen da liegen, um weiterer

Men come to it with a taste formed on quite other models, trying it by laws which were not its laws, by the approximation which it makes to a standard which is so far from being its standard, that the nearer it reaches that, the further removed from any true value it is. They come trying the Gothic cathedral by the laws of the Greek temple, and because they do not find in it that which, in its very faithfulness to its own idea, it cannot have, they treat it as worthy only of scorn and contempt. Nor less have they forgotten, in estimating the worth of this poetry, that much which appears trite and commonplace to us was yet very far from being so at its first utterance. When the Gothic nations which divided the Roman empire began to crave intellectual and spiritual food, in the healthy hunger of their youth there lay the capacity of deriving truest nourishment from that which to us, partly from our far wider range

Ausfuhrung zu bedurfen, die auch nie, selbst in Mittelalter, ver- kannt warden sind, so glauben wir doch dass es zweckmassig und von wesentlichem Nutzen seyn diirfte den Erzeugnissen cbristli- cher Poesie auch auf unseren hoheren Bildungsanstalten eine grossere Aufmerksamkeit zuzuweuden, als diess bisher der Fall war, die Jugend demnach in den obern Classen der Gymnasien und Lyceen mit den vorziiglicheren Erscheinungen dieser Poesie, die ihnen jetzt so ganz fremd ist und bleibt, bekannt zu machen, ja selbst einzelne Stiicke solcher Dichtungen in die Chrestomathien Lateinischer Dichter, in denen sie wahrlich, auch von ande- ren Standpunkten aus betrachtet, eine Stelle neben manehen Productioneu der heidnischen Zeit verdienen, aufzunehmen, um so zugleich den lebendigen Gegensatz der heidnischen und christii- chen Welt und Poesie erkennen zu lassen, und jugendlichen Gemii- thern friihe einzupragen.

Ampere (vol. iii. p. 213) says with truth, and on this very matter: Ce qui est pen important pour l'histoire de l'art peut l'etre beaucoup pour l'histoire de l'esprit humain.

of choice, and partly also from a satiated appetite, seems little calculated to yield it.

But considerations of this kind would lead me too far, and lie too wide of the immediate scope of this

Ferdinand Wolf, in his instructive work, *Ueber die Lais,* p. 281, and James Grimm, have both observed, that a history of this medieval Latin poetry is a book still waiting to be written, and which, when it is written will fill up a huge gap in the literary history of Europe. We have nothing in the kind but Leyser's compendium, *Historia Poetarum et Poematum Medii Mvl,* Halae, 1721, which would have its use for the future labourer in this field, and which he would find especially serviceable in its copious literary notices; but for a book making, as by its title it does, some claim to completeness, absurdly fragmentary and imperfect – and this, even when is added to it another essay, which Leyser published two years earlier, *Diss. de ficta Medii Mvi Barbaric, imprimis circa Poesin Latinam,* Helmstadt, 1719. Less complete than even in his own day he might have made it, it is far more deficient now, when so much bearing on the subject has been brought to light, which was then unknown. The volume, too, is as much at fault in what it has, as what it has not – including as it does vast poems of very slightest merits; and from which an extract or two would have sufficed. Edele- stand du Meril's two volumes, *Poesies populaires Latines ante-rieures au doTtxieme Siecle,* Paris, 1843, and *Poesies populairis Latines du Moyen Age,* Paris, 1847, contain many valuable notices, and poems which had not previously, or had only partially or incorrectly, been printed. But, as the titles indicate, they have only to do with the *popular* Latin poetry of the middle ages. – Whoever undertakes such a work, must be one who esteems as the glory of this poetry, and not the shame, that it seeks to emancipate itself, if not always from the forms, yet always from the spirit, of the classical poetry of the old world – desires to stand on its own ground, to grow out of its own root. Indeed no one else would have sufficient love to the subject to induce him to face the labours and wearinesses which it would involve. The later Latin poetry, that which has flourished since

volume, to allow me to follow them further. Already what I thought to put into a few paragraphs has insensibly grown almost into an essay, having from its length some of the pretensions of an essay, with at the same time little that should justify those pretensions. I may not further encroach upon the room which I would reserve for other men's words, rather than pre-

the revival of learning, and which has drawn its inspiration not from the Church, but from ancient classical literature, has found a very careful and enthusiastic historian; but one who, according to my convictions, has begun his work just where all or nearly all of any true value has ended, leaving untouched the whole period which really offers much of any deep or abiding interest. I mean Budik, in his work, *Leben und Wirken der vorziiglichsten Latein. Dichter des XV – XVIII. Jahrhunderts,* Vienna, 1828. Such, however, was not *his* mind, who could express himself about the Christian middle ages with a fanaticism of contempt, possible some thirty years ago, but hardly so now, when we are in danger rather of exaggerations in the other extreme. He says: " Since the ages of Pericles and Augustus, the perfect creations of which enjoy an everlasting youth, until the middle of the fifteenth century, one sees nothing but a waste, whose dreary and barren uniformity is only broken by some scattered brushwood, and whose most vigorous productions awaken rather astonishment than admiration." For myself, I never so felt the inanity of modern Latin poetry as, when looking over the entire three volumes of Budik (and I have repeated the experiment with much larger collections), I could find no single poem or fragment of a poem which I cared to use, save, indeed, a few lines from Casimir, which I already possessed. It was from no affected preference of the old that my extracts from modern Latin poetry are so few; but three or four is all. If Vida, or Sannazar, or Buchanan, or any other of the moderns, would have offered anything of value, I would gladly have adopted it; but repeatedly seeking for something, I always sought in vain.

occupy with my own : and whatever else might have been said upon the subject, spatiis exclusus iniquis Prsetereo.

Nor do I unwillingly conclude with a word from him, the chiefest in Latin art, for whom our admiration need not in the least be diminished by our ability to admire Latin verse, composed on very different principles from his; and, if possessing, yet needing also, large compensations, for all which *it* has not, but which he with his illustrious fellows has ; and which must leave, in so many aspects, the great masterpieces of Greece and Rome for ever without competitor or peer.

SECTION 2

POEMS.

ADAM OF ST VICTOR.

OF the life of Adam of St Victor, the most fertile, and, as I am inclined to believe, the greatest of the Latin hymnologista of the middle ages, very little is known. He was probably a native of Brittany, although the terms *breton, brito,* which in the early writers indicate his country, leave in some doubt whether England might not have had the honour of giving him birth. The authors of the *Histoire Litteraire de la France,* vol. xv. p. 40 – 45, account this not altogether unlikely ; and it is certain that this illustrious foundation drew together its scholars from all parts of Europe; thus, of its other two chiefest ornaments, Hugh was a Saxon, and Richard a Scot. Yet the fact that France was the great seat of Latin poetry in the twelfth century, and that all the chief composers in this kind, as Hilde- bert, the two Bernards, Abelard, Marbod, Peter the Venerable, were Frenchmen, leaves it more likely that he, the chiefest of all, was such as well. At all events he made his studies at Paris, where he entered the religious foundation of St Victor, then in the suburbs, but at a later day included within the walls, of Paris, in which he continued to his death. The year of his death is unknown; the *Gallia Christiana* places it somewhere between 1172 and 1192. Gautier, of whose edition of Adam's hymns I shall have presently to speak, thinks the latter year to be itself the most probable date (vol. i. p. lxxxviii). His epitaph, graven on a plate of copper in the cloister of St Victor, near the door of the choir, remained till the general destruction of the first Revolution. The ten first verses of it, as Gautier has shown, are his own, and constituted an independent poem, which, with the title *De Miserid Hominis,* is still to be found among his works. The four last were added by a later hand, so to fit them for an epitaph on their author. His own lines possess a grand moral flow, and are very well worthy to be quoted.

Hseres peccati, natura filius irse,
Exiliique reus nascitur omnis homo.
Unde superbit homo, cujus coneeptio culpa,
Nasci poena, labor vita, neeesse mori ?
Vana salus hominis, vanus decor, omnia vana;
Inter vana nihil vanius est homine.
Dum magis alludit prsesentis gloria vite,
Prseterit, immo fugit; non fugit, immo perit.
Post hominem vermis, post vermem fit cinis, heu, hen!
Sic redit ad cinerem gloria nostra sinnil.
Hie ego qui jaceo miser et miserabilis Adam,
Unam pro summo munere posco precem:
Peccavi, fateor, veniam peto, parce fatenti,
Parce pater, fratres parcite, parce Deus.

We may certainly conclude that Adam of St Victor shared to the full in the theological culture of the school to which he belonged. This, indeed, is evident from his hymns, which, like the poetry of Dante, have oftentimes as great a theological, as poetical or even devotional interest, the first indeed sometimes predominating to the injury of the last. The aim of that illustrious school of theology, especially in its two foremost representatives, Hugh, and his scholar Richard, of St Victor, the first called in his own day *Lingua Augustini, Alter Augustinus,* and both of them cotemporaries of Adam, though Hugh belonged to an elder generation, was to unite and harmoniously to reconcile the scholastic and mystic tendencies, the light and the warmth, which had appeared more in opposition in Abelard and Bernard: and to this its noble purpose and aim it long remained true: nor would it be easy to exaggerate the influence for good which went forth from this institution during the twelfth and thirteenth centuries upon the whole Church. (See Liebner, *Hugo von St Victor,* p. 9 – 16.) It long remained faithful to the cultivation of sacred song: for, in later times, Santeuil, a poet, it is true, of a very different rank indeed from him with whom we now have to do, was a Victorine as well.

Very different estimates have been formed of the merits of Adam of St Victor's hymns. His most zealous admirers will hardly deny that he pushes too far, and plays overmuch with, his skill in the typical application of the Old Testament. So too they must own that sometimes he is unable to fuse with a perfect success his manifold learned allusion into the passion of

Calderon is often, consciously or unconsciously, an imitator of Adam of St Victor's manner – knitting together, as he does, a succession of allusions to Old Testament types, and weaving themhis poetry. How full of this learned allusion they are, I have had evidence while preparing this volume, in the amount of explanatory notes which they required, – so far larger than almost any other equal quantity of verse which it contains. Nor less must it be allowed that he is sometimes guilty of *concetti,* of plays upon words, not altogether worthy of the solemnity of his theme. Thus of one martyr he says:

Sub securi stat securus; of another, St Lawrence namely:

Dum torretur, non terretur;

with more or less success into the woof of a single poem. This hymn, drawn from an *Auto* of his, on the Holy Eucharist, will illustrate what I mean:

Honey in the lion's month,
Emblem mystical, divine,
How the sweet and strong combine ;
Cloven rock for Israel's drouth ;
Treasure-house of golden grain,
By our Joseph laid in store,
In hie brethren's famine sore
Freely to dispense again ;
Dew on Gideon's snowy fleece ;
Well from bitter changed to sweet;
Shew-bread laid in order meet,
Bread whose cost doth ne'er increase
Though no rain in April fall;
Horeb's manna, freely given,
Showered in white dew from heaven,
Marvellous, angelical;
Weightiest bunch of Canaan's vine;
Cake to strengthen and sustain
Through long days of desert pain ;
Salem's monarch's bread and wine ; –
Thou the antidote shalt be
Of my sickness and my sin,
Consolation, medicine,
Life and Sacrament to me.

of the blessed Virgin, (for he did not escape, as it was not to be expected that he should, the exaggerations of his time):

0 duleis vena venise;

of heaven:

0 quam beata *curia,*
Quse *cum* prorsus nescia.

Sometimes too he is overfond of displaying feats of skill in versification, of prodigally accumulating, or curiously interlacing, his rhymes, that he may shew his perfect mastery of the forms which he is using, and how little he is confined or trammelled by them.

These faults it will be seen are indeed most of them but merits pushed into excess. And even accepting them as defects, his profound acquaintance with the whole circle of the theology of his time, and eminently with its exposition of Scripture, – the abundant and admirable use, with indeed the drawback already mentioned, which he makes of it, delivering as he thus does his poems from the merely *subjective* cast of those, beautiful as they are, of St. Bernard – the exquisite art and variety with which for the most part his verse is managed and his rhymes disposed – their rich melody multiplying and ever deepening at the close – the strength which often he concentrates into a single linef

Augustine had already shewn him the way to this play of words. Addressing the sinner as the barren fig-tree of Luke xiii. 9, he says: "Dilata est securis, noli esse secura;" and again: " Distulit securim, non dedit securitatem."

t Thus of a Roman governor, who, alternating flatteries with threats, is seeking to bribe one of the early martyrs from her – his skill in conducting a story – and most of all, the evident nearness of the things which he celebrates to his own heart of hearis – all these, and other excellencies, render him, as far as my judgment goes, the foremost among the sacred Latin poets of the middle ages. He may not have any single poem to vie with the austere grandeur of the *Dies Irce,* nor yet with the tearful passion of the *Stabat Mater,* although concerning the last point there might well be a question ; but then it must not be forgotten that these stand wellnigh alone, in the names of their respective authors, while from his ample treasure-house I shall enrich this volume with a multitude of hymns, all of them of considerable, some of the very highest, merit. Indeed were I disposed to name any one who might dispute the palm of sacred

allegiance to Christ, by the offer of worldly dignities and honours :

Offert multa, spondet plura,
Periturus peritura.

Thus with what graceful ease his hymn on the martyrdom of St Catharine commences:

Vox sonora nostri chori Nam perlegit disciplinas
Nostro sonet Conditori, Sfficulares et divinas
Qui disponit omnia ; In adolesoentia.
Per quem dimicat imbellis,
Per quem datnr et puellis Vas electum, vas virtutum,
De viris victoria: Beputavit eicut lutnm
Bona transitoria:
Per quem plebs Alexandrina Et reduxit in contemptum
Foemime non fcEminina Patris opes, et parentum
Stnpuit ingenia ; Larga patrimonia.
Cum beata Catharina
Doctos vinceret doctrina, Vasis oleum includens,
Ferrum patientia. Virgo sapiens et prudens,
Sponso pergit obvia;
Florem teneri decoris Ut adventus ejus hora
Lectionis et laboris Prseparata sine mora
Attrivere studia: Intret ad convivia.

Latin poetry with him it would not be one of these, but rather Hildebert, Archbishop of Tours.

There are readers who may possibly consider that I have set the merits of Adam of St Victor too high; yet fresh from the perusal of his hymn on St Stephen, or his longer one on the Resurrection, or those on Pentecost, they will certainly wonder at the taste and judgment of his countrymen, who could apportion him no higher praise than the following: A l'egard du merite de ses pieces, ce serait outrer l'admiration que d'adopter sans reserve les e'loges qu'on leur a donnes. Elles etaient bonnes pour le temps, et meme les meil- leurs qu'on eut vues jusqu'alors. Mais il a paru depuis des modeles en ce genre, qui les ont fait totalement oublier, et avec lesquelles elles ne peuvent rellement entrer en comparaison. *(Hist. Lift. de la France,* vol. xv. p. 41.) Over against this I will set another and a fairer estimate of the merit of his hymns, the writer, probably John of Toulouse, (he died in 1659, and was himself Prior of St Victor,) seizing, as it seems to me, very happily the character at once learned and ornate, the " decorated" style, which is so characteristic of many of them : Valde multas prosas fecit... quse suc- cincte et clausulatim progredientes, venusto verborum matrimonio subtiliter decorata?, sententiarum flosculis mirabiliter picturatse, schemate congruentissimo com- ponuntur, in quibus et cum interserat prophetias et figuras, qsae in sensu quem praetendunt videantur obscurissimse, tamen sic eas adaptat ad suum proposi- tum manifesto, ut magis videantur historiam texere quam figuram (Martene, *Thes. Anecdot.* vol. vi. p. 222). Eambach calls him, I know not whether very felicitously, " the Schiller of the middle ages," Dora Gue'- ranger, le plus grand poete du moyen age.

Several of the hymns of Adam of St Victor had got abroad, and were in use at a very early date, probably during the author's life: but till very lately we were mainly indebted to the care of Clichtoveus, a theologian of the first half of the sixteenth century for what larger acquaintance with them we could obtain. Among numerous other works which he composed was the *Elucidatorium Ecclesiasticum,* Paris, 1515; Basle, 1517, 1519; Paris, 1540, 1556 (the best edition); Cologne, 1732, and in an abridged form, Venice, 1555 : written for the instruction of the parochial clergy in the meaning of the various offices of the Church. The book, which is rather scarce, was till very lately of absolute necessity for the student of the Christian hyrtmology, above all for the student of Adam of St Victor's hymns. Besides containing grains of gold to be washed from the sands. of a diffuse exposition, it was long a principal source of the text, and had highest authority therein ; Clichtoveus having drawn it, as he himself assures us, from copies of the hymns preserved in the archives of St Victor itself. Recent discoveries, however, have much diminished the importance of this work. Almost until the other day it had been taken for granted that Clichtoveus had published all the hymns of Adam which were in existence in his time, all therefore which could be in existence in ours. No one thought it worth while to call in question his statement to this effect; nor, though it was well known that such of the manuscript treasures of the Abbey of St Victor as had escaped the Revolution were deposited in the ImperialLibrary in Paris, to make researches there, and prove whether this was indeed the case. At length, however, the suspicions of the M. Gautier were aroused, mainly by observing that while we possessed hymns of his in honour of some of the obscurest saints, some of the mightiest events of the Christian Year, Christmas for example, were altogether uncelebrated in them; and he resolved to prove whether other hymns, which he was sure must once have existed, might not still be discovered. The search which he instituted was abundantly rewarded; and he has been able to publish an edition of the poetical works of Adam of St Victor *(CEuvres Poe'tiques d'Adam de S. Victor,* Paris, 1858, 1859), containing one hundred and six hymns, or sixty- nine more than were hitherto ascribed to him. It is true indeed that *all* of these were not unknown before; some were going about the world, but without attribution to their author. Far the larger portion, however, were thus for the first time drawn from their hiding-place of centuries, and not a few of these worthy to take rank with the noblest compositions of Adam himself, or any other among the foremost hymnologists of the medieval Church. I have enriched this second edition of my book with several of these, the beauty and grandeur of which will, I feel sure, be acknowledged by all competent judges.

3

SECTION 3

I. DE SS. EVANGELISTIS.
   TUCUNDARE, plebs fidelis,
   W Cujus Pater est in coelis,
   Recolens Ezechielis
   ProphetEe prasconia:
   Est Joannes testis ipsi, 5
   Dicens in Apocalypsi,
   Vere vidi, vere scripsi
   Vera testimonia.
   Circa thronum majestatis,
   Cum spiritibus beatis, 10
   Qnatuor diversitatis
   Astant animalia.
   Formam primum aquilinam,
   Et secunduni leoninam,
   Sed humanam et bovinam 15
   Duo gerunt alia.

I. Clichtoveus, *Elucidat. Eccles. vol.* ii. p. 218; *Seguentite t!e- Tempore,* Argentinse, 1516, p. 21; Corner, *Promptuarium De- votionis,* Viennse, 1672, p. 346; Daniel, *Thes. Hymnol.* vol. ii. p. 84 ; Gautier, *Adam de S. Victor,* vol. ii. p. 425.

6. *testis ipsi]* Cf. Rev. iv. 6 – 8 with Ezek. i. 4 – 28; x. 9 – 22.

6 – 8. Cf. Rev. xxi. 5 ; xxii. 6.

12. *animalia]* The fwa of Rev. iv. 6, &c., are in our Version " beasts;" – " living creatures " it should have been, as *animalia* in the Vulgate ; and " beast" should have been reserved for the of the 13th and later chapters. The distribution made in Forms e formant figurarum

Formas Evangelistarum,
Quorum imber doctrinarum
Stillat in Ecclesia : 20
Hi sunt Marcus et Matthseus,
Lucas, et quem Zebedseus
Pater tibi misit, Deus,
Dum laxaret retia.

this hymn of these four to the four Evangelists is St Jerome's, *(Comm. in Ezek* c. 1 ; *Prol. in Matt.; Ep.* 50), is that of St Ambrose *(Prol. in Luc.),* of Gregory the Great *(Hom.* 4 *in Ezek.; Mar.* xxxi. 47), and through his influence became the prevailing though not the exclusive one (for Bede has another), during the middle ages. In earlier times there was much fluctuation in the application of the four to the four; and, strangely enough, even the eagle was not by universal consent attributed to St John: Irenseus, the first who makes the application at all, giving the lion to him, and the eagle to St Mark *(Con. Har.* iii. 2. 8); his other two are as in this hymn ; and so Juvencus. Athanasius *(Opp.* vol. ii. p. 155), shifts them in another fashion. Leaving St Matthew untouched, he gives the calf to St Mark, the lion to St Luke, and the eagle to St John. Augnstine *(De Cons. Evany.* 1. 7), whom Bede follows, makes yet another transposition. With him the lion belongs to St Matthew, the man to St Mark, the calf and eagle respectively to St Luke and St John. One might be tempted by these variations to dismiss the whole matter as an idle play of the fancy; and yet there was more than this, and indeed a deep insight into the nature of the Gospels, in the desire which thus manifested itself of claiming for them to be at once four and one, an *eva. yyfuv rcrpdpopQov* (Irenseus), *rarfdyuvov* (Origen), setting forth, in four cardinal aspects, the inexhaustible fulness of the life of Christ. The subject in its artistic aspect is fully treated by Mrs. Jameson, *Poetry of Sacred and Legendary Art,* vol. i. pp. 98 – 110.

Formam viri dant Matthaao, 25
Quia scripsit sic de Deo,
Sicut descendit ab eo,
Quem plasmavit, homine.
Lucas bos est in figura,
Ut pnemonstrat in Scriptura, 30
Hostiarum tangens jura
Legis sub velamine.
Marcus, leo per desertum

Clamans, rugit in apertum,
Iter fiat Deo certum, 35
Mundum cor a crimine.
Sed Joannes, ala bina
Caritatis, aquilina
Forma fertur in divina
Puriori lumine. 40
Quatuor describunt isti
Quadriformes actus Christi,
Et figurant, ut audisti,
Quisque sua formula.
Natus homo declaratur, 45
Vitulus sacrificatur,

25 – 28. Mat. i. 1 – 16.

29 – 32. For explanation of these lines see ver. 37 – 42 in the next hymn.

37. *ald. Una]* The love of God, and of our neighbour. Thus H. de S. Victore *(Serm.* 97): Columba sancta Ecclesia est: quse duas alas habet per dilectionem Dei et proximi, a dextris dilec- tionem Dei. a sinistris dilectionem proximi.

41, 42. Clichtoveus: Scilicet Matthaeus Nativitatem, Lucas Passionem, Marcus Resurrectionem, et Johannes Ascensionem Christi.

Leo mortem deprasdatur,
Et ascendjt aquila.
Ecce forma bestialis,
Quam scriptura prophetalis r-o
Notat; sed materialis
Hsec est impositio.
Currunt rotis, volant alls;
Inest sensus spiritalis;
Rota gressus est sequalis, 55
Ala contemplatio.
Paradisus his rigatur,
Viret, floret, foecundatur,
His abundat, his lastatur
Quatuor fluminibus: eo
Fons est Christus, hi sunt rivi,
Fons est altus, hi proclivi,
Ut saporem fontis vivi
Ministrent fidelibus.

53 – 56. *currant... volanf]* Wheels *run on earth,* wings *soar to heaven.* In these symbolic representations of the Evangelists we hear of both ; for they now tell of the *earthly* life of the Saviour *(currunt rotis);* they now ascend to the contemplation of the *heavenly* world *(volant alis).* The *gressus aqualis* is the mutual consent of the four; they keep step. But the allusions to the medieval typology in this and the next following hymns are so . infinite and complex, that I should exhaust my room long before I had exhausted them. I must be content but to touch on a few, only observing

that the key to a multitude of them lies in Gregory the Great's homilies on Ezekiel
(Opp. vol. i. p. 1183, sqq. Bened. ed.).

57 – 64. Irenaeus, in his famous passage (iii. 11. 8), the foundation of so much
which has followed in the same line, does not refer to the four streams of Paradise, as
prefiguring the four F

> Horum rivo debriatis 65
> Sitis crescat caritatis,
> Ut de fonte pietatis
> Satiemur plenius.
> Horum trahat nos doctrina
> Vitiorum de sentina, 70
> Sicque ducat ad divina
> Ab imo superius.

Evangelists, near as such an application lay to him, and likening as he does the four
to the four principal winds, *iravraxSe" Trvfovras r]V afiOapffiay, Kai avaairvpovvras
rovst a. vQp&xovs.* Nor does St. Ambrose *(De Paradise,* c. 3), though finding a
mystical meaning in the four streams, find this one. We meet it in Jerome *(Ep. ad
Euseb.):* Quemadmodum unus fluvius erat Paradisi, qui in quatuor capita dmditnr;
ita unica Christi evan- gelica doctrina per quatuor ministros ad irrigandum et foecun-
dandum ecclesiss hortum est distributa; cf. *Prol. in Matt.;* Augustine, *De Civ. Dei,*
xiii. 21, and Durandus, *Rational.* vii. 46. The image has passed into the region of
Christian Art (Aringhi, vol. i. pp. 181, 183, 195), where we often find in the early
mosaics a hill surmounted by a cross, or by a lamb holding a cross, and four streams
flowing out in several ways from its sides ; in the words of Paulinus of Nola:

> Petram superstat Ipse, petra ecclesiss,
> De qu& sonori quatuor f ontes meant,
> Evangelistse, viva Christi flumina :

or, as we may express the thought in an English quatrain:

> As those four streams that had in Eden birth,
> And did the whole world water, four ways going, –
> With spiritual freshness fill our thirsty earth
> Four streams of grace from one cleft mountain flowing.

Sometimes, as in the magnificent mosaic filling the cupola of St. Mark's, at Venice,
the Evangelists appear as four aged men, each with his urn, from which a stream of
water flows.

65. *debriatis]* In some editions *ebrietatis;* but thus, plainly in ignorance of there
being such a word as *debrio.* It is a medieval form of *inebrio* (see Du Cange, s. v.); I
find it as early as Gregory the Great *(Hom.* 6. *in*

ADAM OF ST VICTOR.

II. DE SS. EVANGELISTIS.

> T)SALLAT chorus corde mundo,
> J- Hos attollat, per quos mundo
> Sonant Evangelia;
> Voce quorum salus fluxit,
> Nox recessit, et illuxit 5

Sol illustrans omnia.
Curam agens sui gregis
Pastor bonus, auctor legis,
Quatuor instituit,
Quadri orbis ad medelam ; 10
Formam juris et cautelam
Per quos scribi voluit.

II. Clichtoveus, *Elucidat Eccles.* vol. ii. p. 221 ; Daniel, *Thrs. Hymnol.* vol. ii. p. 88 ; Mone, *Hymn. Lat. Med, Mm.,* vol. iii. p. 130 ; Gautier, *Adam de 8. Victor,* vol. ii. p. 417.

I. This first line Gautier reads:
Plausu chorus lsetabundo.

9, 10. Augustine *(De Cons. Evany,* i. 2): Quatuor Evange- listse,... ob hoc fortasse quatuor, quoniam quatuor sunt partes orbis terrse, per eujus universitatem Christ! Eeclesiam dilatari ipso sui numeri sacramento quodammodo declararunt.

II. *cautelam]* A juristic word. Ducange explains it perfectly: *Cautdce* sunt instrumenta et charbe, quibus privilegia, jura, possessiones, etc.. asseruntur; hinc *cautela* dicta, quod sint veluti *cautio* (oo-ifiiAiira) res illas ita se habere.

Circa thema generale
Habet quisque speciale
Stili privilegium ; 15
Quod prsesignat in propheta
Forma pictus sub discreta
Vultua animalium.
Supra coelos dum oonscendit,
Summi Patris comprehendit 20
Natum ante secula;
Pellens nubem nostrse molis,
Intuetur jubar solis
Joannes in aquila.
Est leonis rugientis 25
Marco vultus. resurgentis
Quo claret potentia:
Voce Patris excitatus
Surgit Christus, laureatus
Immortali gloria. 20
Os humanum est Matthaei,
In humana form& Dei
Dictantis prosapiam :
Cujus genus sic contexit,
Quod a stirpe David exit 35
Per carnis materiam.

'25. *ntgientis]* The legend, frequent in the middle ages, and indeed already alluded to by Origen *(Hom.* xvii. *in Gen.* xlix. 9). that the lion's whelps were born dead, and first roused to life on the third day by the roar of their sire, was often contemplated as a natural type of the resurrection : so is it here. The subject will recur in a note on Adam of St Victor's Resurrection hymn, *Zyma veins expurgctur,* later in this volume.

Ritus bovis Lucae datur,
In qua forma figuratur
Nova Christus hostia :
Ara crucis mansuetus 40
Hie mactatur, sicque vetus
Transit observantia.
Paradisi hsec fluenta
Nova pluunt sacramenta,
Quse descendant coelitus. 45
His quadrigis deportatur

37. *Ritus]* So Clichtoveus, and this reading has manuscript authority (see Mone); but Daniel, Mone, and Gautierreadn'ciw; in favour of which may be urged that it is the rarer word, less likely therefore to find its way into a text to which it did not belong : yet *ritus* seems preferable after all.

40. *Ar& crucis]* Elsewhere he has a beautiful stanza on the cross *as the altar* on which Christ was offered:

Oh, quam felix, quam pneclara Agni sine macula,
Fuit bsee salutis ara, Qui mundavit specula
Rubens Agni sanguine, Ab antique crimine!

46. *His quadrigis]* Clichtoveus sees here, but wrongly, an allusion to Zech. vi.: Zacharias vidisse ipse dicit in spiritu quatuor quadrigas egredientes de medio duorum montium, et equos in eis varies, quibus jussum est ut totam terram perambu- larent: Hae autem quadrigae figura sunt SS. quatuor Evangelis- tarum, quibus Dei cognitio per universum orbem defertur et promulgatur. The traces are very slight among the. Fathers of any such application of Zechariah's vision of the four chariots : St Jerome (in loc.) giving a whole series of mystical interpretations of these, does not give this; while elsewhere he makes abundantly plain that the poet is still drawing his imagery from that grand vision of Ezekiel *(Ep. 60):* Matthaeus, Marcus, Lucas, et Johannes, *quadriga Domini* et verum Cherubim, per totum corpus oculati sunt, scintillae emicant, discurrunt fulgura, pedes habent rectos et in sublime tendentes, terga pennata et ubique

Mundo Deus, sublimatur
Istis area Vectibus.
Non est domus ruitura
Hac subnixa quadrature, 50
Hsec est domus Domini:
Gloriemur in hac domo,
Qua beate vivit homo
Deo junctus Homini.

volitantia. Tenent se mutuo, sibique perplexi sunt, et quasi rota in rota volvuntur, et pergunt quoquumque eos flatus S. Spiritus perduxerit. Cf. Augustine, *De Cons. Evang, i.* 7 ; and Durandus, *Rationale,* vii. 46, who indeed suggests quite another allusion, namely to Cant. v. 11.

48. *vectibus]* Cf. Exod. xxv. 13 – 15. The *vectes,* of shittim- wood overlaid with gold, were the staves which lifted the ark from the ground. They passed through the four golden rings at the four corners of the ark ; and, though being only in fact *two,* had *four* extremities. Sometimes these, but oftener the four golden rings through which they pass, are made symbolic of the four Evangelists. Thus Hugh of St Victor: Quatuor annuli, qui arcae inhaerent, quatuor sunt Evangelionim libri. Clichtoveus unites both : Per hos autem quatuor circulos et vectes illis in- sertos, quibus deferebatur area, intelliguntur Evangelistae, quorum narratione Christus, area mystica et spiritualis, in omnem mundi partem, quantum ad sui notitiam, est delatus.

50. *quadratura]* The allusion is to Rev. xxi. 16. The house stands firm which stands on a foursquare foundation: in this shape is the greatest strength and stability of all. See the symbolic use of the *iSos -rtrpdyuros* in the *Tabula* of Cebes, c. 18. Even so the fourfold history of the Lord's life, the euayye'Aioi' *rtrpdywvov,* is the strong foundation on which the faith of the Church reposes. Thus Durandus *(Rational.* vii. 46): Sicut enim inter cseteras formas quadratum, sic inter cseteras doctrinas Evangelium solidius et sta-bilius persevorat; nam illud undique stat, et ideo legitur (Apocal. c. 21) quod civitas in quadro posita eat.

4

SECTION 4

ADAM OF ST VICTOR.
  III. DE S. JOANNE EVANGELISTA.
  TTERBI vere substantivi,
  T Caro cum sit in declivi
  Temporis angustisi,
  In asternis verbum annis
  Permanere nos Johannis 5
  Docet theologia.
  Dum Magistri super pectus
  Fontem haurit intellects,
  Et doctrinse flumina,
  Fiunt, ipso situ loci, 10

  III. Gautier, *Adam de S. Victor,* vol. i. p. 241. This grand poem, a noble addition to our Latin hymnal, was by him published for the first time.

  1 – 6. I cannot but think that Dr Neale, to whom we are indebted for a translation of this hymn *(Mediaval Hymns,* 1863, p. 125), has failed to seize the true meaning of this first stanza. He renders it thus :
  That substantive Word, united

To the flesh, and therein plighted
To a life of misery sore,
Him to be the Co-eternal,
John's theology supernal
Testifieth evermore.

By *caro* he understands that flesh which the Word assumed at the Incarnation, and the contrast which the poet, so understood, would find taught in the theology of St John is that between

Verbo fides, auris voci,
Mens Deo contermina.
Unde mentis per excessus,
Carnis, sensus super gressus,
Errorumque nubila, 15
Contra veri soi!s lumen
Visum cordis et acumen
Figit velut aquila.
Verhum quod non potest dici,
Quod virtute creatrici 20
Cuncta fecit valde bona,
Iste dicit ab seterni
Patris nexu non secerni
Nisi tantum in persona.
Quem Matthseus de intactas 25
Matris alit casto lacte

Christ's human nature and his divine. But what then is made of tho *verbum Vcrbi* of the original, not to speak of other objections ? I take the passage altogether differently, and find a key to its meaning at 1 John ii. 16, 17 ; John xii. 48 ; cf. 1 Pet. i. 24, 25; understanding the poet to say as follows: The theology of John teaches us that while the flesh (that is, all which is in the world and of the world), declines, wastes, and decays, the word of the Word *(verbum Verbi),* all which Christ utters, endures for everlasting years, shall never pass away,, i

12. *Mentis per excessus].* Cf. Rev. i. 10, 19 – 18.' The poet urges that the *theology,* properly so called, belongs to St John. The other Evangelists set forth Christ's earthly ministry of labour and toil and passion ; St John rather the relation of Him, the creative Word, to the Father (Johni. 3; Gen. i. 1), and his return, at the end of time, *cum ultrici framed* (ver. 48) – these last words containing an allusion to that sublimest of all visions, Rev. xix. 11 – 16.

Cum labore et serumna,
Quem exaltat super cruce
Cornu bovis, penna Luck,
Ut serpentem in columna ; 30
Quem de mortis mausoleo
Vitse reddit Marci leo,
Scisais petris, terra mota,
Hunc deDeo Deum verum,

Alpha et *Q.,* patrem rerum 33
Solers scribit idiota.
Cujus lumen visuale
Vultus anceps, leves alse,
Rotas stantes in quadriga,
Sunt in coelo visa, prius
Quam hie esset vel illius
Forma capax, vel auriga.

36. *idiota].* A reference to Acts iv. 15, where Peter and John are described as homines sine litteris et *idiots* (Vulg.).

37 – 42. A difficult stanza. Gautier, who is prodigal of un- needed help, gives not a word of assistance here. The first throe lines contain no serious difficulty, or at any rate none which an accurate study of Ezekiel, chap. i. and x . will not remove. Thus we can explain *lumen visuale* by aid of Ezek. i. 18 ; z. 12 (Macarius calling the living creatures of the prophet *iott,9iip-a* fin); the *vultus anceps* by Ezek. i. 6, 10; the *leves alte* by i. 6, 9 ; und the *rota stantes* by i. 21. But what is exactly the force of the last three lines is harder to Bay. I take however Adam to mean that St John's eagle glance *(lumen visuale),* with all else ascribed to him here, was seen in heaven, anticipated in Ezekiel's vision, before John himself, or his Lord, the charioteer *(auriga)* of that wondrous chariot which John, with the other " living creatures," upbore, took form and shape on earth.

Illi scribunt Christum pati
Dolum, inde vim Pilati,
Cum coronS, spineS,. 45
Hie sublimis tractu pennse
Tractat Christi jus perenne
Cum ultrici framea.
Pennis hujus idiotee
Elevantur regis rotas, 50
Secus animalia ;
Et coelestes citharoedi
Se prosternunt Patris sedi
Canentes, Alleluia.

49, 50. Cf. Ezek. i. 19 : Cumque ambularent animalia, ambulabant pariter et rote juxta ea, et cum elevarentur animalia de terra, elevabantur simul et rotse (Vulg.).

5

SECTION 5

IV. DE S. JOANNE EVANGELISTA.

TTEKBUM Dei, Deo natum,
T Quod nee factum, nee creatum,
Venit de coelestibus,
Hoc vidit, hoc attrectavit,
Hoc de coelo reseravit
Joannes hominibus.
Inter'illos primitivos
Veros veri fontis rivos

IV. *Sequentia de Tempore,* Argentinse, 1516, p. 2 ; Clich- toveus, *Elucidat. Eccles.* Paris, 1556, p. 213 (not in the earlier editions); Rambach, *Anthol. Christl. Gesange,* Altona u. Leipzig, 1817, p. 340; Daniel, *Thes. Hymn.* vol. ii. p. 166; Mone, *Hymni IM. Med. Mvi,* vol. iii. p. 118. – This sublime hymn, though not Adam of St Victor's, proceeds from one formed in his school, and on his model, and is altogether worthy of him. It is, indeed, to my mind grander than his own, which has just preceded it. Daniel ascribes it to the thirteenth or fourteenth century, but has nothing certain to say about its authorship.

4 – 6. Cf. 1 Joh. i. 1.

6. It is seldom that we meet in Christian sapphics so fine a stanza as this, which occurs in a hymn of Damiani's to St John : and which may here be brought into comparison :

Fonte prorumpens fluvius pcrenni
Curris, arentis satiator orbis ;
Hausit ex pleno modo quod propinat
Pectore pectus.

7 – 9. See note on no. I. 57 – 64.

Joannes exsiliit;
Toti mundo propinare 10
Nectar illud salutare,
Quod de throno prodiit.
Coelum transit, veri rotam
Solis vidit, ibi totam
Mentis figens aciem ; 15
Speculator spiritalis
Quasi Seraphim sub alis
Dei vidit faciem.

12. *de throno]* Of. Rev. xxii. 1.

13. *Coelum transit]* Ambrose *(Prol. in Exp. in Luc.* c. 3): Nemo enim, audeo dicere, tanta sublimitate sapientise majestatem Dei vidit, et nobis proprio sermone reseravit. Transcendit nubes, transcendit virtutes coelorum, transcendit argelos, et *Verbum in principio* reperit, et *Verkum apud Deum* vidit.

15. *figens aciem]* Augustine *(In Joh., Tract.* 36) : Aquila ipse est Johannes, sublimium prsedicator, et lucis internse atque seternse fixis oeulis contemplator. Dicuntur enim et pulli aqui- larum a parentibus sic probari, patris scilicet ungue suspend!, et radiis solis opponi; qui firme contemplatus fuerit, filius agno- scitur; si acie palpitaverit, tanquam adulterinus ab ungue di- mittitur.

17, 18: These verses can only be fully understood by reference to Isai. vi. 2 (Vulg.), where "with twain he covered his face," i. e. the seraphim with two wings covered their (own) face, (faciem *suam,* as it should have been), is given: Duabus velabant faciem *(jus,* i. e. Domini. This was referred to the obscure vision of God vouch'safsd under the Old Covenant, so that even prophets saw but Si" tViJTrrpou, *(v cuviypari:* the wings of the seraphim being as a veil between God and them. Thus H. de S. Victore *(De Area Mor.* i. 3): Quod autem in Esaia scriptum est, Vela- bant faciem ejus, eo modo intelligi debet, quo dictum est ad Moysem: Non poteris videre faciem meam : non enim videbit me homo, et vivet. But St John, the poet would say, lookingAudiit in gyro sedis

Quid psallant cum citharoedis 20
Quater seni proceres :
De sigillo Trinitatis
Nostrse nummo civitatis
Impressit characteres.
Volat avis sine meta 2/j
Quo nee vates nee prophets

Evolavit altius :
Tam implenda, quam impleta,
Nunquam vidit tot secreta
Purus homo purius. so
Sponsus rubra veste tectus,
Visus, sed non intellectus,

beneath these covering wings *(seraphim sub alis)* saw the unveiled glory of God. A passage in St Bernard *(Opp.* 1, 955, Bened. ed.) shews that even in the middle ages they were aware *suam* would have been a more accurate translation.

19 – 21. Cf. Rev. iv. 4 ; xiv. 2. – 22 – 24. I said in the first edition, that by the "money of our city" we must understand the mind of man. This, as I am now convinced, was a mistake. Language is the money by aid of. which the moral and intellectual business of the world is carried on between man and man. On this St John set his stamp. Thus the Greek Logos, our English " Word," since they have past under his hands, mean something quite else, and something far higher and deeper- than they ever did, before he put a heavenly stamp, the *sigillum Trinitatis,* upon them.

25 – 30. *Volat avis]* Olshausen has taken this stanza, than w-hich sacred Latin poetry does not possess a grander, as the motto of his *Commentary on St John.* The *implenda* are tho Apocalypse, the *impleta* the Gospel.

31. Cf. Isai. Ixiii. 1 – 3; Rev. six. 11.

32. *non intellectus]* Cf. Isai. Hii. 2 – 4.

Redit ad palatium:
Aquilam Ezechielis
Sponsse misit, quse de coelis 35
Referret mysterium.
Dic, dilecte, de Dilecto,
Qualis adsit, et de lecto
Sponsi sponsse nuncia :
Die quis cibus angelorum, 40

34. *Aquilam Ezechielis]* Cf. Ezek. i. 10 ; Rev. iv. 7. 38, 39. So Clichtoveus; but Daniel and Mone:

Qualis sit, et ex dilecto
Sponsus sponsse nuncia:

But, not to say that, so read, the lines yield no tolerable sense, the reading violates the laws of rhyme which the Latin medieval poets observe. They allow themselves, it is true, greater freedom than we do : with us a syllable may not rhyme with itself, even when in the second line it belongs to an entirely different word from that to which it belonged in the first. Thus *vine* and *divine* are faulty as rhymes, though many – Spenser in particular – frequently admit them. But the medieval Latin poets, permitting rhymes such as these, so that a word may even rhyme with itself, if different senses be attached to it, as *mundus* the world, with *mundus* clean ; yet would not rhyme *mundus* to itself, the word in both places signifying the world. And rightly: such rhymes contradicting the fundamental idea of rhyme, which is that of likeness *with difference* – difference, if possible, in the sound, since that is the region in which rhyme moves ; but if not there, at least in the sense. Moreover the mystics had much to say of the *lectus Domini,* the deep rest and joy of perfected souls in innermost communion with their Lord ; deriving, as is needless to observe, the image from the Canticles.

40. *cibus angelorum]* Allusion to the Incarnation was often found in the words of the Psalmist (Ixxviii. 25), " Man did eat angels' food." The Eternal Word, from the beginning the food of angels, in the Incarnation became also the food of men. Thus Augustine *(In Ep. Joh. Tract.* 1): Erat enim [Vita] ab initio;

Qus e sint festa superorum
De Sponsi prsesentia.
Veri panem intellectus,
Coenam Christ! super pectus
Christ! sumptam resera: 45
Ut cantemus de Patrono,
Coram Agno, coram throno,
Laudes super sethera.

sed non erat manifestata hominibus ; manifestata autem erat angelis videntibus, et tanquam pane suo cibantibus. Sed quid ait Scriptura? Panem angelonun manducavit homo. Ergo manifestata est ipsa Vita in carne. So too Hildebert:

Quam felix Panis, caro felix, hostia dives,
In terns homines, qui pascit in a; there civee.

And Damiani yields a fine stanza here:

En ilia felix aquila Queg cteli cives vegetat,
Ad escam volat avida, Et nos in via recreat.

44, 45. That he who was named *iiriffrfiffios,* drew, from his greater nearness to that bosom (John xiii. 23), the deeper depths of his wisdom, has been often urged. Thus, to rescue the best lines from a poem otherwise of no eminent merit:

Hie, enjus alse virtutum scake, Prseminens scientise,
Hora cojnEe hausit plene Figens visum non elisum
Mese fontem gratise; In me, Solem glorise.
Ales alls spiritalis

46. *Patrono]* Led away by this word, Clichtoveus will have it, that the end to which the enraptured poet aspires is, that he may sing the praises of St John before the throne and the Lamb ! A reference to Rev. v. 9 should have taught him better. That *Patronus* may be used of a divine Person the following quotation makes abundantly plain *(Hymn, de Temp.* Argent.

p. 25):

Prsesta, Pater et Patrone,
Prsesta Fili, Pastor bone,
Prsesta, Spiritus amborum,
Medicinam peccatorum. V. LAUS S. SCRIPTUK. E.
STRINGERE pauca libet bona carminis hujus, et ipsum
Laude vel exili magnificare libet.
Hie ea triticea est pannisque allata farina
Hebrseo populo de Pharaonis humo.
Hie illud missum de coelo manna aaporum, 5
Omnem gustanti qui sapit ore cibum :

lit brevius curram per singula; praminet auro
In pretio; soli luce; sapore favo.
I lie facit humano generi quod sol facit orbi;
Sol terne lucet; luce cor ipse replet. 1 o
Tons est hortorum, puteus vel abyssus aquarurn,
Quarum potus alit pectora, corda rigat.

V. Leyser, *Hist. Poett. Med. Mvi,* p. 748. – It is the *Aurora,* a *metrical* version of the larger part of Holy Scripture, which, as Leyser informs us, the anonymous author of this poem has immediately in his eye. This is the explanation of the *carminis* in the first line, which would not otherwise be intelligible. He passes, however, at once from it to the praise of Scripture itself.

3, 4. Cf. Exod. xii. 34.

5, 6. The Jewish legend, that the manna tasted to every man like that which he liked the best, is well known (Wisd. xvi. 21). Even such heavenly manna, meeting every man's'desires, is Scripture. Gregory the Great *(Mor.* xxxi. 15): Manna quippe est verbum Dei, et quidquid bene voluntas suscipientis appetit. hoc profecto in ore comedentis sapit.

11. *Fons . . . puteus]* The words of Cant. iv. 15 (Vulg.): Fons hortorum; puteus aquarum viventium, quse flunnt impetu

Pascua coelestis, cellaria regia, coelum
Tot signis fulgens quot sacramenta tegens.
Hie calamus Scribse subito scribentis; hie arcus, 15
Qui curativo vulnere corda ferit.
Hie rota sive rotas, quarum ut mare visio mira,
In medioque rotse fertur inesse rota.

de Libano ; were applied to Scripture, a fountain for its abundance, a well for its depth. Thus a mystical expositor of the Canticles *(Bernardi Opp.* vol. ii. p. 125): Accipiamus in fonte sufficientiam doctrinse, in puteo secretum: in illo abundantiam, in isto alta mysteria.

13. *cellaria regia]* Cf. Cant. i. 3 (Vulg.): Introduxit me rex in cellaria sua. For the sense in which Scripture is thus the king's cellar, see St Bernard, *In Cant. Serm.* 23.

15. The old exposition of Ps. xlv. 2, namely, that the Holy Spirit was " the ready writer," and that the Psalmist would say his tongue did but utter, and his hand set down, that which was suggested by that Spirit, must explain this line. The poet transfers to all Scripture what had been spoken of a single Psalm.

Ibid, *arcus]* Gregory the Great, speaking of the different uses of the word "bow" in Scripture, observes *(Mor.* xix. 30): Aliquando autem per arcum etiam Sacra Seriptura signatur. Ipsa quippe arcus est Ecclesise, ipsa arcus est Domini, de qua ad corda hominum, sicut ferientes sagitte, sic terrentes sententise veniunt.

17. *Hie rota sive rota]* Cf. Ezek. i. 15, 16. At ver. 15, the prophet sees *"one* wheel;" apparuit *rota una* (Vulg.), while immediately in the next verse it is said, Et aspectus *rotarum* quasi visio maris. The wheel or wheels is Holy Scripture; and the wheel within wheel, of which the same verse presently speaks (quasi sit rota in medio rotse), is the New Testament; which is contained and shut up in the Old. Gregory the Great *(Hom.* 6 *in Ezek.): Rota ergo in medio rotse est; quia inest Testamento Veteri

Testamentum Novum. Quod Tt-stamentum Vetus promisit, hoc Novum exhibuit; et quod G

  Quatuor his facies, species est una: levantur,
  Stant, vel eunt, prout has Spiritus intro regit.   20 Hie liber in dextra regnantis scriptus et intus
    Et foris; intus habens mystica, plana foris. Hie Moysi facies, quse velo tecta, videri
    Non valet; at Christi luce retecta patet. Per Moysen typico, per Christum sanguine vero 25
  Hie liber aspersus, remque typumque gerit. Lex nova, res; antiqua, typus: diffusior illa,
  Hsec brevior: retegit ista, quod illa tegit.

illud occulte annunciat, hoc istud exhibitum aperte clamat. Prophetia ergo Testamenti Novi, Testamentum Vetus est; et expositio Testamenti Veteris, Testamentum Novum. Cf. Anselm, *Dial. Christ. et Jud.* iii. p. 539. – *Quarum ut mare visio mira]* Et aspectus rotarum et opus earum, quasi visio maris; (Ezek. i. 16, Vulg.) on which Gregory the Great *(ibid.):* Recte sacra eloquia visioni maris similia narrautur, quia in eis magna sunt volumina sententiarum, cumuli sensunm. These words have nothing answering to them in our text, or in the Hebrew.

    19. *Quatuor . . . una]* Gregory the Great *(ibid.):* Eota quatuor facies habere deseribitur [Ezek. i. 15], quia Scriptura Sacra per utraque Testamenta in quatuor partibus est distiucta. Vetus enim Testamentum in Lege et Prophetis, Novum vero in Evangeliis atque Apostolorum Actibus et Dictis. Una similitude ipsarum est quatuor (Ezek. i. 16), quia divina eloquia, etsi temporibus distincta, sunt tamen sensibus unita.

    21, 22. *intus et foris]* Richard of St Victor *(In Apoc.* v. 1): Liber qui in dextera Dei tenetur, est Sacra Scriptura. Intus scriptus est per spiritualem intelligentiam, foris per literam. Cf. Gregory the Great, *Hom. 9 in Ezek.* § 30.

    23, 24. Cf. Exod. xxxiv. 33 ; 2 Cor. iii. 13-16.

    25, 26. Cf. Exod. xxiv. 8 ; Heb. ix. 19. There is no mention, as is well known, in the former passage, of a sprinkling *oj the took* with blood.

    28. *retegit]* The lengthening of the last syllable of *retegit*Dumque rei testis typus exstat, abyssus abyssum
  Invocat. Utraque lex nomen abyssus habet. 30 Sic brevitate libri geminse clauduntur abyssi;
  Utraque magna nimis, nullus utramque capit. Jugiter hie legem meditari, inquirere, nosse,
    Quid nisi coelesti luce ciboque frui?
    Nil homini melius, quam si divina legendo 35
    Figat ibi vitam, quo sibi vita venit.
    Felix qui sitit hsec, et eodem fonte saporem
    Attrahit, ut vitam condiat inde suam.
    Nam nisi sic sapiat, sapientem non puto, quando
    Nil sibi, quod didicit codice, corde sapit. 40
    Qui studet Ms, vel propter opes vel propter honores,
    Non sapit; it prorsus a sapiente procul. Non nisi propter se vult se Sapientia quseri;

Qui colit hanc, audi, quse metit inde bona. Purior affectus, sensus fit clarior, et mens 45

Liberior mundo, carneque pressa minus. Lectio jugis alit virtutes, lucida reddit Intima, declinat noxia, vana fugat.

here, by the force of the arsis and on the strength of the two *mora* which must here be made, is not without its parallels among the best writers of elegiac verse. It was another sign of the way in which accent was penetrating into the domain of quantity, that the later Latin poets, most of all the medieval, assumed the entirest liberty of making short a long syllable – even a short vowel – at this place, whenever it was convenient to them. They used the same freedom with the hexameter, where, when the csesura occurred immediately after the arsis in the third foot, the syllable on which the pause thus fell, was always, and on this ground alone, considered long. The reader will find examples of both kinds in this volume, and should not regard them as neglects or ignorances, but as parts of a system.

6

SECTION 6

ST AMBROSE.

ST AMBROSE, born about 340, and probably at Treves, was intended by his father, who was prefect of Gaul, for a secular career. He practised as an advocate at Milan ; and was already far . advanced on the way to the highest honours and offices of the state, Laving been appointed about 370 Consular Prefect of Liguria, when it became plain that for him other and more lasting honours were in store. For, having won the affections alike of Catholics and Arians by the mildness and justice of his rule, on the death of Auxentius, bishop of Milan, A. d. 374, he was chosen as by a sudden inspiration, and under circumstances which are too well known to need being repeated, his successor, being as yet only a layman and unbaptized. He died in 397.

The hymns which are current under the name of *Ambrosian* are very numerous, yet are not all his; the name having been freely given to as many as were formed after the model and pattern of those which he composed, and to some in every way unworthy of him. The Benedictine editors do not admit more than twelve as with any certainty of his composition: and even these some in later times have affirmed to be " ascribed to him upon doubtful authority ; " so the *Dictionary of Greek and Roman Biography;* although no evidencecan well be stronger than that which in regard of some of them we possess.

After being accustomed to the softer and richer strains of the later Christian poeCs, to the more ornamented style of a Bernard or an Adam of St Victor – to the passionate sinking of himself in the great objects which he contemplates, that marks the first of these great poets of the Cross – to the melodies long drawn out and the abundant theological lore of the second, – it is some little while before one returns with a hearty consent and liking to the almost austere simplicity which characterizes the hymns of St Ambrose. It is felt as though there were a certain coldness in them, an *aloofness* of the author from his subject, a refusal to blend and fuse himself with it. The absence too of rhyme, for which the almost uniform use of a metre, very far from the richest among the Latin lyric forms, and with singularly few resources for producing variety of pause or cadence, seems a very insufficient compensation, adds to this feeling of disappointment. The ear and

This evidence is well brought together by Cardinal Thoma- sius in a preliminary discourse, *Ad Lectorem* (unpaged), prefixed to the *Hymnarium,* in the second volume of his *Works (J. M. Thomasii, S. R. E., Cardinalis, Opera Omnia,* Romse, 1747, vol. ii. p. 351 – 434). This book, of rare occurrence in England, is important in fixing the text, especially of the earlier hymns. The Cardinal's position gave him access to the oldest Vatican and other Italian MSS., of all which he made diligent and careful use. Ex illo libro, says Daniel, tanquam fonte primario hauriendum est. For an estimate of St Ambrose's merits in promoting the new Christian psalmody, see Rambach, *Anthol. Christl. Gesiinge,* vol. i. p. 58 – 60.

the heart seem alike to be without their due satisfaction.

Only after a while does one learn to feel the grandeur of this unadorned metre, and the profound, though it may have been more instinctive than conscious, wisdom of the poet in choosing it; or to appreciate that confidence in the surpassing interest of his theme, which has rendered him indifferent to any but its simplest setting forth. It is as though, building an altar to the living God, he would observe the Levitical precept, and rear it of unhewn stones, upon which no tool had been lifted. The great objects of faith in their simplest expression are felt by him so sufficient to stir all the deepest affections of the heart, that any attempt to dress them up, to array them in moving language, were merely superfluous. The passion is there, but it is latent and represt, a fire burning inwardly, the glow of an austere enthusiasm, which reveals itself indeed, but not to every careless beholder. Nor do we fail presently to observe how truly these poems belonged to their time and to the circumstances under which they were produced – how suitably the faith which was in actual conflict with, and was just triumphing over, the powers of this world, found its utterance in hymns such as these, wherein is no softness, perhaps little tenderness; but in place of these a rock-like firmness, the old Roman stoicism transmuted and glorified into that nobler Christian courage, which encountered and at length overcame the world.

7

SECTION 7

VI. DE ADVENTU DOMINI.
VENI, Redemptor gentium,
Ostende partum Virginis;
Miretur omne sseculum:
Talis decet partus Deum.
Non ex virili semine, 5
Sed mystico spiramine,
Verbum Dei factum est caro,
Fructusque ventris floruit.
Alvus tumescit Virginis,
Claustrum pudoris permanet, Id
Vexilla virtutum nlicant,
Versatur in templo Deus.

VI. *8. Ambrosii Opp.* Paris, 1836, vol. iv. p. 201 ; *Card. Thomasii Opp.* Romse, 1747, vol. ii. p. 351; Mone, *Hymn. Lat. Med. JEvi,* vol. i. p. 42. The German hymn-book is indebted to this immortal hymn of St Ambrose for one of its choicest treasures – I mean John Frank's Advent hymn, commencing:
Komm, Heidenheiland, Lbsegeld,

Komm, schbnste Sonne dieser Welt,
Lass abwarts flammen deinen Schein,
Denn so will Gott geboren sein.

It is not a translation, but a free recomposition of the original, beside which it is wellnigh worthy to stand, even though we may not count it, as Bunsen does, noch tiefer und lieblicher als das Lateinische.

Procedit e thalamo suo,
Pudoris aula regia,
Gemmse Gigas substantisB, 15
Alacris ut currat viam.

13. So Thomasius, on good MS. authority. The line is oftener read, *Procedens de thalamo suo,* which is quite inadmissible, no single instance in the genuine hymns of St Ambrose occurring of a line beginning with two spondees; invariably the second foot is an iambic. *Talis partus decet Deum,* which Daniel prints as the fourth line of this present hymn, is a transposition of words of which the older MSS. know nothing.

15. *Gigas]* The "giants" of Gen. vi. 4, were, according to the interpretation of the early Church, *gemina substantia ;* the ' "sons of God" who begot them (ver. 2) being angels, who formed unions with the " daughters of men." This scripture, so understood, must be brought into connexion with Ps. xviii. 6, (Vulg.), xix. 5 (E. V.), before we can enter into the full meaning of this line. In the "double substance" of the giants, thus born of heaven and of earth, Ambrose sees a resemblance to Him who in like manner was of twofold nature, divine and human. He might hardly have dared trace an analogy, but for the words of the Psalmist, referred to above, in which he saw an undoubted reference to the earthly course of the Lord. Elsewhere *(De Incarn. Dom.* c. 5) he unfolds his meaning at full: Quem [Christum] quasi gigantem Sanctus David propheta de- scribit, eo quod biformis geminseque naturse unus sit cousors divinitatis et corporis: qui tanquam sponsus procedens de thalamo suo exsultavit tanquam gigas ad currendam viam. Sponsus animse secundum Verbum: gigas terrse, quia usus nostri officia pereurrens, cum Deus semper esset seternus, Incarnationis sacra- menta suscepit. Thus too in another hymn he sings : Processit aula Virginis, Suse Gigas Ecclesise.

And Adam of St Victor, in a Christmas hymn:

Gigas velox, gigas fortis, Ad currendam venit viam,
Gigas nostrse victor mortis, Complens in se prophetiam
Accinctus potentia, Et legis mysteria.
Egressus ejus *v.* Patre,
Kegressus ejus ad Patrem,
Excursus usque ad inferos,
Recursus ad sedem Dei. 20
. lEqualis seterno Patri,
Carnis tropseo cingere,
Infirma nostri corporis
Virtute firmans perpeti.

17 – 20. He still draws his imagery from the 18th Psalm (19th, E. V.). It is written there of the sun : A summo coelo igressio ejus: et occursus ejus usque ad summum

ejus (Vulg.). This he adapts to Him who said concerning Himself: Exivi a Patre, et veni in mundum: iterum relinquo mundum et vado ad Patrem (John xvi. 28); who was acquainted with the deepest depths of humiliation, and afterwards with the highest heights of glory. In one of Augustine's *Sermons* (372, 3) he quotes this stanza as having just been sung in the Church: Hunc nostri Gigantis excursum brevissime ac pulcherrime cecinit beatus Ambrosius in hymno quem paulo ante cantastis.

22. *trofeo* I preferred *stropheo (strophium* or *stropheum = ffrptituy)* in the first edition; and defended the reading, though supported by inferior MS. authority, at some length; but erroneously, I am now convinced, and from insufficient acquaintance with the language of the Fathers. For them the risen flesh of Christ is constantly a *tropaum* which He erected in witness of his completed victory over death, and him that had the power of death; a rpdiraioc Kara Sai; iiiWj', with reference to the heathen custom of claiming and celebrating a victory by the erection of a *rpAirtuov* Kor' *ixf"""*- Thus Clichtoveus : Christus per carnem assumptam debellato diabolo victor evasit, ipsamque glorificatam carnem tandem coelo intulit.

Ibid, *cingere]* This is commonly read *oecingere* . but Mone, after Thomasius and the best MSS., as in the text. What, however, Mone means, when he remarks here, Ambrosius brauchtPrassepe jam fiilget tuum, 25

Lumenque nox spirat novum,

Quod nulla nox interpolet,

Fideque jugi luceat.

manchmal *den Infinitiv* mit dem Partieip wie die Griechen den Aorist, namlich als historischen Aorist, it ia difficult to guess. He can hardly take *eingere* as the infinitive active. What I understand St Ambrose to say is this: " Equal to the Eternal Father, Thou clothest Thyself with the trophy of redeemed flesh, so strengthening with everlasting strength the infirmities of our body."

25. *fulgef]* Thus in the *Evangel. Infant.* oh. 3, some enter the cave where the new-born child is laid, – et ecce repleta erat illa luminibus, lucernarum et caudelarum fulgoribus exce- dentibus, et solari luce majoribus. .

27. *nox interpolet)* Gregory the Great *(Moral.* iv. 6): Anti- quns hostis dies est, per naturam bene conditus; sed nox est, per meritum ad tenebras delapsus.

8

SECTION 8

PISTOR.

THF. only notice which I have of the probable author of the following hymn is drawn from Clichtoveus, p. 198 : Atictor ejus fuisse traditur eximius pater Henricus Pistor, doctor theologus Parisiensis, et in religiosO, domo Sti Victoris juxta Parisios monasticam vitam professus, qui etiam Concilio Constantinensi [1414 – 1418] inter-iuit, eaque tempestate, doctrina et virtute mirifice floruit. Referring to the histories of the Council of Constance, I can find no notice of his having taken any prominent share in its deliberations. Yet the internal evidence of the poem itself, as far as it reaches, is all in favour of this statement. That the writer was an accomplished theologian is plain ; and no less so that he was trained in the school, and formed upon the model, of Adam of St Victor, as indeed we have just been told that he was himself a Victorine as well.

9

SECTION 9

VII. DE S. JOHANNE BAPTISTA.
  et Baptista e
  -I- Diem istum chorus iste
  Veneretur laudibus.
  Vero die jam diescat,
  Ut in noatris elucescat 5
  Verus dies mentibus.
  Przecursore nondum nato,
  Nondum partu reserato,
  Reserantur mystica.
  Nostro sole tune exclusus, 10
  Verioris est perfusus
  Solis luce typica.
  Prius novit diem verum,
  Quam nostrorum sit dierum
  Usus beneficio. 15
  Hie renascens noadum natus
  Nondum nascens est renatus

Coelesti mysterio.
Clausa pandit, ventre clausus ;
Gestu plaudens, fit applausus 20
Messise prsesentias.
VII. CHchtoveus, *Etucidat. Eccles.* p. 198; Eambach, *Anthol. Christl. Gesdnge,*
p. 364; Daniel, *Thes. Hymnol.* vol. ii. p. 169.
20,21. Cf. Lukei. 41.
Linguse gestus obsequuntur;
Dum pro lingua sic loquuntur,
Serviunt infantise.
Tori fructus matri dantur, 25
Et jam matris excusantur
Sterilis opprobria.
Ortus tanti prsscursoris
Multus terret, sed terroris
Comes est lsetitia. 30
Se a mundo servans mundum,
Munde vivit intra mundum
In setate tenerL
Ne formentur a convictu
Mores, loco, veste, victu 35
Mundi fugit prospera.
Quem dum replet lux superna,
Vene lucis fit lucerna,
Veri solis lucifer;
Novus pra3co novse legis, 40
Immo novus novi regis
Pugnaturi signifer.
27. Cf. Luke i. 26.
29. *terret]* Luke i. 69. Daniel *has tenet;* one of the serious misprints with which his
book, in many respects so carefully and conscientiously prepared, too much abounds.
36. Cf. Luke i. 60; Matt. iii. 4.
38. *lucerna]* In the words of the Psalmist, Paravi lucernam Christo meo (Ps.
cxxxi. 7, Vulg.), it was very common to find an express prophecy of the Baptist. The
application was helped on by the reappearance of *lucerna* in the Lord's words about
him: Jlle erat lucerna ardens, et lucens (John v. 35, Vulg.). Cf. Augustine, *Serm.*
293, 4; Tertullian, *Adv. Jud.* 9.
39, *lucifer]* This title of the light-bringer, the morningSingular! prophetia
Prophetarum monarchia
Sublimatur omnium. 45
Hi futurum, hie . prsesentem,
Hi venturum, venientem
Monstrat iste Filium.
Dum baptizat Christum foris,
Hie a Christo melioris 50

Aquse tactu tingitur:
Duos duplex lavat flumen,
Isti nomen, illi numen
Baptistse conceditur.
Dum baptizat, baptizatur, 55
Dumque lavat, hie lavatur
Vi lavantis omnia.

star, was a nomen proprium applied to the Baptist: *Ti* c/uv?; *Rov Atyov, 6 vxms Rov itarts, (t* , Wc$iS/jos *i Rov fitov irpo&poftos,* as he was called in the Greek Church. Durandus: Ideo autem Joannes dictus est Lucifer, quia obtulit novum tempus. To remember this, explains St Bernard's comparison of him and that other 'son of the morning,' or *Lucifer* (Isai. xiv. 12, 13, Vulg.), who sought not to go before the true Sun, but to usurp his place: Lucet ergo Johannes, tanto verius quanta minus appetit lucere. Fidelis Lucifer, qui Solis justitise non usurpare venerit, sed prsenuntiare splendorem.

43 – 45. *sublimatur]* Clichtoveus sees here allusion to Christ's word concerning John, that he was a prophet, ' and more than a prophet' (Matt. xi. 9); compare Gregory the Great *(Hom.* 6 *in Evang.).* But it was often urged as a prerogative of the Baptist, that he was the only prophet who was himself prophesied of before his birth; thus by Augustine *(Serm.* 288, 3): Hie propheta, immo amplius quam propheta, prsenuntiari meruit per prophetam. De illo namque dixit Isaias,

Aquse lavant et lavantur,
His lavandi vires dantur
Baptizati gratia. 60
O lucerna Verbi Dei,
Ad coelestis Dos diei
Ducat luminaria,
Nos ad portum ex hoc fluctu,
Nos ad risum ex hoc luctu 65
Christ! trahat gratia.

Vox clamantis in deserto; and this is possibly the *singularis prophetia,* which the poet would say lifted him above all his fellows.

68 – 60. *lavantur]* So Marbod, in a leonine couplet:

Non eguit tergi, voluit qni flumine mergi :
Lotus aquas lavit, baptismaque sanctificavit.

66. Other hymns upon John the Baptist, though inferior to this, have much merit. Thus hi Daniel's *Thes. Hymnol.* vol. ii. p. 217, an anonymous one beginning thus, but not at all maintaining the merits of its opening:

In occursum prsscursoris Quaro nobis hebetatis
Concurrenti cordis, oris, Sol supernse veritatis
Curramus obsequio ; Prseluxit in sidere.
In lucerna Lux laudetur,
In prsecone veneretur Hie prsecursor et propheta,
Judex, Sol in radio. Immo prophetarum meta,
Legi ponens terminum,
Solem solet repentinum, Mire crepit, per applausum

Vel quid grande vel divinum Ventre matris clausus clausum
Tulgus segre capere : Bevelando Dominum.
Another by Adam of St Victor (Gautier, vol. ii. p. 28), yield these stanzas:
Ad honorem tuum, Christe, Laus est Regis in prseconis
Becolat Ecclesia Ipsius prseconio,
Prsecursoris et Baptistie Quem virtutum ditat donis,
Tui natalitia. Sublimat offlcio.
Agnnm monstrat in aperto Malta dooet millia.
Vox clamantis in deserto, Non lux iste, sed luceraa,
Vox Verbi prsenuncia. Christus vere lux seterna,
Ardens fide, verbo lucens, Lux illustrans omnia.
Et ad veram lucem ducens,

These stanzas swarm with patristic and Scriptural allusion. And first, the poet brings out the exceptional circumstance, that, while for all other saints it is the day of their death, it is that of *his* birth, his *natalitia,* which the Church celebrates – the *Uativity* of the Baptist. Augustine gives the reason *(Serm.* 290, c. 2): Denique quia in magno Sacramento natus est Johannes, ipsius solius justi natalem diem celebrat Ecclesia. Et natalis Domini celebratur, sed tanquam Domini. Date mihi alium servum, prseter Johannem, inter Patriarchas, inter Pro- phetas, inter Apostolos, cujus natalem diem celebret Ecclesia Christi. Passionum diem servis plurimis celebramus ; nativitatis diem nemini nisi Johanni. The reasons thus touched on by Augustine, Durandus *(Rationale,* vii. 14) gives at full. They are found in the words of the angel, that many should rejoice *at his birth* (Luke i. 14); that he should be filled with the Holy Ghost *from his mother's womb* (i. 15); and in his relation to his Lord as the morning star, whose appearing heralded the rising of the true Sun; Cant. ii. 12 being in like manner applied to him; and his the voice of the turtle, which, being heard in the land, told that winter was past, and the rain was over and gone. Nor should the reader miss, in the second stanza, the play with the words *Vox* and *Verbum,* which is indeed much more than a play – John a *sound,* a startling cry in that old world to which he himself belonged, a *voice* crying in the wilderness ; but Christ a new utterance out of the bosom of the Eternal, an articulate *Word.* Compare Origpn *(In Joan.* ii. 26); and Augustine *(Serm.* 288, 3). The next line, *Ardens fide, verbo lucens,* is a commentary on the Saviour's words: Ille erat lucerna *ardens* et *lucens.* VIII. DE NATIVITATE DOMINI.

PUER natus in Bethlehem,
Unde gaudet Jerusalem.
Hie jacet in prsesepio,
Qui regnat sine termino.
Cognovit bos et asinus
Quod puer erat Dominus.

VIII. Corner, *Prompt. Devot.* p. 278; Daniel, *Thes. Hymnol.* vol. i. p. 334. – This hymn, of a beautiful simplicity, and absorbing easily so much theology in its poetry, continued long a great favourite in the Lutheran Churches of Germany; surviving among them till wellnigh the present day.

5. bos et asinus] Two passages in the Old Testament supplied the groundwork to that wide-spread legend which painters have so often made their own, and to which here the poet alludes, viz. that the ox and the ass recognized and worshipped that Lord whom the Jews ignored and rejected. The first, Isai. i/3: Cognovit bos possessorem suum, et asinus prsesepe domini sui: Israel autem me non cognovit, et populus meus non intel- lexit (Vulg.); in which was seen a prophetic reference to the manger at Bethlehem; and no less at Hab. iii. 2, where the Septuagiut has strangely enough, *in peffif* 5iio *tyav yvnurBfioTi:* and the old Italic: lu medio duorum animalium innotesceris. The *bos* and *asinus* were further mystically applied to the Jew and Gentile, who severally, in the persons of the shepherds and the wise men, were worshippers at the cradle of the new-born King.

6. There is some merit in these lines from the *Musa Angli-* U
Reges de Saba veniunt,
Auram, tus, myrrham offerunt.
Intrantes domum invicem
Novum salutant Principem. 10
De matre natus Virgine
Sine virili semine;
Sine serpentis vulnere
De nostro venit sanguine;
In carne nobis similis, 15
Peccato sed dissimilis;
Ut redderet nos homines
Deo et sibi similes.
In hoc natali gaudio
Benedicamus Domino: 20
Laudetur sancta Trinitas,
Deo dicamus gratias.

canes, vol. i. p. 115. Christian alcaics, which are not wholly profane, are so rare, that on this score they are worth quoting :
Doloris expers, Mater amabilem
Enixa prolem gramineo in toro
Deponit immortale pignus,
Arma timens pecorumque vultus.
Ast ille cunas fortiter occupat,
Faasusque numen, et jubare anreo
Perfusus, absterret paventes
Quadrupedes animosus infans.

7. *Rcges]* The old Church legend – the Roman Church makes it almost a matter of faith – that the wise men from the East were kings, rests on Isai. be. 3; Ps. Ixxii. 10, 15- To this last passage also we owe *Saba,* as the interpretation of the iraToAtii of Matt. U. 1.

10

SECTION 10

PETER THE VENERABLE.

PETER the Venerable, born 1092 or 1094, of a noble – family of Auvergne, was elected in 1122 abbot of Clugny – being constituted thereby the chief of that reformed branch of the Benedictine order, the headquarters of which were at Clugny in Burgundy. This admirable man, one of that wonderful galaxy of illustrious men who adorned France in the first half of the twelfth century, was probably only second, although second by a very long interval, to St Bernard in the influence which, by his talents and virtues, and position at the head of a great and important congregation, he was able to exercise upon his time. His history is in more ways than one bound up with that of his greater cotemporary. He is indeed now chiefly known for his keen though friendly controversy with St Bernard, on the respective merits of the "black" and "white" monks, the Clugnian, and the yet later Cistercian, who now in their fervent youth were carrying the world before them. The correspondence is as characteristic in its way as that with which it naturally suggests a comparison, between St Augustine and St Jerome; casting nearly as much light on the characters of the men, and far more on that of their times. But besides this, it was with him that Abelard found shelter, after the condemnation of his errors, and to his good offices the reconciliation which was effected before Abelard's

1 /I G 53 1 A death, between him and St Bernard, was owing. Nor ought it to be forgotten, that to Peter the Venerable western Christendom was indebted for its first accurate acquaintance with the Koran. Travelling in Spain, he was convinced how important it was that the Church should be thoroughly acquainted with that system with which it was in hostile contact, and at a great cost he caused a translation of the Koran into Latin to be made. That he should have done this, is alone sufficient to mark him as no common man. He has also himself written a refutation of Mahometanism. He died in 1156.

The poems which bear his name are not considerable in bulk, nor can they be esteemed of any very high order of merit. Yet apart from their interest as productions of one who played so important a part in the history of his age, these lines which immediately follow, and another hymn occupying a later place in this volume, possess a sufficient worth of their own to justify their insertion.

IX. DE NATIVITATE DOMINI.

/(CELUM gaude, terra plaude,
-' Nemo mutus sit in laude:
Auctor rerum creaturam
Miseratus perituram,

IX. *BiUiotheca Cluniacensis,* Paris, 1614, p. 1349.

Praebet dextram libertatis 5
Jam ab hoste captivatis.
Coelum terras fundit rorem,
Terra gignit Salvatorem.
Chorus cantat angelorum,
Cum sit infans Rex eorum. 10
Venter ille virginalis,
Dei cella specialis,
Fecundatur Spiritu. Et ut virga parit florem, Sic et Virgo Redemptorem, 15
Carnis tectum habitu. Matris alitur intactas Puer-Deus sacro lacte,
Res stupenda sseculis !
Esca vivit alien& 20
Per quem cuncta manent plena;
Nullis par miraculis!
Pastu carnis enutritur
Vitam carni qui largitur :
Matris habet gremium, 25
Quem et Patris solium':
Virgo natum consolatur,
Et ut Deum veneratur.

ALANUS.

ALANUS de Insulis, or of Lille, in Flanders, called Doctor Universalis from the extent of his acquirements, was born in the first half of the twelfth century,' and died at the beginning of the next. His life is as perplexed a skein for the biographer to disentangle as can well be imagined, abundantly justifying the axiom of Bacon : Citius emergit veritas ex errore quam ex confusione – the main perplexity arising here from the difficulty of determining whether he and Alanus, also de Insulis, the friend of St Bernard and bishop of Auxerre, be one and the same person. The *Biographie Universelle* corrected this as an error, although a generally received one ; Oudinus, it is true, having already shewn the way *(De Script. Eccles.* vol. ii. p. 1389 – 1404) ; but Guericke and Neander again identify the two. The question, however, does not belong to this volume. The Doctor Universalis is undoubtedly the poet, and it is only with the poet we are here concerned.

The only collected edition of his works was published by Charles de Visch, Antwerp, 1654 ; a volume so rare that only in the Imperial Library at Paris was I able to get sight of it, and to obtain a perfect copy of a very beautiful Ode, inserted later in this volume. His *Parables* were a favourite book before the revival of learning ; but the work of his which enjoyed the highest reputation was a long moral poem, entitled *AntiClaudianus,* it does not very clearly appear why. (See Leyser, p. 1017, who gives copious extracts from it.) I know not whether it will bear out the praises which have been bestowed upon it and on its author. One says of him (Leyser, p. 1020): Inter sevi sui poetas facile familiam duxit; and Oudinus (vol. ii. p. 1405), characterizes the poem as singulari festivitate, lepore, et elegantia conscriptum; see also Rambach, *Antliol. Christl. Gesange,* vol. i. p. 329. Certainly, in the following lines, the description of a natural Paradise, Ovidian both in their merits and defects, we must recognize the poet's hand.

Est locus ex nostro secretus climate, tractu
Longo, nostrorum ridens fennenta locorum:
Iste potest solus quidquid loca csetera possunt.
Quod minus in reliquis, melius suppletur in uno;
In quo pubescens tenera lanugine florum,
Sideribus stellata suis, succensa rosarum
Muriee, terra novum contendit pingere coelum.
Non ibi nascentis exspirat gratia floris,
Nascendo moriens; nee enim rosa, mane puella,
Vespere languet anus, sed yultu semper eodem
Gaudens interni juvenescit munere veris.
Hunc florem non urit hyems, non decoquit sestas,
Non ibi bacchantis Borese furit ira, nec illic
Fulminat aura noti, nec spicula grandinis instant.
Ambit silva locum, muri mentita figuram:
Non florum prsedatur opes, foliique capillum
Tondet hyeras, teneram florum depasta juventam.
Sirenes nemorum, eitharistse veris, in illum
Convenere locum, mellitaque carmina sparsim
Elsewhere he has this couplet:
Ver, quasi fullo novus, reparando pallia pratis
Horum suocendit muricis igne togas. Commentantur aves, dum gutturis organa
pulsant.
In medio lacrymatur humus, fletuque beato
Producens lacrymas, fontem sudore perenni

Parturit, et dulces potus singultat aquarum.
Exuit iugemitas (?) facies argenteus amnis ;
Ad purl remeans elementi jura, nitore
Fulgurat in proprio, peregrina fsece solutus.

The following lines form part, or, as Oudinus asserts, the whole, of the genuine epitaph of Alanus. The last of them is striking enough :

Alanum brevis hora brevi tumulo sepelivit,
Qui duo, qui septem, qui totum scibile scivit;
Scire eunm moriens dare vel retinere nequivit.

X. DE NATIVITATE DOMINI.

TTIC est qui, carnis intrans ergastula nostras,
J-J- Se poenas vinxit, vinctos ut solveret; seger
Factus, ut asgrotos sanaret; pauper, ut ipsis
Pauperibus conferret opem; defunctus, ut ipsa
Vita donaret defunctos: exsulis omen 5
Passus, ut exilio miseros subduceret exul.
Sic livore perit livor, sic vulnere vulnus,
Sic morbus damnat morbum, mors morte fugatur :
Sic moritur vivens, ut vivat mortuus ; hasres
Exulat, ut servos hasredes reddat; egenus 10
Fit dives, pauperque potens, ut ditet egenos.
Sic liber servit, ut servos liberet ; imum
Summa petunt, ut sic ascendant infima summum ;
X. *Alani Opera,* ed. C. de Visch, Antwerp, 1654, p. 377.
Ut nox splendescat, splendor tenebrescit; eclipsi
Sol verus languescit, ut astra reducat ad ortum. 15
Egrotat medicus, ut sanet morbidus segrum.
Se coelum terrse conformat, cedrus hysopo,
Ipse gigas nano, fumo lux, dives egeno,
JEgroto sarms, servo rex, purpura sacco.
Hie est, qui nostram sortem miseratus, ab aula 20
./Eterni Patris egrediens, fastidia nostrse
Sustinuit sortis; sine crimine, criminis in se
Defigens ptcnas, et nostri damna reatfts. io6

HILDEBERT.

TTILDEBERT, born in 1057, shared as the scholar of ."- Berengarius, in all the highest culture of his age ; and having himself taught theology for a while at Mans, was in 1097 consecrated bishop of that see, and in 1125 became archbishop of Tours. A wise and gentle prelate, although not wanting in courage to dare, and fortitude to endure, when the cause of truth required it, he must ever be esteemed one of the fairest ornaments of the French Church. In his *Letters* he more than once seeks earnestly to check some of the superstitions of his time, as, for instance, the exaggerated value attributed to pilgrimages made to the Holy Land, and to the shrines of saints. He died in 1134. There is an interesting sketch of his character and of his work in Neander's *Life of St Bernard,* pp. 447 – 458.

His verses amount, as the Benedictine editors calculate, to ten thousand or more. The enforced leisure of imprisonments and exiles may have given him opportunity for composing so many. Of these a great number consist of versifications of scriptural history, or of the legends of saints, in heroic or elegiac verse, sometimes rhyming and sometimes not, and possess a very slight value. More curious than these is a legendary life of Mahomet, whereof Ampere (vol. iii. p. 440) has given a brief analysis; and his lines on the death of his master Berengarius display true feeling, and a verydeep affection : however hard we may find it to go along, in every particular, with praise such as this:

Cujus cura sequi naturam, legibus uti, .
Et mentem vitiis, *ora negare dvlis ;*
Virtutes opibus, verum prseponere falso,
Nil vacuum sensu dicere, nil facere.

Two or three further specimens of his poetry will shew that he could versify with considerable elegance and ease, as the following lines from a poem in praise of England'.

Anglia, terra ferax, tibi pax diuturna quietem,
Multiplicem luxum merx opulenta dedit.
Tu nimio nec stricta gelu, nee sidere fervens,
dementi coelo temperieque places.
Cum pareret Natura parens, varioque favore
Divideret dotes omnibus una locis,
Elegit potiora tibi, matremque professa,
Insula sis locuples, plenaque pacis, ait,
Quidquid luxus amat, quidquid desiderat usus,
Ex te proveniet, aut aliunde tibi.
Te siquidem, licet occiduo sub sole latentem,
Quseret et inveniet merce beata ratis: &c.

And the following have a real energy. They make part of the soul's complaint against the tyranny of the flesh:

Angustse fragilisque domus jam jamque ruentis
Hospita, servili conditione premor.
Triste jugum cervice gero, gravibusque catenis
Proh dolor! ad mortem non moritura trahor.
Hei mihi! quam docilis falli, quam prompta subire
Turpia, quam velox ad mea danma fui.

But grander still are the lines which follow. I have not inserted them in the body of this collection, lest Imight seem to claim for them that entire sympathy which I am very far from doing. Yet, believing as we may, and, to give any meaning to a large period of Church history, we must, that Papal Rome of the'middle ages had a work of God to accomplish for the taming of a violent and brutal world, in the midst of which she often lifted up the only voice which was anywhere heard in behalf of righteousness and truth – all which we may believe, with the fullest sense that her dominion was an unrighteous usurpation, however overruled for good to Christendom, which could then take no higher blessing, – believing this, we may freely admire these lines, so nobly telling of that true strength of spiritual power, which may be perfected in the utmost weakness of all other power. It is the city of Home which speaks :

Dum simulacra mihi, dum numma vana placerent,
Militia, populo, moenibus alta fui:
At simul effigies, arasque superstitiosas
Dcjiciens, uni sum famulata Deo ;
Cesserunt arces, cecidere palatia divum,
Servivit populus, degeneravit eques.
Vix scio quse fuerim : vix Romse Roma recordor;
Vix sinit occasus vel meminisse mei.
Gratior hsec jactura mihi successibus illis,
Major sum pauper divite, stante jacens.
Plus aquilis vexilla cracis, plus Csesare Petrus,
Plus einctis ducibus vulgus inerme dedit.
Stans domui terras ; infernum diruta pulso ;
Corpora stans, animas fracta jacensque rego.
Tune miserse plebi, nunc principibus tenebrarum
Impero ; tune urbes, nunc mea regna polus :
Quod ne Csesaribus videar debere vel armis,
Et species rerum meque meosque trahat,
Armorum vis illa perit, ruit alta Senatus
Gloria, procumbunt templa, theatra jacent.

11

SECTION 11

Rostra vacant, edicta silent, sua prsemia desunt
  Emeritis, populo jura, colonus agris.
Ista jacent, ne forte meus spem ponat in illis
  Civis, et evacuet spemque bonumque crucis.

As modern Rome builds in here and there an antique frieze or pillar into her more recent structures, so the poet has used here, as will be observed, three or four lines that belong to the old Latin anthology.

XI. DE NATIVITATE CHRISTI.

'VTECTAREUM rorem terris instillat Olympus,
-L' Totam respergunt flumina mellis humum,
Aurea sanctorum rosa de prato Paradisi
Virginia in gremium lapsa, quievit ibi.
Intra virgineum decus, intra claustra pudoris,
Colligit angelicam virginis aula rosam. Flos roseus, flos angelicus, flos iste beatus
Vertitur ill foenum, fit caro nostra Deus.

XI. *Hildeberti et Marbodi Opp.* p. 1313. – These very beautiful lines – for their violation of some ordinary rules of the classical hexameter and pentameter ought not to conceal their beauty from us – form part of a longer poem ; but gain much through being disengaged from verses of an inferior quality.

7. *Flos roseus]* Elsewhere Hildebert has some lines on Christ, the rose of Paradise, of which in like manner the real grace is not affected by some metrical and other faults. After a long description of the loveliness of this world, he turns suddenly round:

At quia flos mundi cito transit et aret, ad illam
Quse nunquam marcet currite, quseso, rosam :
Vertitur in carnem Verbum Patris, at sine damno,
Vertitur in matrem virgo, sed absque viro. 10
Lumine plena suo manet in nascente potestas,
Virgineum florens in pariente decus,
Sol tegitur nube, foeno flos, cortice granum,
Mel cerS, sacco purpura, carne Deus. yEtheris ac terrse sunt hsec quasi fibula, sancto 15
Foederis amplexu dissona regna ligans.
Est rosa quse dicit, Ego flos campi; rosa certe
Aurea, principii nescia, fine carens.
Floruit in coelis, in mundo marcuit; illic
Semper olens, istic pallida facta parum.
Hunc florem Paradisus habet, Seraphim videt, orbis
Non capit, infernus nescit, adorat homo.

11. *Lumine]* Should we not read *Numine 1* ADAM OF ST VICTOR

XII. IN NATIVITATE DOMINI.

POTESTATE, non natura
J- Fit Creator creatura,
Reportetur ut factura
Factoris in gloria.
Prsedicatus per prophetas, 5
Quem non capit locus, aetas,
Nostrae sortis intrat metas,
Non relinquens propria.
Ctelum terris inclinatur,
Homo-Deus adunatur, 10
Adunato famulatur
Coelestis familia.
Rex sacerdos consecratur
Generalis, quod monstratur

XII. Mone, *Hymni Lat. Med. Mm,* vol. ii. p. 85 (but without ascription to the author); Gautier, *Adam de S. Victor,* vol. i. p. 10. – Dr. Neale, who before Mone had printed this grand hymn from a MS. missal *(Seqwntia,* p. 80), had rightly divined Adam of St Victor to be its author. It is certainly the richest and fullest of his Nativity hymns ; although the *Jubilemus Salvatori,* first rescued by Gautier from oblivion (vol. i. p. 32), for which I have been unable to find room, does not fall very far behind it

3. *Rtj, ortetur]* Mone reads *Reparetur.*

11, 12. Cf. Luke ii. 10, 13; Matt. iv. 11; Luke xxii. 43; Matt. xxviii. 2.

7. *metas]* So in the Greek theology,
Cum pax terris nuntiatur 15
Et in altis gloria.
Causam quseris, modum rei ?
Causa prius omnes rei,
Modus justum velle Dei,
Sed conditum gratia. 20
O quam dulce condimentum,
Nobis mutans in pigmentum
Cum aceto fel cruentum,
Degustante Messia!
O salubre sacramentum, 25
Quod nos ponit in jumentum,
Plagis nostris dans unguentum,
Ille de Samaria.
Ille alter Elisxus,
Reputatus homo reus, 30
Suscitavit homo-Deus
Sunamitis puerum.

23, 24. Cf. Matt. xxvii. 34; Ps. Ixix. 21.

26 – 28. The poet claims here, as so many have done before him, the good Samaritan of the parable as the type of Christ. He does so more at length in a sequence on the Circumcision (Gautier, *Adam de S. Victor,* vol. i. p. 49) :

Dum cadit secus Jericho vir Hierosolomita,
Samaritanus affuit, quo lapso datur vita.
Perduxit hunc in stabulum dementia divina,
Vinum permiscens oleo suavi medicina.
Curantis segri vulnera sunt dulcia f omenta,
Dum cunctis prenitentia (uit reis inventa.
Bini dati denarii suut duo Testamenta,
Bum Christus, finis utriusque, complet sacramenta.

29 – 32. Cf. 2 Kin. iv. 7 – 37 ; and on Elisha as a type of Christ, Bernard, *In Cant. Serm.* 15, 16.

Hie est gigas currens fortis,
Qui, destructa lege mortis,
Ad amoena primae sortis 35
Ovem i'ert in humerum.
Vivit, regnat Deus-homo,
Trahens Oreo lapsum pomo;
Coelo tractus gaudet homo,
Denum complens numerum. *40*

39, 40. An allusion to that interpretation of the parable of the ten pieces of silver (Luke xv. 8 – 10), which makes the nine pieces which were *not* lost to be the nine ranks of angels who stood in their first obedience, and the one lost to be the race of mankind.

12

SECTION 12

MAUBUKN.

JOHN Mauburn was born at Brussels in 1460, and died abbot of the Cloister of Livry, not far from Paris, in 1502. He was the author of several ascetic treatises, among others the *Rosetum Spirituale,* from which the following hymn is derived.

XIII. DE NATIVITATE DOMINI.

HETJ ! quid jaces stabulo,
Omnium Creator,
Vagiens cunabulo,
Mundi reparator ?

XIII. Mauburnus, *Rosetmn Spirituale,* Duaci, 1620, p. 416; Corner, *Prompt. Devot.* p. 280; Daniel, *Thes. Hymnol.* vol. i. p. 335. – Those three stanzas are taken from a longer poem, consisting of thirteen in all, which commences:

Eja, mea anima,
Bethlehem eamus.

I have not selected them, for they had long since been separated from the context, and constituted into a Christmas hymn – a great favourite in the early reformed Churches, so long as the practice of singing Latin compositions survived among them.

It still occasionally retains a place in the German hymnals, but now in an old translation which commences thus :

Warum liegt im Krippelein – As this hymn sometimes appears with a text differing not a littleSi rex, ubi purpura, 5

Vel clientum murmura,
Ubi aula regis ?
Hie omnis penuria,
Paupertatis curia,
Forma novse legis. 10
Istuc amor generis
Me traxit humani,
Quod se noxa sceleris
Occidit profani.
His meis inopiis 15
Gratiarum copiis
Te pergo ditare:
Hocce natalitio,
Vero sacrificio,
Te volens beare. 20
O te laudum millibus
Laudo, laudo, laudo ;
Tantis mirabilibus
Plaudo, plaudo, plaudo :
Gloria, sit gloria, 25
Amanti memoria
Domino in altis:
Cui' testimonia
Dantur et prseconia
Coelicis a psaltis. 30

from that here presented, I may say that mine has been obtained, cot from any secondary source, but from the *Rosetum* itself; not indeed from the original edition, Basle, 1491, which lay not within my reach, but from that referred to above, which has much appearance of having been carefully edited, XIV. DE NATIVITATE DOMINI.

OTER foecundas, o ter jucundaa
Beatse noctis delicias,
Quae suspiratas e coelo datas
In terris paris delicias!
Gravem primaevse ob lapsum Evse 5
Dum jamjam mundua etnoritur,
In carne meus, ut vivat, Deus,
Sol vitas, mundo suboritur.
Sternum Lumen, immensum Numen
Pannorum vinculis stringitur ; 10
In vili caula, exclusus aula,
Rex cceli bestiis cingitur.

In cunis jacet, et infans tacet
Verbum, quod loquitur omnia;
Sol mundi friget, et flamma riget: 15
Quid sibi volunt haec omnia ?

XIV. [Walraff,] *Corolla Hymnorum,* Colonise, 1806, p. 8; Daniel, *Thes. Hymnol.*
vol. ii. p. 339. – This pretty poem, for it can claim no higher praise, is certainly
not old, can scarcely be earlier than the fifteenth century; and thus belongs, if I am
right in my conjecture, to a period when the fountains of inspiration, at least of that
inspiration which has given us th great medieval hymns, were very nearly exhausted.

13

SECTION 13

XV. SEQUENTIA DE TRIBUS REGIBUS.
  MAJESTATI sacrosanctie
  Militans cum triumphante
  Jubilet Ecclesia:
  Sic versetur laus in ore,
  Ne gravetur cor torpore, ' 5
  Quod degustat gaudia.
  Novum parit virga florem,
  Novum monstrat stella solem;
  Currunt ad prsesepia
  Reges magi, qui non vagi, 10
  Sed prsesagi, gaudent agi
  Stella duce prsevi&.
  Trium regum trinum munus;
  Christus, Homo-Deus, unus
  Cum carne et anima; *in*
  Deus trinus in personis
  Adoratur tribus donis,

Unus in essentia.

XV. Corner, *Prompt. Devot.* p. 367; Daniel, *Thes. Hymnol.* vol. v. p. 48.

14. Compare on these Eastern Magi the grand lines of Pru- dentius (*Cathemer.* xii. 1 – 76), which rank among the noblest passages of his poetry.

Myrrham ferunt, tus, et aurum,
Plus pensantes, quam thesaurum, 20
Typum, sub quo veritas;
Trina dona, tres figure :
Rex in auro, Deus in ture,
In myrrha mortalitas.
Turis odor deitatem, 25
Auri splendor dignitatem
Regalis potentise:
Myrrha caro Verbo nupta,
Per quod manet incorrupta
Caro carens carie. $0
Tu nos, Christe, ab hue valle
Due ad vitam recto calle
Per regum vestigia;
Ubi Patris, ubi Tui,
Et Amoris Sacri, frui 35
Mereamur gloria. Amen.

36. The following lines, blending into a single stanza the twofold homage of the Jewish shepherds and the Gentile sages, were great favourites at and after the Reformation. They belong probably to the fourteenth century (Rambach, *Anthol. Christl. Gesdnge,* p. 333).

Quem pastores laudavere,
Qnibus angeli dixere,
' Absit vobis jam timere'
Natua est Rex gloriEe:
Ad quem reges ambulabant,
Aurum, tus, myrrham, portabant;
Hsec sincere immolabant
Leoni victoriss.

PRUDENTIUS.

A URELIUS Clemens Prudentius was born, as there -Li- is good reason to suppose, in Spain. But the evidence from certain expressions which he uses, in favour of Saragossa as his birth-place, is equally good in favour of Tarragona, and of Calahorra ; and therefore, since he could not have been born in more places than one, is worthless in regard of them all. All that we know with any certainty about him, is drawn from a short autobiography in verse, which he has prefixed to his poems, and which contains a catalogue of them. From this we gather that he was born A. d. 348 ; that, having enjoyed a liberal education, and for a while practised as a pleader, he had filled important judicial posts in two cities which he does not name, and had subsequently received a high military appointment at the Court; but that now, in his fifty-seventh year, in which this sketch of his life was given, he looked back with sorrow and shame to the sins and follies of his youth, to the worldliness of his middle age, and desired to dedicate what remained of his life to an earnest and devoted service of God. The year of his death is not known.

Earth, who in his *Adversaria* is always prodigal in his commendations of the Christian poets, is most prodigal of all in regard of Prudentius. Poeta eximius
eruditissimus et sanctissimus scriptor – nemo divinius
de rebus Christianis unquam scripsit – such is theordinary language which he uses about him : and even Bentley, who for the most is not at all so lavish of admiration, calls him " the Horace and Virgil of the Christians." Extravagant praises, compensated on the other side by as undue depreciation ! For, giving, as it must be owned he does, many and distinct tokens of belonging to an age of deeply sunken taste, yet was his gift of sacred poetry a most true one ; and when it is charged against him in the *Dictionary of Greek and Roman Biography,* that " his Latinity is not formed, like that of Juvencus and Victorinus, upon the best ancient models, but is confessedly impure," this is really his praise, – namely, that, whether consciously or unconsciously, he did act on the principle, that the new life claimed new forms in which to manifest itself, – that he did not shrink from helping forward that great transformation of the Latin language, which it needed to undergo, now that it should be the vehicle of truths which were altogether novel to it, having not yet risen up above the horizon of men's minds, at the time when it was in its first growth and formation. Let any one compare his poems with those of Juvencus or Sedulius, and his vast superiority will be at once manifest – that superiority mainly consisting in this, that he does not attempt, as they did, to pour the new wine into old bottles; but has felt and understood that the new thoughts and feelings which Christianity has brought into the world, must of necessity weave new garments for themselves.

The poems on which the reputation of Prudentius as a poet mainly rests, are his Cathemerinon=Diurnorum. The tenth, Deus, ignee fons animarum, is confessedly the grandest of them all. The first also, on Cockcrow, and the twelfth, an Hymn for Epiphany, though they attain not to the grandeur of this, may well share with it in our admiration.

XVI. DE SS. INNOCENTIBUS.
OALVETE, flores martyrum,
J Quos lucis ipso in limine
Christi insecutor sustulit,
Ceu turbo nascentes rosas.
Vos, prima Christi victima, 5
Grex immolatorum tener,
Aram ante ipsam simplices
Palma et coronis luditis.
Aiidit tyrannus anxius
Adesse regum Principem, 10
Qui nomen Israel regat,
Teneatque David regiam.

XVI. *Prudentii Carmina,* ed. Obbarius, Tubingse, 1845, p. 48 ; Daniel, *Thes. Hymnol.* vol. i. p. 124. – This hymn, as given in the text above, is not exactly as Prudentius wrote it; rather is it a piece of mosaic, constructed from his twelfth *CathemerinSn.* It has, however, been so long current in the form in which it here appears, and is so skilfully put together, that I have neither excluded it, nor attempted to restore it to the form in which it appears in the text of the poet.

1. *flores mnrtyrum]* Augustine, or rather one in the name of Augustine, says, and with manifest reference to this hymn (*Serm.*Exclamat amens nuncio :

Successor instat, pellimur;
Satelles, i, ferrum rape, 15
Perfunde cunas sanguine.
Mas omnis infans occidat,
Scrutare nutricum sinus,
Fraus nequa furtim subtrahat
Prolem virilis indolis. 20
Transfigit ergo carnifex,
Mucrone districto rurens,
Effusa nuper corpora,
Animasque rimatur novas.
O barbarum spectaculum ! 25
Vix interemptor invenit
Locum minutis artubus
Quo plaga descendat patens.
Quid proficit tantum nefas ?
Quid crimen Herodem juvat ? 30
Unus tot inter funera
Impune Christus tollitur.
Inter cosevi sanguinis
Fluenta solus integer,
Ferrum, quod orbabat nurus, 35
Partus fefellit Virginis.

220, Appendix): Jure dicnntur *martyrumflores,* quos in medio frigore infidelitatis exortos, velut primas erumpentis Ecclesis? gemmas, qusedam persecutionis pruina decoxit.

14

SECTION 14

ADAM OF ST VICTOR.
  XVII. IN EPIPHANIA.
  dona reges femnt :
  Stella duce regem quserunt,
  Per quam certi semper erunt
  De superno lumine.
  Auro regem venerantes, 5
  Ture Deum designantes,
  Myrrha mortem memorantes,
  Sacro docti Flamine.
  Dies iste jubileus
  Dici debet, quo Sabaeus, 10
  Plene credens quod sit Deus,
  Mentis gaudet requie ;
  Plebs Hebraa jam tabescit ;
  Multa sciens, Deum nescit;
  Sed gentilis fide crescit, 15
  Visa Christi facie.

XVII. Gautier, *Adam de S. Victor,* vol. ii. p. 341. – It was by him edited for the first time. I regret to have no choice but to omit the first stanza of this truly noble poem.

10. *SatxBvs]* This is to be explained by Ps. Ixxi. 10 (Vulg.): Reges Arabum *et Saba* dona adducent, which was always interpreted as having its fulfilment in the coming of the wise men (kings they were often, therefore, assumed to be), from the East. Thus, in a Nativity Hymn (see p. 98) we find this line : Reges de Sab4 veniunt.

Synagoga pridem cara,
Fide fulgens et preclara,
Vilis jacet et ignara
Majestatis parvuli; 20
Seges Christi prius rara,
Mente rudis et amara,
Contemplatur luce clarS,
Salvatorem eseculi.
Synagoga coeca, doles, 25
Quia Sarse crescit proles.
Cum ancillse prolem moles
Gravis premat criminum.
Tu tabescis et laboras;
Sarah ridet dum tu ploras, 30
Quia novit quem ignoras,
Redemptorem hominum.
Consecratus patris ore,
Jacob gaudet cum tremore:

25 – 32. The poet follows up the hint of St Paul (Gal. iv. 22 – 31), to the effect that in Isaac, the child of the free woman, we have the type of the Church; that in Ishmacl, the son of the bondwoman, we have the type of the Synagogue, serving in the oldness of the letter, not in the newness of the spirit. Every line almost contains its own scriptural allusion; thus, 25 – 28 to Gen. xxi. 8, 9 ; 29, to ver. 6, 16 of the same chapter.

33 – 39. He now shifts the types from Isaac and Ishmael to Jacob and Esau; and again, as will be seen, is extraordinarily rich in his allusions to Scripture.

33. *Consecratus]* Cf. Gen. xxvii. 27 – 29; xxviii. 1 – 4.

34. *cum tremore]* Cf. Gen. xxxii. 7.

Tu rigaris coeli rore 35
Ex terra pinguedine;
Delectaris in terrenis
Rebus vanis et obscenis,
Jacob tractat de serenis,
Et Christi dulcediue. 40
Unguentorum in odore
Sancti currunt cum amore,
Quia novo fragrat flore
Nova Christi venia.

Ad peccatum prius proua 45
Jam percepit sponsa dona,
Sponsa recens, et coron&
Decoratur aurea.

35. *Tu rigaris]* This *tu* is addressed to Esau, as representing the Jewish Synagogue, and he is here reminded that he did but receive earthly promises from his father's mouth (in pinguedine terrse et in rore coeli desuper erit benedictio tua, Gen. xxvii. 39, 40, Vulg.), the heavenly having been all anticipated by his brother. Not to him, delighting in earthly things, but to his brother, it was given to behold the marvellous ladder reaching from earth to heaven, and with angels ascending and descending upon it (Gen. xxviii. 11 – 22); for, though it is not very clear, I must see an allusion to this at ver. 39.

41. *Unguentorum]* So the Bride in the Canticles (i. 3, Vulg.) : Trahe me. Post te curremus in odorem unguentorum tuorum.

45. *Ad peccatum]* Cf. Hos. ii. 2 – 24; Ephes. v. 26, 27. This line is alone sufficient to refute Gautier's assertion that the Blessed Virgin, and not the Church, is contemplated as the Bride of these latter stanzas.

Adstat sponsa regi nato,
Cu'i ritu servit grato SO
In vestitu deaurato,
Aureis in fimbriis :
Orta rosa est ex spinis,
Cujus ortus sive finis
Semper studet in divinis, 5fl
Et regis deliciis.
Hasc est sponsa spiritalis,
Vero Sponso specialis;
Sponsus iste nos a malis
Servet et eripiat; 60
Mores tollat hie ineptos,
Sibi reddat nos acceptos,
Et ab hoste sic ereptos
In coelis recipiat. Amen.

49 – 52. Cf. Ps. xliv. 10, 14 (Vulg.): Astitit regina a dextris tuis in vestitu deaurato, ... in fimbriis aureis.

15

SECTION 15

XVIII. IN EPIPHANIA.
  TRIBUS signis Deo dignis
  Dies ista colitur;
  Tria signa laude digna
  Coetus hie persequitur.
  Stella magos duxit vagos 5
  Ad praesepe Domini,
  Congaudentes omnes gentes
  Ejus psallunt nomini.
  Novum minim, aqua vinum
  Factum est ad iraptias: 10
  Mundus credit, Christus dedit
  Signorum primitias.
  XVIII. *BiU. Max. Patrum,* Lugduni, 1677, vol. xxvii. p. 617. – This little poem,
sometimes ascribed to Hartmann, a monk of St Gall, brings together well the three
events of the Lord's life, the three *maniftstations* of His glory, which the Western
Church brought into connexion with the feast of Epiphany, and commemorated upon
that day. Thus Maximus Taurinensis, at the beginning of the fifth century *(Hom.*

23): In hac celebritate multiplici nobis est festivitate lsetandum. Ferunt enim hodie Christum Dominum nostrum vel Stella duce a gentibus adora- tum: invitatum ad nuptias aquas in vinum vertisse: vel suscepto a Johanne baptismate consecrasse fluenta Jordanis. Oportct itaque nos ad honorem Salvatoris nostri, cujus nativitatem debita nuper cum exultatione transegimus, etiam hunc virtutum ejus celebrare natalem. Cf. Durandus, *Rational.* vi. 16.

A Johanne in Jordane
Christus baptizatus est:
Unde lotus mundus totus 15
Et purificatus est.
Lector, lege; a summo Rege
Tibi benedictio
Sit in coelis: plebs fidelis
Psallat cum tripudio. Amen. 20 FORTUNATUS.

T7ENANTIUS Fortunatus, an Italian by birth, whose *m* life, however, was chiefly spent in Gaul, belongs to the latter half of the sixth century. He was born ia the district of Treviso, in the year 530, but passed the Alps a little before the great invasion of the Lombards and the desolation of Northern Italy, and is memorable as one of the last, who, amid the advancing tide of barbarism, retained anything of the old classical culture. A master of *vers de socie'te,* which he made with a negligent ease, yet not without elegance, he wandered, a highly favoured guest, from castle to cloister in Gaul, repaying the hospitalities which he everywhere received, with neatly-turned compliments in verse. Such was the manner of his life, until Queen Rhadegunda, now separated from her husband Clotaire, persuaded him to attach himself to her person, and, having received ordination, to settle at Poitiers, in the neighbourhood of which she was presiding over a monastic institution that had been founded by herseE Here he remained till his death, which some place in the year 609, having become, during the latter years of his life, bishop of Poitiers.

There is a chapter of singular liveliness in Thierry's *Recits des Temps Merovingiens, Recit bme,* on the character of Fortunatus, and on his relations, which, though intimate, even Thierry does not pretend to consider otherwise than perfectly innocent, and removed from all scandal, with the Queen. It is impossible to deny that there is some truth in the portraiture of the poet which he draws. Even Guizot *(Civilisation en France,* 18me Le9on) must be taken to allow it. Yet had Fortunatus been merely that clever, frivolous, self- indulgent and vain character, which Thierry describes, he would scarcely have risen to the height and elevation which, in two or three of his poems, he has certainly attained; – poems, it is true, which are inconceivably superior to the mass of those out of which they are taken. In Barth's *Adversaria* there is the same exaggerated estimate of Fortunatus which there is of Pru- dentius, and with far less in his poetry to justify or excuse it. It would indeed have been otherwise, had he often written as in the lines which follow.

XIX. DE ClHJCE CHRISTI.

benedicta nitet, Dominus qua carne pependit, Atque cruore suo vulnera nostra lavat; Mitis amore pio pro nobis victima factus,

Traxit ab ore lupi qua sacer agnus oves; Transfixis palmis ubi mundum a clade redemit, 5

Atque suo clausit funere mortis iter.

XIX. Thomasius, *Hymnarium, Opp.* vol. ii. p. 433; Daniel, *Thes. Hymnol.* vol. i. p. 168. – These lines are only the portion of a far longer poem; yet have a completeness in themselves which has long caused them to be current in their present shape, till it is almost forgotten that they only form part of a larger whole.

Hie manus ilia fuit clavis confixa cruentis,

Quse eripuit Paulum crimine, morte Petrum. Fertilitate potens, o dulce et nobile lignum,

Quando tuis ramis tam nova poma geris; 10

Cujus odore novo defoncta cadavera surgunt,

Et redeunt vitse qui caruere die;

Nullum uret sestus sub frondibus arboris hujus,

Luna nee in nocte, sol neque meridic.

Tu plantata micas, secus est ubi cursus aquarum, 15

'Spargis et ornatas flore recente comas. . Appensa est vitis inter tua brachia, de qua

Dulcia sanguineo vina rubore fluunt.

8. *Paulum – Petrum)* Cf. Acts is. 5; xii. 7.

13. 14. Cf. Ps. cxx. 6.

14. The double false quantity of *meridie,* which it would be impossible to ascribe to ignorance, must be taken as a token of the breaking up of the metrical scheme of verse which had already begun, and the coming in of quite another in its room.

15. *secus]* The use of *secus* as a preposition governing an accusative (here understand *loca),* and equivalent to *secundum,* though unknown to Augustan Latinity, belongs alike to the anterior and the subsequent periods of the language, at once to Cato and to Pliny. And thus we have Ps. i. 3 (Vulg.), words which doubtless were in the poet's mind when he wrote this line: Kt erit tanquam lignum, quod plantatum est secus decursus aquarum, quod fructum suum dabit in tempore suo.

17. *vitis]* The cross as the tree to which the vine is clinging, and from which its tendrils and fruit depend, is a beautiful weaving in of the image of the true Vine with the fact of the Crucifixion. The blending of one image and another comes perhaps yet more beautifully out, though not without a certain incoherence in the images, in that which sometimes appears in ancient works of Christian Art, – namely, Christ set forth as the Lamb round which the branches of a loaded vine arc clustering and clinging.

16

SECTION 16

XX. DE PASSIONE DOMINI.

QUISQUIS ades, mediique subis in limina templi,
Siste parum, insontemque tuo pro crimine passum
Respice me, me conde ammo, me in pectore serva.
Ille ego qui, casus hominum miseratus acerbos,
Hue veni, pacis promissse interpres, et ampla 5
Communis culpse venia: hie clarissima ab alto
Reddita lux terris, Me alma salutis imago;
Hie tibi sum requies, via recta, redemptio vera,
Vexillumque Dei, signum et memorabile fari.
Te propter vitamque tuam sum Virginis alvum 10
Ingressus, sum factus homo, atque horrentia passus
Funera, nee requiem terrarum in finibus usquam
Inveni, sed ubique minas, et ubique labores.

XX. Fabricius, *Poett. Vett. Christ. Opp.* Basilese, 1562, p. 759; *Lactantii Opp.* Antverpise, 1555, p. 589. – This poem, consisting of about eighty lines, of which I have here given something less than half, appears in Fabricius, with the title *De Beneficiis suis Christus.* It is there ascribed to Lactantius, in most editions of whose works it in like manner appears, with the title *De Passione Domini.* Although Earth (*Advers.* xxxii. 2) maintains the correctness of this its ascription to Lactantius, there cannot be any doubt that it pertains to a somewhat later age. But whoseever it may be, it does, in Bahr's words (*Die Christl. Dichter Rom's,* p. 22), " belong to the more admirable productions of Christian poetry, and in this respect would not be unworthy of Lactantius," having something of the true flow of the Latin hexameter, which so few of the Christian poets, or indeed of any of the poets who belonged to the silver age, were able to catch.

Nunc me, nunc vero desertum, extrema secutum
Supplicia, et dulci procul a genetrice levatum, 15
Vertice ad usque pedes me lustra; en aspice crines
Sanguine concretos, et sanguinolenta sub ipsis
Colla comis, spinisque caput crudelibus haustum,
Undique diva pluens vivum super ora cruorem;
Compressos speculare oculos et luce carentes, 20
Afflictasque genas, arentem suspice linguam
Felle venenatam, et pallentes funere vultus.
Cerne manus clavis fixas, tractosque lacertos,
Atque ingens lateris vulnus; cerne inde fluorem
Sanguineum, fossosque pedes, artusque cruentos. 25
Flecte genu, innocuo terramque cruore madentem
Ore petens humili, lacrymis perfunde subortis,
Et me nonnunquam devoto in corde, meosque
Per monitus, sectare mes e vestigia vitse,
Ipsaque supplicia inspiciens, mortemque severam, 30
Corporis innumeros memorans animique dolores,
Disce adversa pati, et proprise invigilare saluti.
. Tsec monumenta tibi si quando in mente juvabit
VcVere, si qua fides animo tibi ferre, meorum
Debita si pietas et gratia digna laborum 35
Surget, erunt vera stimuli virtutis, enintque
Hostis in insidias clypei, quibus acer in omni
Tutus eris victorque feres certamine palmam.

XXI. MEDITATIONES.

DESERE jam, anima, lectulum soporis,
Languor, torpor, vanitas excludatur foris,
Intus cor efferveat facibus amoris,
Recolens mirifica gesta Salvatoris.
Mens, aifectus, ratio, simul convenite,
Occupari frivolis ultra jam nolite;
Discursus, vagatio, cum curis abite,
Dum pertractat animus sacramenta vite.

XXI. *Bibl. Max. Patrum,* vol. xxvii. p. 444. – These stanzas form part of a very long rhymed contemplation of our Lord's life and death, sometimes ascribed to Anselm, bishop of Lucca, a cotemporary of his more illustrious English namesake. He died 1086. – These trochaic lines of thirteen syllables long, disposed in mono-rhymed quatrains, were great favourites in the middle ages, and much used for narrative poems; and though, when too long drawn out, wearying in their monotony, and in the necessity of the pause falling in every line at exactly the same place, are capable both of strength and beauty. These *Meditations* have both ; and Du Meril has lately published, for the first time, a long poem on the death of Thomas a Becket *(Poesies Popul. Lat.* 1847, p. 81), which will further yield a stanza or two, if such were wanted, in proof. They relate to the feigned reconciliation of Henry with the archbishop, by which he drew him from his safer exile in France:

jEgras dat inducias latro viatori,
Sabulo vis turbinis, vis procellse flori;
Lupi cum ovicula ludus est dolori ;
Vere lupus lusor est qui dat dolo mori.
Ut post syrtes mittitur in Charybdim navis,
Ut laxatis laqueis iuescatur avis,
Sic remisit exulem male pax suavis,
Miscens crucis poculum sub verborum fa vis.
Jesu 'mi dulcissime, Domine coelorum,
Conditor omnipotens, Rex universorum, 10
Quis jam actus sufficit mirari gestorum,
Queb te ferre compulit salus miserorum ?
Te de coelis caritas traxit animarum,
Pro quibus palatium deserens prseclarum,
Miseram ingrediens vallem lacrymarum, 15
Opus durum suscipis, et iter amarum.
Tristatur Isetitia, salus infirmatur,
Panis vivus esurit, virtus sustentatur;
Sitit fons perpetuus, quo cesium potatur;
Et ista quis intuens mira, non miratur ? 20
Oh mira dignatio pii Salvatoris,
Oh vere mirifica pietas amoris;
Expers culpse nosceris, Jesu, flos decoris,
Ego tui, proh dolor ! causa sum doloris.
Ego heu ! superbio, tu humiliaris; 25
Ego culpas perpetro, tu poena mulctaris ;
Ego fruor dulcibus, tu felle potaris;
Ego peto mollia, tu dure tractaris.

17

SECTION 17

ST BERNARD.

ST BERNARD, born in 1091, of a noble family, at Fontaine in Burgundy, became in 1113 a monk of Citeaux, and in 1115 first abbot of Clairvaux. He died Aug. 20, 1153. There have been other men, Augustine and Luther for instance, who by their words and writings have ploughed deeper and more lasting furrows in the great field of the Church, but probably no man during his lifetime ever exercised *a. personal* influence in Christendom equal to his; who was the stayer of popular commotions, the queller of heresies, the umpire between princes and kings, the counsellor of popes, the founder, for so he may" be esteemed, of an important religious Order, the author of a crusade. Besides all deeper qualities which would not alone have sufficed to effect all this, he was gifted by nature and grace with rarest powers of persuasion, (Doctor mellifluus as he was rightly called, though the honey perhaps was sometimes a little too honied,) and seems to have exercised a Wellnigh magical influence upon all those with whom he was brought into contact. The hymns which usually go by his name were judged away from him on very slight and insufficient grounds, by Mabillon, in his edition of St Bernard's works. But with the exception of the *Cur mundus militat,* there is no reason to doubt the correctness of their attribution to him. All internal evidence is in favour of him as their author. If he did not write, it is not easy to guess who could have written, them; and Indeed they bear profoundly the stamp of his mind, being only inferior in beauty to his prose.

XXII. ORATIO RHYTHMICA AD CHRISTUM A CRUCE PENDENTEM.

1. Ad Pedes.

SALVE, mundi salutare,
Salve salve, Jesu care !
Cruci tuse me aptare
Vellem vere, tu scis quare,
Da mihi tui copiam. 5
Ac si prassens sis, accedo,
Immo te prsesentem credo ;
O quam mundum hie te cerno !
Ecce tibi me prosterno,
Sis facilis ad veniam. 10
Clavos pedum, plagas duras,
Et tam graves impressuras

XXII. *Bernardi Opp.* ed. Bened., Paris, 1719, vol. ii. pp. 916, 919; Mone, *Hymn. Lat. Med. Mvi,* vol. i. p. 162. – The full title of the poem from which two of its seven portions, each however complete in itself, are here drawn, is commonly as follows : Rhythmica oratio ad unum quodlibet membrorum Christi patientis, et a cruce pendentis. I have chosen these two, the first and the last, because in a composition of such length, extending to nearly four hundred lines, it was necessary to make some selection ; yet its other divisions are of no inferior depth or beauty: quse omnia, as Daniel says with merest truth, omnes divini amoris spirant sestus atque incendia, ut nil possit suavius dulciusque excogitari.

Circumplector cum affectu,
Tuo pavens in aspectu,
Meorum memor vulnerum. 15
Grates tante caritati
Nos agamus vulnerati:
O amator peccatorum,
Reparator constratorum,
O dulcis pater pauperum! '20
Quidquid est iu me confractum,
Dissipatum aut distractum,
Dulcis Jesu, totum sana,
Tu restaura, tu complana,
Tam pio medicamine. , 25
Te in tua cruce qusero,
Prout queo, corde mero ;
Me sanabis hic, ut spero,
Sana me et salvus ero,
In tuo lavans sanguine. 30
Plagas tuas rubicundas,
Et fixuras tam proftmdas,

Cordi meo fac inscribi,
Ut configar totus tibi,
Te modis amans omnibus. 35
Quisquis hue ad te accessit,

15. *Meorum]* So Mone, on good MS. authority. It is a wonderful improvement on *tuorum,* the ordinary reading; and at once carries conviction with it.

36 – t0. So Mone; but more commonly the latter half of this strophe is read as follows:

Dulcis Jesu, pie Deus,
Ad te clamo, licet reus,
Et hos pedes corde pressit
./Eger, sanus hinc abscessit,
Hie relinquens quidquid gessit,
Dans osculum vulneribus. 40
Coram cruce procumbentem,
Hosque pedes complectentem,
Jesu bone, me ne spernas,
Sed de cruce sancta cernas
Compassionis gratia. 45
In hac cruce stans directe
Vide me, o mi dilecte,
Ad te totum me converte;
Esto sanus, die aperte,
Dimitto tibi omnia. 50
2. Ad Faciem.
Salve, caput cruentatum,
Totum spinis coronatum,
Prsebe mihi te benignum,
Ne repellas me indignum
De tuis sanctis pedibus.

51. *Salve, caput cruentatum]* I have observed already how these great hymns of the early or medieval Church served as the foundation of some of the noblest post-Reformation hymns; the later poet, no slavish copyist nor mere translator, yet rejoicing to find his inspiration in these earlier sources. It has been so in the present instance. Paul Gerhard's Passion

Hymn –
O Haupt voll Blut und Wunden,
Voll Schmerz und voller Tloiin !

is freely composed upon the model of what follows now.

Conquassatum, vulneratum,
Arundine verberatum,
Facie sputis illita. 55
Salve, cujus dulcis vultus,
Immutatus et incultus,
Immutavit suum florem,

Totus versus in pallorem,
Quem coeli tremit curia. 60
Omnis vigor atque viror
Hinc recessit, non admiror,
Mors apparet in adspectu,
Totus pendens in defectu,
Attritus zegra macie. 65
Sic affectus, sic despectus,
Propter me sic interfectus,
Peccatori tam indigno
Cum amoris intersigno
Appare clara facie. 70
In hac tua passione
Me agnosce, Pastor bone,
Cujus sumpsi mel ex ore,
Haustum lactis cum dulcore,
Prse omnibus deliciis. 75
' Non me reum asperneris,
Nee indignum dedigneris;
Morte tibi jam vicina
Tuum caput hie inclina,
In meis pausa brachiis. 80
73. Cf. Judg. xiv. 8, 9.
Tuse sanctee passion!
Me gauderem interponi,
In hac cruce tecum mori
Prsesta crucis amatori,
Sub cruce tua moriar. 85
Morti tuse tam amarse
Grates ago, Jesu care,
Qui es clemens pie Deus,
Fac quod petit tuus reus,
Ut absque te non finiar. 90
Dum me mori est necesse,
Noli mihi tune deesse;
In tremenda mortis hora
Veni, Jesu, absque mora,
Tuere me et libera. 95
Cum me jubes emigrare,
Jesu care, tune appare;
O amator amplectende,
Te'metipsum tune ostende
In cruce salutifera. 100 BONAVENTURA.

T)ONAVENTURA, a Tuscan by birth, was born in J-) 1221, and educated at Paris, which was still the most illustrious school of theology in Europe. Upon entering the

Franciscan Order, he changed his family name, John of Fidanza, to that by which he is known to the after world. In 1245 he became himself professor of theology at Paris, in 1256 General of his Order, and in 1273 cardinal-bishop of Alba. He died in 1274 at Lyons, during the Council which was held there, to which he had accompanied Pope Gregory the 10th. At once a master in the scholastic and mystical theology, though far greater in the last, he received from the Church of the middle ages the title Doctor Seraphicus, and his own Order set him against the yet greater Dominican, Thomas Aquinas. His *Biblia Pau- perum* is an honourable testimony to his zeal for the spread of Scriptural knowledge through the ministry of the Word among the common people : nor can any one have even that partial knowledge of his writings, which is all that I myself would claim, without entirest conviction that he who could thus write, must have possessed a richest personal familiarity with all the deeper mysteries of that spiritual life whereof he speaks. Yet this ought not to tempt us to deny, but rather the more freely to declare, that he shared, and shared largely, in the error as well as in the truth of his age. At the same time, if we except the *Psaltery of the Virgin,* there is no work of his by which he could be so unfavourably known as his *Meditations on the Life of Jesus Christ,* of which some may remember a most offensive reproduction some years ago in England. If indeed that *Psaltery of the Virgin* be his, of which happily there are considerable doubts, it is too plain that he did not merely acquiesce in that amount of worship of the creature which he found, but was also its enthusiastic promoter to a yet higher and wilder pitch than before it had reached. His Latin poetry is good, but does not call for any especial criticism.

XXIII. IN PASSIONE DOMINI.

QUAM despectus, quam dejectus,
Rex coelorum est effectus,
Ut salvaret Sasculum;
Esurivit et sitivit,
Pauper et egenus ivit 5
Usque ad patibulum.
Recordare paupertatis,
Et extremse vilitatis,
Et gravis supplicii.
Si es compos rationis, 10
Esto memor passionis,
Fellis, et absinthii.
XXIII. *Bonaventurs Opp.* Lngduni, 1668, vol. vi. p. 423.
Cum deductus est immensus,
Et in cruce tune suspensus,
Fugerunt discipuli. 15
Manus, pedes perfoderunt,
Et aceto potaverunt
Summum Regem sjeculi;
Cujus oculi beati
Sunt in cruce obscurati, 20
Et vultus expalluit:

Suo corpori tune nudo
Non remansit pulcritudo,
Decor omnis aufugit.
Qui hsec audis, ingemisce, 25
Et in istis planctum misce,
Et cordis moestitias:
Corpus ange, corde plange,
Mentem frange, manu tange
Christi mortis ssevitias. ao
Virum respice dolorum,
Et novissimum virorum,
Fortem ad supplicia.
Tibi gratum sit et sequum
Jam in cruee mori secum, 35
Compati convicia.

35. *secum]* All are aware that there are, even in the Latin of the best age, some slight anticipations of the breaking down of the distinction between the demonstrative and the reflective pronouns (Zumpt, *Lat. Gramm.* § 550). In medieval Latin they are continually confounded, and the reflective put instead of the demonstrative, as here, and again in the next stanza.

Bone frater, quicquid agas,
Crucifix! vide plagas,
Et sibi compatere ;
Omni tempore sint tibi 40
Quasi spiritales cibi;
His gaudenter fruere.
Crucifixe, fac me fortem,
Ut libenter tuam mortem
Plangam, donee vixero. *45*
Tecum volo vulnerari,
Te libenter amplexari
In cruce desidero.

18

SECTION 18

BONAVENTURA.
   XXIV. DE PASSIONE DOMINI.
   QUANTUM hamum caritas tibi prasentavit,
   Mori cum pro homine te solicitavit;
   Sed et esca placida hamum occupavit,
   Cum lucrari animas te per hoc monstravit.
   Te quidem aculeus hami non latebat, s
   Sed illius punctio te non deterrebat,
   Immo liunc impetere tibi complacebat,
   Quia desiderium escse attrahebat.
   Ergo pro me misero, quem tu dilexisti,
   Mortis in aculeum sciens impegisti, 10
   Cum te Patri victimam sanctam obtulisti,
   Et in tuo sanguine sordidum lavisti.
   Heu! cur beneficia Christi passionis
   Penes te memoriter, homo, nou reponis ?
   Per hanc enim rupti sunt laquei priedonis, l. T
   Per hanc Christus maximis te ditavit bonis.

Suo quippe corpore languidum te pavit,
Quem in suo sanguine gratis balneavit,
Demum suum dulce cor tibi denudavit,
Ut sic innotesceret quantum te amavit. 20
XXIV. *Bonaventura Opp.* vol. vi. p. 424; Corner, *Prompt. Devot. p.* 117.
Oh ! quam dulce balneum, esca quam suiivis,
Quse sumenti digne fit Paradisi clavis:
Est ei quem reficis nullus labor gravis,
Licet sis fastidio cordibus ignavis. .
Cor ignavi siquidem minime perpendit 25
Ad quid Christus optimum suum cor ostendit.
Super alas positum crucis, nee attendit
Quod reclinatorii vices hoc prsetendit.
Hoc reclinatorium quoties monstratur
Pise menti, toties ei glutinatur, *SO*
Sicut et accipiter totus inescatur
Super carnem rubeam, per quam revocatur.

19

SECTION 19

XXV. DE CORONA SPINEA.
  SI vis vere gloriari,
  Et a Deo coronari
  Honore et gloria,
  Hanc Coronam contemplari
  Studeas, atque sectari 5
  Portantis vestigia.
  Hanc coelorum Rex portavit,
  Honoravit et sacravit
  Sacro suo capite;
  In hac galea pugnavit, 10
  Cum antiquum hostem stravit,
  Triumphans in stipite.
  Hsec pugnantia galea,
  Triumphantis laurea,
  Tiara pontificis: 15
  XXV. Cliehtoveus, *Elucidat. Ecdes.* Paris, 1556 (not in the
earlier editions) Balde has a series of brief poems on the

several instruments of the passion. This on the thorn-crown:

Hoc quale vides pressit Begem
Diadema tuum : fulget acutus
Utrinque lapis. Ferus in mediis
Sentibus istas reperit gemmas
Lictor, et alto vulnere flxit.
En ut radiant 1 rhamnus iaspis,
Faliurus onyx, spina smaragdos,
Tanto posthac vcrius omncs,
Homo, divitias regnaque mundi
Opulenta potcs dicere *Spinas*.

13 – 18. There appeared a very good translation of some of

Primum fuit spinea,
Postmodum fit aurea
Tactu sancti verticis.
Spinarum aculeos
Virtus fecit aureos 20
Christi passionis;
Quse peccatis spineos,
Mortis seternse reos,
Adimplevit bonis.
De malis colligitur, 25
Et de spinis plectitur
Spinea perversis :
Sed in aurum vertitur,
Quando culpa tollitur,
Eisdem conversis. 30
Jesu pie, Jesu bone,
Nostro nobis in agone
Largire victoriam;
Mores nostros sic compone,
Ut perpetuse coronas *3S*
Mereamur gloriam.

these stanzas in *Fraser's Magazine,* May, 1849, p. 530. This stanza was rendered thus:

Helm on soldier's forehead shining,
Laurel, conqueror's brows entwining,
High Priest's mitre dread 1
'Twas of thorns ; but now, behold,
'Tis become of purest gold.
Touched by that blest head.

20

SECTION 20

XXVI. DE PASSIONE DOMINI.
  ECQUIS binas columbinas
  Alas dabit animae ?
  Ut in almam crucis palmam
  Evolet citissime,
  In qua Jesus totus lsesus, 5
  Orbis desiderium,
  Et immensus est suspensus,
  Factus improperium !
  Oh cor, scande; Jesu, pande
  Caritatia viscera, 10
  Et profunde me reconde
  Intra sacra vulnera;
  In superna me caverna
  Colloca macerise;
  Hie viventi, quiescenti 15
  Finis est miserias!

XXVI. [Walraff,] *Corolla Hymnorwm,* p. 16 ; Daniel, *Thes. Hymnol.* vol. ii. p. 345. – Of this graceful little poem, which, to judge from internal evidence, is of no great antiquity, I am not able to give any satisfactory account. I have only met it twice, as noted above, and in neither case with any indication of its source or age. It is certainly of a very rare perfection in its kind.

8. *improperium]* = *convicium, derisio,* and probably connected with *probrum,* is a word peculiar to Church Latin. It occurs several times in the Vulgate, as Hom. xv. 3 ; Heb. xi. 26. The verb *improperare* (= *ortiSltiv*) is used by Petronius.

13, 14. *oavemd... macerit8]* He alludes to Cant. ii. 14 (Vulg.):O mi Deus, amor meus !

Tune pro me pateris ?
Proque indigno, crucis ligno,
Jesu mi, suffigeris ? 20
Pro latrone, Jesu bone,
Tu in crucem tolleris?
Pro peccatis meis gratis,
Vita mea, moreris ?
Non sum tanti, Jesu, quanti 25
Amor tuus sestimat;
Heu ! cur ego vitam dego,
Si cor te non redamat ?
Benedictus sit invictus
Amor vincens omnia; ao
Amor fortis, tela mortis
Reputans ut somnia.
Iste fecit, et refecit
Amor, Jesu, perditum;
O insignis, Amor, ignis, 35
Cor accende frigidum !
O fac vere cor ardere,
Fac me te diligere,
Da conjungi, da defungi
Tecum, Jesu, et vivere ! 40

Columba mea in foraminibus petrse, *in cavcrn5 maceria:* on which words St Bernard writes *(In Cant. Serm.* 61): Foramina petrse, vulnera Christi. In his passer invenit sibi domum et turtur nidum, ubi reponat pullos suos: in his se columba tutatur, et circumvolitantem intuetur accipitrem.

21

SECTION 21

'5

FORTUNATUS.
XXVII. DE RESURRECTIONE DOMINI.
SALVE, festa dies, toto venerabilis sevo,
Qua Deus infernum vicit, et astra tenet.
Ecce renascentis testatur gratia mundi
Omnia cum Domino dona redisse suo.
Namque triumphanti post tristia Tartara Christo 5
Undique fronde nemus, gramina flore favent. Legibus inferni oppressis super astra meantem
Laudant rite Deum lux, polus, arva, fretum. Qui crucifixus erat, Deus ecce per omnia regnat,
Dantque Creator! cuncta creata precem. 10
XXVII. Creuzer, *SymboWt,* vol. iv. p. 742; Daniel, *Thes. ttymnot.* vol. i. p. 170.

22

SECTION 22

ADAM OF ST VICTOR.
  XXVIIL DE RESURRECTIONS DOMINI.
  MUNDI renovatio
  Nova parit gaudia,
  Resurgente Domino
  Conresurgunt omnia :
  Elementa serviunt, 5
  Et Auctoris sentiunt
  Quanta sint sollemnia.
  Ignis volat mobilis,
  Et aer volubilis,
  Fluit aqua labilis, 10
  Terra manet stabilis,
  Alta petunt levia,
  Centrum tenent gravia,
  Renovantur omnia.
    XXVIII. Clichtoveus, *Elucidat. Ecdes.* p. 168; Daniel, *Thes. Symnol.* vol. ii. p.
68; Gautier, *Adam de S. Victor,* vol. i. p. 82. – The thought of the coincidence of

the natural and spiritual spring, the falling in of the world's Easter and the Church's, and of the iiropxal of both, which is the underlying thought of this and the last poem, comes beautifully out in a noble Easter Sermon by Gregory of Nazianzum, in which he exclaims: Nw *lap v, lap* 7ri/eu; iiari/ciii/ ' fop il uxuf, tap *ira/minu . lap*

Coelum fit serenius, 15
Et mare tranquillius,
Spirat aura levius,
Vallis nostra floruit;
Revirescunt arida,
Recalescunt frigida, 20
Quia ver intepuit.
Gelu mortis solvitur,
Princeps mundi tollitur,
Et ejus destruitur
In nobis imperium; C5
Dum tenere yoluit
In quo nihil habuit,
Jus amisit proprium.
Vita mortem superat;
Homo jam recuperat 30
Quod prius amiserat
Paradisi gaudium.
Viam prasbet facilem
Cherubim, versatilem
Amovendo gladium. 85
23. *tollitur]* Some MSS. read *fallitur.* 34. *versatilem)* Cf. Gen. jii. 24 (Vulg.).

SECTION 23

XXIX. DE RESURRECTIONS DOMINI.
    H./EC est dies triumphalis,
    Mundo grata perdito,
    Dans solamen nostris mai!s,
    Hoste jugo subdito.
    Hssc est dies specialis, 5
    Tanto nitens merito,
    Quod peccati fit finalis,
    Mali malo irrito.
    Duce fraudis demolito
    Terris pax indicitur, 10
    Et exhausto aconite
    Salus segris redditur:
    Morte mortis morsu trito
    Vitse spes infunditur,
    Claustro pestis inanito 15
    Nefas omne pellitur.
    Cum nos Christus feoundare

Tanto vellet foedere,

XXIX. Flacius Illyricus, *Poemm. de Comipto Ecclesia Statu,* Basle, 1556, p. 71.

8. *Mali malo]* The first *mali* is probably *malum,* and a play intended on the word; such it often provoked, as in Quarles' Totus mundus jacet in *mali-ligno.*

17, 18. *fecundare-.. foedere]* This at first sight seems a strange mixture of metaphors ; but by *fadus* doubtless the poet means the marriage-union betwixt the Church or single soul and its

Et se morti gratis dare
Pro reorum scelere, 20
Jure decet hunc laudare,
Et ei consurgere,
Pascha novum celebrare
Corde, voce, et opere.

Lord, whereby the former is made fruitful (fecundata), and enabled to bring forth spiritual children to him. Thus Hugh of St Victor: Quatuor sunt propter quse anima dicitur sponsa . . . and then among these four: proles virtutum, quibus fecundata est divini Verbi dogmate.

24

SECTION 24

PETER THE VENERABLE.
XXX. DE RESURRECTIONE DOMINI.

MORTIS portis fractis, fortis
Fortior vim sustulit;
Et per crucem regem trucem
Infernorum perculit.
Lumen clarum tenebrarum 5
Sedibus resplenduit;
Dum salvare, recreare,
Quod creavit, voluit.
Hinc Creator, ne peccator
Moreretur, moritur; 10
Cujus morte nov& sorte
Vita nobis oritur.
Inde Sathan victus gemit,
Unde victor nos redemit;
Illud illi fit letale, 15
Quod est homini vitale,

Qui, dum captat, capitur,
Et, dum mactat, moritur.
Sic decenter, sic potenter
Rex devincens inferos, *20*
Linquens ima die primS,,
Rediit ad superos.

XXX. *Kbliotheca Cluniacensis,* Paris, 1614, p. 1349.
Resurrexit, et revexit
Secum Deus hominem,
Reparando quam creando 2. j
Dederat originem.
Per Auctoris passionem
Ad amissam regionem
Primus redit nunc colonus :
Unde lsetus fit hie sonus. 30XXXI. IN RESURRECTIONE DOMINI.
PONE luctum, Magdalena,
Et serena lacrymas;
Non est jam Simonis coena,
Non cur fletum exprimas;
Causse mille sunt Isetandi, 5
Causse mille exultandi:
Alleluia resonet.
Sume risum, Magdalena,
Frons nitescat lucida;
Demigravit omnis poena, 10
Lux coruscat fulgida;

XXXI. [Walraff,] *Corolla Hymnorum,* p. 36 ; Daniel, *Thes. Hymnol.* Vo!, ii. p. 365.

3. *Simonis cana]* This identification of Mary Magdalene and " the woman that was a sinner" (Luke vii. 37) runs through all , the theology of the Middle Ages; constantly recurring in the hymns; thus in the *Dies Ira ;* and in another hymn, published, I believe, for the first time in the *Missale de Arbuthnott,* 1864, p. 176 ; where of Mary Magdalene it is said:

Hsec est ilia fcemina,
Cujus cuncta crimina
Ad Christi vestigia
Ejus lavit gratia.
Queg dum plorat, et mens orat,
Facto clamat quod cor amat
Jesum super omnia;
Non ignorat quem adorat,
Quid precetur ; sed deletur
Quod mens timet conscia.
Christus mundum liberavit,
Et de morte triumphavit:

Alleluia resonet.
Gaude, plaude, Magdalena, 15
Tumba Christus exiit,
Tristis est peracta scena,
Victor mortis rediit;
Quem deflebas morientem,
Nuno arride resurgentem : 20
Alleluia resonet.
Tolle vultum, Magdalena,
Redivivum obstupe;
Vide irons quam sit amoena,
Quinque plagas aspice; 25
Fulgent sicut margaritas,
Ornamenta novae vitae:
Alleluia resonet.
Vive, vive, Magdalena,
Tua lux reversa est, 3d
Gaudiis turgescat vena,
Mortis vis abstersa est;
Mcesti procul sunt dolores,
Lseti redeant amores:
Alleluia resonet. 35 ADAM OF ST VICTOR.
XXXII. DE RESURRECTIONE DOMINI.
BCCE dies celebris!
Lux succedit tenebris,
Morti resurrectio.
Lsetis cedant tristia,
Cum sit major gloria, 5
Quam prima confusio.
Umbram fugat veritas,
Vetustatem novitas,
Luctum consolatio.
Pascha novum colite ; I n
Quod prseit in capite,
Membra sperent singula;
Pascha novum Christus est,
Qui pro nobis passus est,
Agnus sine macula. IS
Hostis, qui nos circuit,
Prsedam Christus eruit:

XXXII. Clichtoveus, *Elwidat. Eccles.* p. 173; Daniel, *Thus. Hymnol.* vol. v. p. 194; Gautier, *Adam de S. Victor,* vol. i. p. 54.

16. *gni not circuit]* Cf. 1 Pet. v. 8 (Vulg.). M
Quod Samson prsecinuit,
Dum leonem lacerat.

David fbrtis viribus 20
A leonis unguibus,
Et ab ursi faucibus,
Gregem Patris liberat.
Qui in morte plures stravit,
Samson, Christum figuravit, 25
Cujus mors victoria:
Samson dictus *Sol eorum ;*
Christus lux est electorum,
Quos illustrat gratia.
Jam de crucis sacro vecte so
Botrus fluit in dilectas
Penetral Ecclesise.

18, 19. Cf. Judg. xiv. 6.

20 – 23. Cf. 1 Sam. xvii. 34 – 36.

24 – 26. *mars victoria]* Gregory the Great *(Mor.* xxix. 14): Pauci enim ex plebe Israelitica ipso prsedicante credidcrunt: innumeri vero gentium populi viam vitae moriente illo secuti sunt. Quod bene Samson in semetipso dudum figuraliter expressit, qui paucos quidem, dum viveret, interemit; destructo autem templo, hostes innumeros, cum moreretur, occidit.

27. *Sol eorum]* This etymology of Samson's name is derived from Jerome, who *(De Nam. Heb.)* explains Samson: *Sol eorum,* vel solis fortitudo – *their* light, or, the light of them that are his. So too Augustine *(Enarr. in Ps.* lxxx. 10) : Undo Samson noster, qui etiam interpretatur *Sol ipsorum,* eorum scilicet quibus lucet; non omnium, sicuti est oriens super bonos et malos, sed sol quo- rundam, sol justitiae, figuram enim habebat Christi. They may haye been right in seeing *shemesh,* or the sun, in Samson's name ; but' sol *eorum'* is of course a mistake.

31. *Sotrus']* Among the Old Testament types of Christ and his cross, that of Num. xiii. 23, 24, was ever counted as one :

Jam calcato torculari,
Musto gaudent ebriari
Gentium prioritise. 35
Saccus scissus et pertusus
In regales transit usus;
Saccus fit soccus gratise,
Caro victrix miserise.
Quia regem peremerant, 40
Rei regnum perdiderunt:

thus Hugh of St Victor *(Inst. Mor.* i. 4): Christus est Botrus de terra promissionis in desertum translates; the type of the cross being the pole (vectis is the word of the Vulgate), on which this bunch of grapes was suspended. Augustine *(Enarr. in Ps.* viii. 1): Nam et Verbum divinum potest *Uva* intelligi. Dictus est enim et Dominus botrus uvse, quem liguo suspensum, de terra promissionis, qui prsemissi erant a populo Israel, tanquam cru- cifixum, attulerunt. In Christ's passion this bunch of grapes was trodden as in the winepress (Isai. Ixiii. 3, 6), and his blood as the wine flowed into the *penetral* or *imo4ivuv* of the Church.

In ligno botrus est pendens, in cruce Christus;
Profluit hinc vinum, profluit inde salus.
Ejicitur prselo de botro gratia vini;
Prselo pressa cruois sanguis et unda flult. – *Put. de Riga.*

36 – 38. *Saccits scissus]* The poet has in his eye Ps. xxix. 12 (Vulg.), xxx. 11 (E. V.): Conscidisti saccum meum, et cir- cumdedisti me lsetitia; upon which words Augustine *(Scrm.* 336, c. 4): Saccus ejus erat similitudo carnis peccati. In passione conscissus est saccus. And then presently, with allusion to the *saccus* as the purse or bag of money: Conscidit saccum lancea persecutor, et fudit pretium nostrum Redemtor [John xix. 34]. – Clichtoveus; *In regales transit usus,* quando per resurrec- tionem immortalitatis stola corpus est indutum, et incorruptibili- tatis virtute prsecinctum.

41. *Rei]* A far better reading, as it seems to me, than *Dei,* which Gautier has. We may compare Augustine: Ut possi- derent, occiderunt; et quia occiderunt, perdiderunt.

Sed non deletur penitus
Cain, in signum positus.
Reprobatus et abjectus
Lapis iste, nunc electus, *45*
In tropseum stat erectus,
Et in caput anguli.
Culpam delens non naturam,
Novam creat creaturam,
Tenens in se ligaturam 50
Utriusque populi.
Capiti sit gloria
Membrisque concordia! Amen.

43. *in signum positus]* The poet with only the Vulgate before him, in which he found (Gen. iv. 15), Posuitque Domi- nus Cain signum (Cain being undeclined), understood the passage thus: " The Lord set Cain for a sign," instead of " The Lord set a sign upon Cain." In his application of these words to the Jewish people, the great collective Cain, the murderer of Him whose blood spake better things than that of Abel, he had many forerunners. They too, it was said, were not destroyed, but, while other nations were fused and absorbed and lost in the great Roman world, abode apart, being not slain, despite their sin, but set for an everlasting sign. Thus Augustine ; who even in his time found a wonderful significance in this continued and separate existence of the Jews, and therein a prophetic fulfilment of these words of Genesis, as also of those of the Psalmist: "Slay them not, lest my people forget it" *(Con. Faust.* 12, 13; *Enarr. in Ps.* Iviii. 12).

ADAM OF ST VICTOR.

XXXIII. DE RESURRECTIONS DOMINI.

F7YMA vetus expurgetur,
Ut sincere celebretur
Nova resurrectio.
Hsec est dies nostrae spei,

Hujus mira vis diei 5
Legis testimonio.
Hsec JEgyptum spoliavit,
Et HebriEos liberavit
De fornace ferreu:
His in arcto constitutis 10
Opus erat servitutis
Lutum, later, palea.

XXXIII. Clichtoveus, *Elucidat. Eccles.* p. 169 ; Rambach, *Antlwl. Christl. Gesange,* p. 290; Daniel, *Thes. Hymnol.* vol. ii. p. 69; Gautier, *Adam de S. Victor,* vol. i. p. 88. – Clichtoveus says truly here : Sane hsec prosa admodum diviua est, paucis multa comploctens, et tota ex sacris litcris prseclare desumpta, cujus et historias ct sententias congruenter copioseque adaptat proposito, ut hoc suo opiflcio auctor ipsius liqnido prodat se in divinis Scripturis apprime oxercitatum et promptum iuissc.

1 – 3. Cf. 1 Cor. v. 7, 8; Exod. xii. 19.

4 – 6. Cf. Exod. xii. 41, 42.

12. *Lutum, later, palea]* Cf. Exod. i. 11; v. 12. In the "mortar, "brick," and "straw" were often seen, as here, the works of the old man, while still serving sin in the spiritual Egypt. Thus Hugh of St Victor *(Allra.* iii. 1): Lutum, in quo servierunt filii Israel Pharaoni, eo quod lutum inquinat, luxuriamJam divinas laus virtutis,

Jam triumphi, jam salutis
Vox erumpat libera: 15
Hsec est dies quam fecit Dominus,
Dies nostri doloris terminus,
Dies salutifera.
Lex est umbra futurornm,
Christus fmis promissorum, 20
Qui consummat omnia. '
Christi sanguis igneam
Hebetavit rhomphaaam,
Amota custodia.
Puer, nostri forma risus, 25
Pro quo vervex est occisus,
Vitae signat gaudium.

designat. Palea, eo quod levis est, et cito transvolat, vanam gloriam significat. Later quoque, qui de molli terra confectus, per decoctionem ignis durescit, humani eordis duritiam, per longam sive concupiscentise, sive libidinis, aut avaritise consuetudinem decoctam ostendit.

15. Cf. Ps. cxvii. 24 (Vulg.).

25. *risus]* Daniel has made this verse unintelligible, printing *visus,* whether by mistake, or intending a correction. The omendation, if such, and no mere error of the press, rests on ignorance of that ever-recurring thought in early and medieval theology, of Christ as our Isaac, in that He made us to laugh, and thus, our *laughter,* with allusion to Gen. xxi. 6 (Vulg.): Risum fecit mihi Deus: quicumque audierit, corridebit mihi.

Thus Ambrose *(De Isaac et Anlma,* c. 1): Ipso nomine gratiam signat, Isaac etenim *risus* Latine significatur, risus autem insigne laetitise est. Quis autem iguorat quod is universorum Isetitia sit, qui mortis formidolosse vel pavore compresso, factus omnibus est

Joseph exit de cisterns,
Christus redit ad superna
Post mortis supplicium. 30
Hie draconea Pharaonis
Draco vorat, a draconis
Immunis malitia,
Quos ignitus vulnerat,
Hos serpentis liberat 35
. jEnei prassentia.
Anguem forat in maxilla-
Christus, hamus et armilla;

remissio peceatorum ? That the thought was a familiar one with our poet we have proof in another poem of his, in which he expresses himself thus:

Prole sera tandem fceta,
Anus Sara ridet Iaeta-
Nostrum lactans Gaudium.

The use *of forma* here *as=figura,* Rutoj, is frequont; thus Hugh of St Victor: Melchisedek, qui *est forma* Christi.

31 – 33. Cf. Exod. vii. 10 – 12.

38. *hamus et armiUa]* Cf. Job xl. 20, 21 (Vulg.); xli. 1, 2, (E. V.), where the Lord asks Job, An extrahere poteris Leviathan hamo, et fune ligabis linguam ejus ? Numquid pones circulum in naribus ejus, aut armilla perforabis maxillam ejus ? This question, by the help of Isai. xxvii. 1 ("Leviathan, that crooked serpent") was mystically interpreted, Wilt thou dare to contend with Satan and the powers of spiritual wickedness ? (cf. Jerome on Isai. xxvii. 1). But this, which a mortal man like Job could not do, Christ did. He did " draw out Leviathan with a hook." It is a favourite thought with the old Fathers, that Christ's humanity was as the bait which Satan seized, not perceiving the hook for his jaws, which lay beneath, in Christ's latent Divinity. Thus Gregory the Great *(Mor.* xxxiii. 7): In hamo ergo ejus inIn cavernam reguli

Manum mittit ablactatus, 40
Et sic fugit exturbatus
Vetus hospes saculi.
Irrisores Helissei,
Dum conscendit domum Dei,
Zelum calvi sentiunt. 45
David arreptitius,

carnationis eaptus est, quia dum in illo appetit escam corporis, transfixus est aculeo divinitatis. Ibi quippe inerat humanitas, quae ad se devoratorem duceret: ibi divinitas quse perforaret: ibi aperta infirmitas quse provocaret: ibi occulta virtus, quse raptoris faucom transfigeret. In hamo igitur eaptus est, quia inde interiit undo devoravit.

39. *reguli] Regulus,* the diminutive of *rex,* exactly answers to *fiafftlffKos,* mid to *basilisk,* a name we give to a serpent with crownlike, and so *kingly,* marks upon its head; Pliny *(H. N.* viii. 33): Caudid& in capite macula, ut quodam diademate insignis; cf. Gregory the Great *(Mor.* xv. 15): Regulus namque serpontum rex dicitur. These lines must be explained by Isai. xi. 8 (Vulg.): Et in cavernam reguli qui ablactatus est, manum suam mittet. Christ, according to a favourite interpretation, was " the weaned child ;" this evil world the cockatrice's hole into which He thrust in his hand, dragging out Satan from his lurking-place and den. Thus Jerome *(in loc.),* and Gregory the Great *(Mor.* xxvi. 32).

43 – 45. Cf. 2 Kin. ii. 23 – 25. Hugh of St Victor: Eliseus in- terpretatur salus Dei. Huic, id est, Christo, illuserunt Judsei exaltato in cruce... Sed postquam Christus ascendit in Bethel, id *est,* in domum Dei, in quadragesimo anno immisit duos ursos de filiis gentium, Vespasianum et Titum, qui crudeli strage eos dujeccrunt. Cf. Augustine, *Enarr. in Ps.* xliv. in init.

46. *arreptitius]* = arreptus furore. The word occurs in Augustine, *De Civ. Dei,* ii. 4. The allusion is to 1 Sam. xxi. 14, where instead of the Vidistis hominem *insanum* ? of the Vulgate, the older Latin version must have had *arrcptitium;* as is plain

Hircus emissarius,
Et passer effugiunt.
In maxilla mille sternit,
Et de tribu sua spernit 50
Samson matrimonium:
Samson Gazae seras pandit,
Et asportans portas scandit
Montis supercilium.
Sic de Juda -Leo fortis, 55
Fractis portis dirae mortis,
Die surgit tertia.
Rugiente voce Patris,
Ad supernas sinum matris
Tot revexit spolia. 60

from Augustine, *Enarr.* 1" *in Ps.* xxxiii., where he expounds at length the mystery of David's supposed madness, and of the prophecy which was herein of Christ, of whom the people said, " He is mad, and hath a devil." David's escape from the presence of Achish represents to him Christ's escape at his resurrection from the Jews.

48. *Et passer]* The allusion is not to Ps. xi. 1: Transmigra in montem sicut passer (Daniel); but to Lev. xiv. 49 – 53.

52. *Gaza seras]* Thus Hugh of St Victor: Samson apportans portas Gazae ascendit mentis supercilium, et Christus, fractis portis inferni, ascendit in coelum. The typical character of Samson's feat is brought out at length and with admirable skill by Gregory the Great *(Horn.* 21 *in Eoang.* and by Augustine *(Serm.* 364).

58. *Rugiente)* I have touched already, p. 68, on the medieval legend of the lion's whelps born dosd, but roused on the third day by the roar of their sire. Thus Hugh of St Victor *(De Best.* ii. 1): Cum lesena parit, suos catulos mortuos parit, et ita custo- dit tribus diebus, donec venicns pater eorum in faciem eorumCetus Jonam fugitivum,

Veri Jonse signativum,
Post tres dies reddit vivum
De ventris angustia.
Botrus Cypri reflorescit, 65
Dilatatur et excrescit:
Synagogse flos marcescit,
Et floret Ecclesia.
Mors et vita conflixere,
Resurrexit Christus vere, 70
Et cum Christo surrexere
Multi testes glorise.
Mane novum, mane la; tum,
Vespertinum tergat fletum ;

exhalet, ut vivificentur. Sic omnipotens Pater Filium suum tertia die suscitavit a mortuis. And Hildebert *(De Leone)*; Natus non vigilat dum sol se tertio gyrat, Sed dans rugitum pater ejus suscitat ilium : Tuhc quasi vivescit, tune sensus quinque capescit; Et quotiens dormit sua nunquam lumina claudit.

This last line expresses another belief, namely that the lion slept with its eyes open: these open eyes being an emblem of that divine life of Christ which ran uninterrupted through the three days' sleep of his body in the grave. Cf. Cant. v. 2, often quoted in this sense: " I sleep, but my heart waketh.", – It need hardly be said that the *mater* (ver. *59*) is the New Jerusalem, " the *nwther* of us all."

65. *Botrus Cypri]* Cf. Cant. i. 13 (Vulg.), i. 14 (E. V.): Botrus Cypri dilectus mihi, in vineis Engaddi; on which Bernard *(In Cant., Serm.* 44) with allusion to the verse preceding ("A bundle of myrrh is my beloved unto me "): Dominus meus Jesus myrrha mihi in morte, botrus in resurrectione.

72. Cf. Matt. xxvii. 62.

73, 74. The allusion is to Ps. xxix. 6 (Vulg.), xxx. 5 (E. V.):Quia vita vicit letum, 75

Tempus est Isetitise.
Jesu victor, Jesu vita,
Jesu, vitse via trita,
Cujus morte mors sopita,
Ad paschalem nos invita 80
Mensam cum fiducia.
Vive panis, vivax unda,
Vera vitis et foecunda,
Tu nos pasce, tu nos munda,
Ut a morte nos secunda 85
Tua salvet gratia.

Ad vesperum demorabitur fletus, et ad matutinum Itetitia ; words often regarded as a prophecy of Him who turned by his resurrection the night of sorrow into the morning of joy. Thus Jerome: Ad vesperum demorabitur fletus, quia passo et sepulto Domino Apostoli et mulieres in fletu et gemitu demorabantur. Et ad matutinum Isetitia, quia mane [cf. Marc. xvi. 9] venientes ad sepulcrum gloriam resurrectionis ab angelis acceperunt. And compare Augustine *(in loc.),* who carries on his thought to yet another morning of joy, after a yet longer night of weeping: Matutinum, quo exsultatio resurrectionis futura est, quse in ma- tutina Domini resurrectione prsefloruit.

25

SECTION 25

XXXIV. DE MYSTERIO ASCENSIONIS DOMINI.
  PORTAS vestras seternales,
  Triumphales, principales,
  Angeli, attollite.
  Eja, tollite actutum,
  Venit Dominus virtutum, 5
  Rex seternse glorise.
  Venit totus latabundus,
  Candidus et rubicundus,
XXXIV. Corner, *Pro/tip. Devot.* p. 788. Kothing is poorer throughout the whole Christian Church than the hymnology of the Ascension. Even the German Protestant hymn-book, so incomparably rich in Passion and Resurrection and Pentecost hymns, is singularly ill-furnished with these. It is not here the place to enquire into the causes of this poverty, which certainly is not the effect of chance, but only to observe that the Latin forms no exception ; it does not possess a single first-rate hymn on the Ascension. At the same time the following stanzas are not without a real merit of their own ; and strangely enough, they have never found their way into any of the more modern collections of Latin hymns.

1 – 6. Of. Ps. xxiii. 9, 10 (Vulg.): Attollite portas principes vestras, et elevamini, portse seternales: et introibit rex gloriEe. Quis est iste rex gloriaB ? Dominus virtutum, ipse est rex glorisr,.

8. Cf. Cant. v. 10 (Vulg.): Dilectus meus candidus et rubicundus. A few words from Richard of St Victor *(in Cant.* c. 36) will shew in what sense the epithets were continuallv applied to the Lord : Candidus, quia immunis est ab omni peccato; et rubicundus, quia in Passione sanguine suo est perfusus.

Tinctis clarus vestibus.
Nova gloriosus stola, 10
. Gradiens virtute sola,
Multis cinctus millibus.
Solus erat in egressu,
Sed ingentem in regressu
AiFert multitudinem. 15
Fructum suse passionis,
Testem resurrectionis,
Novam coeli segetem.
Eja, jubilate Deo,
Jacent hostes, vicit leo, 20
Vicit semen Abrahse.
Jam ruintE replebuntur,
Coeli cives aujebuntur,
Salvabuntur animse.
Regnet Christus triumphator, 25
Hominumque liberator,
Rex misericordise:
Princeps pacis, Deus fortis,
Vitse dator, victor mortis,
Laus coelestis curise. SO
Tu, qui coelum reserasti,
Et in illo prsoparasti

9 – 11. Cf. Isai. briii. 1 (Vulg.): Quis est iste, qui venit de Edom, tinctis vestibus de Bosra, iste formosus in stol& su&, gradiens in multitudine fortitudinis suse ?

32, 33. Cf. John xiv. 3.

Locum tuis famulis,
Fac me tibi famulari,
Et te piis venerari
Hie in terra jubilis;
Ut post actum vitse cursum,
Ego quoque scandens sursum
Te videre valeam,
Juxta Patrem considentem,
Triumphantem et regentem
Omnia per gloriam.

42. I have spoken in no high terms of the hymns on the Ascension. I must not however leave unsaid that one of these, first published by Dr. Neale *(Ecclesiologist,* Feb. 1854), yields the following noble stanzas:

Intrat tabernaculum
Hoyses, et populum
Trahit ad spectaculum
Tantse virtus rei:
Stant suspensis vultibus,
Intendentes nubibus
Jesum subducentibus,
Viri Galilaa.
Dum Elias sublevatur,
Elisseo duplex datur
Spiritus et pallium.
Mia Christus dum conscendit,
Servis suis mnas appendit
Gratiarum omnium.
Transit Jacob hunc Jordanem,
Luctum gerens non inanem,
Crucis usus baculo.
Redit tnrmis cum duabus,
Angelis et animabus,
Et thesauri sacculo.

In the last line I have ventured to substitute *sacculo* for *saculo*.   XXXV. DE SPIRITU SANCTO.

T7ENI, Creator Spiritus,
Spiritus recreator,
Tu dans, tu datus coelitus,
Tu donum, tu donator :
Tu lex, tu digitus,
Alens et alitus,
Spirans et spiritus,
Spiratus et spirator.

XXXV. Flacius Illyricus, *Poemm. de Corrupto Ecclesiae Statu,* p. 66.

4. *Tu donum]* Medieval theology made much of the term *donum,* as a *nomen proprium* of the third Person of the Holy Trinity. He was not *a* gift, but *the* gift, of God, in so high and exclusive a sense, that the term competed only to Him, and thus became his proper name. See an interesting discussion by Aquinas *(Summ. Theol., pars* 1, *Qu.* 38): Spiritui S. donum est proprium nomen, et personale. But this application of the term *donum Dei* is indeed as old as Augustine *(Enchir.* 12).

5. *lex] Sex* in the volume of Flacius Illyricus, where only I have seen this hymn; yet I cannot doubt that *lex* is the right reading. In the two preceding and two following lines there is an evident antithesis, and plainly one intended also here; but what such would there be between *rex* and *digitus* ? not to say that *rex is* a title nowhere specially applied to the Holy Spirit. But the antithesis comes excellently out when we read : *Tu*

lex, tu, digitus: " Thou the law, the living law, and the finger which writes that law,"
– with allusion to such promises as that contained Heb. viii. 10.

Tu septiformis gratiae
Dans septiforme donum, 10
Virtutis septifarise,
Septem petitionum.
Tu nix non defluens,
Ignis non destruens,
Pugil non metuens, 15
Propinator sermonum.
Ergo accende sensibus,
Tu, te, lumen et flamen,
Tu te inspira cordibus,
Qui es -vitas spiramen. 20
Tu -sol, tu radius,
Mittens et nuncius,
Persona tertius,
Salva nos. Amen.

9 – 12. We find continually in medieval theology the sevenfold grace of the Holy
Spirit (Isai. xi. 2) brought as here into connection with the seven beatitudes (the
virtus septifaria), and with the seven petitions of the Lord's Prayer. Thus Gregory
the Great, *Mor.* xxxv. 15; *in Ezck. Hom.* 2. 6, 7; and Anselm, in a sermon
on the Beatitudes *(Hom.* 2): Superna Gratia saluti nostrae providens orationem
nobis contulit, in qua septiformi prece Spiritum septiformem possemus impetrare; ut
suffragio gratise septiformis septem supradictas virtutes asse- quamur: et per eas ad
beatitudinem pertingere mereamur. So too Hugh of St Victor: Septem ergo petitiones
in Dominica Oratione ponuntur, ut septem dona mereamur Spiritus Sancti, quibus
recipiamus septem virtutes, per quas, a septem vitiis liberati, ad septem perveuiamus
beatitudines. 16. *Propinator sermonum]* Cf. Luke xxi. 15.

ADAM OF ST VICTOR.
XXXVI. DE SPIRITU SANCTO.
H IMPLEX in essentia,
J Septiformis gratis,
Nos illustret Spiritus:
Cordis lustret tenebras,
Et carnis illecebras,
Lux emissa ccelitus-
Lex prsecessit in figura,
Lex poenalis, lex obscura,

XXXVI. Clichtoveus, *Elucidat. Eecles.* p. 178 ; Gautier, *Adam de S. Victor,* vol.
i. p. 124.

7 – 28. These stanzas are in the true spirit of St Paul and St Augustine, and hardly
to be fully understood without reference to the writings of the latter, above all to his
Anti-pelagian tracts ; wherein he continually contrasts, as Adam does here, the killing
letter of the Old, and the quickening spirit of the New, Covenant. A few chapters of

his treatise *De Spiritu et Littera*, c. 13 – 17, would furnish the best commentary on these lines which could be found. Their first point is the contrast between the giving of the law *de monte*, and of the Spirit *in axnanilo*. In other words, *there* was a God far off who uttered His voice, and that which He spake only set men further from Him (Exod. xx. 18), while *here* it was a God coming into the very midst of them, yea, into that upper-chamber itself. Thus Augustine, c. 17 : In hac mirabili congruentia illud certe pluri- mum distal, quod ibi populus accedere ad locum ubi lex dabatur, N

Lumen evangelicum.
Spiritalis intellectus, 10
Literali fronde tectus,
Prodeat in publicum.
Lex de monte populo,
Paucis in coenaculo
Nova datur gratia : 15
Situs docet nos locorum
Pnsceptorum vel donorum
Quse sit eminentia.

horrendo terrore prohibetur: hic autem in eos supervenit Spiritus Sanctus, qui eum promissum expectantos in unum fuerant congregati, This, the poet adds, still in the spirit of his great teacher, shews whether are better, *precepts* or *gifts* (ver. 17), the precepts of the old law, or the gifts of the new – a God requiring as of old, or a God giving as now – requiring indeed still, but only what He Himself has first given. The fearful accompaniments of the law's promulgation, he goes on to say (ver. 19 – 24), were but the outward clothing of the eternal truth, " The law worketh wrath." A law of fear, it may restrain acts of sin, the *illicita,* but cannot beget that love which alone is the fulfilling of the commandment (ver. 25 – 28). That can only be through the Holy Ghost, whose descent we on this day commemorate.

13 – 28. A few stanzas from one of Abelard's recently discovered hymns will shew how entirely Adam of St Victor is here falling in with the typical interpretation of his time:

Tradente Iegcm Domino Horrendsc sonum bucclnse
Mons tremens metum attulit; Pavebat illic populus;
Spiritus in cosnaculo Verbum intelligentise
Susceptus ilium abstulit. Sonus hie fuit Spiritus.
Micabant illic fulgura, Fumus illic caliginem
Mons caligabat fumigans ; Obsenne signat litcrse ;
Hie est flamma multifida, Splendentis ignis speciem
Xuti urens, sed illuminans. Clare signum hie accipd
Ignis, clangor buccinae,
Fragor cum caligine, 20
Lampadum discursio,
Terrorem incutiunt;
Nee amorem mitriunt,
Quem efiudit unctio.
Sic in Sina lex divina 25

Reis est imposita,
Lex timoris, non amoris,
Puniens illicita.
Ecce patres praaelecti
Dii recentes sunt effecti, 30
Culpse solvunt vincula:
Pluunt verbo, tonant minis,
Novis linguis et doctrinis
Consonant miracula.

19, 20. Cf. Exod. xix. 16 (Vulg.).

21. *Lampadum]* Cf. Exod. xx. 18 (Vulg.): Cunctus autem populus videbat voces et lampades. This word, signifying, as it may, the bickering meteoric flames, perhaps better expresses what is meant than the " lightnings," by which the E. V. has rendered the original.

30. *Dii recentes]* Such the Apostles might be said to have been made, when attributes properly divine, such as the forgiveness of sins, were made over to them.

32. *Pluunt – tonanf]* Augustine *(Enarr. in Ps.* lxxxviii. 7): Prsedieatores nubes esse dictas ex illa prophetia intelligimus, ubi Deus iratus vineae suse dicit, Mandabo nubibus meis n pluant super eam imbrem, Isai. v. 6: which words Augustine found fulfilled when the Apostles said, "Lo, we turn to the Gentiles" (Acts xiii. 46); cf. Gregory the Great, *Mor.* xxvii.

Exhibentes asgris curam, 35
Morbum damnant, non naturam ;
Persequentes scelera,
Reoa premunt et castigant;
Modo solvunt, modo ligant,
Potestate libera. 40
Typum gerit jubilsei
Dies iste, si diei
Requiris mysteria,
In quo tribus millibus
Ad fidem currentibus 45
Pullulat Ecclesia.

24. And thus in another hymn on St Peter and St Paul, Adam of St Victor has these noble stauzas:

Hi sunt nubes coruscantes, Ipsi monies appellantur,
Terrarn cordis irrigantes Ipsi prius illustrantur
Nunc rore, nunc pluvtt: Veri Solis lumine.
Hi pnecones novse legis, Mira virtus est eorum,
Et ductores novi gregis Firmamenti vel coelorum
Ad Christ! prsesepia. Designantur nomine.

We may compare Damiani:

Paule, doctor egrcgie, Nobis potenter intona,
Tuba clangens Ecclesue, Ruraque cordis irrfga;
Nubes volans ac tonitrum Coelestis imbre gratise

Per amplum mundi circulum : Mentes virescant aridse.

41. *jubttai]* The poet has a true insight into the typical significance of the year of jubilee, the great Pentecostal year, the year of restitution and restoration, in which every man came to his own, all yokes were broken, and all which any Israelite had forfeited and alienated, was given back to him once more (Lev. xxv.). He sees in it rightly a type and a prophecy of that great epooh of recreation and restoration which at Pentecost began. Durandus *(Rational-* vi. 107): Similiter in diebus Pentecostes hunc numerum post Domini resurrectionem obseiJubilaras est vocatus

Vel *dimittens* vel *mutatus,*
Ad priores vocans status
Res distractas libere. 50
Nos distractos sub peccatis
Liberet lex caritatis,
Et perfectse libertatis
Dignos reddat munere.

vamus, suscipientes advenientem in nos Spiritus Sancti gratiam, per quem efficimur filii Dei, et virtutum posssssio nobis resti- tuitur, et remissa culpa, et totius debit! chirographo evacuate, ab omni servitutis nexu liberi efficimur.

47, 48. *Vel dimittens vel mutatus]* These etymologies of "jubilee," that it is so called either as the year of *remission (dimittens)* or the year when all things are *changed* for the better *(mutatus),* have long' been given up.

26

SECTION 26

18

HILDEBEKT.
XXXVII. IN LAUDEM SPIRITUS SANCTI.
SPIRITDS Sancte, pie Paraclite,
Amor Patris et Filii, nexus gignentis et geniti,
TJtriusque bonitas et caritas, et amborum essentise pu-
ritas,
Benignitas, suavitas, jocunditas,
Vinculum nectens Deum homini, virtus adunans ho-
minem Numini; 5
Tibi soli digno coli cum Patre Filioque
Jugis cultus, honor multus sit semper procedenti ab
utroque.
Tu mitis et hilaris, amabilis, laudabilis,
Vanitatis mundator, munditias amator,
Vox suavis exulum moerentium, melodia civium gau-
dentium, 10
Istis solamen ne desperent de te,

Istis juvamen ut suspirent ad te;
Consolator piorum, inspirator bonorum, consiliator moes-
torum, Purificator errorum, eruditor ignotorum, declarator
perplexorum,
Debilem erigens, devium colligens, errantem corrigens, Sustines labantem, pro-
moves conantem, perficis aman-
tem; 15
XXXVII. *Hildeberti tt Marlodi Opp.* p. 1340.
Perfectum educis de lacu fsecis et miseriss,
Deducis per semitam pacis et lsetitise,
Inducis sub nube in aulam sapientise.
Fundamentum sanctitatis, alimentum castitatis, 20
Ornamentum lenitatis, lenimentum paupertatis,
Supplementum largitatis, munimentum probitatis,
Miserorum refugium, captivorum suffragium,
Illis aptissimus, istis promptissimus,
Spiritus veritatis, nodus fraternitatis, 25
Ab eodem missus a quo et promissus,
Tu crederis omnium judex qui crederis omnium opi- fex;
Honestans bene meritos pnemio,
Onustans immeritos supplicio,
Spiras ubi vis et quando vis; docea quos vis et quantum vis: so
Imples et instrais certos in dubiis,
Firmas in subitis, regis in licitis:
Tu ordo decorans omnia, decor ordinans et ornans omnia,
Dicta, facta, cogitata,
Dicta veritate, facta honestate, cogitata puritate; 35
Donum bonum, Bonum perfectum,
Dans intellectual, dans et affectum,
Dirigens rectum, formans afFectum, firmans provectum,
Et ad portas Paradisi coronans dilectum.

27

SECTION 27

XXXVni. DE SPIRITU SANCTO.
  VENI, Creator Spiritus,
  Mentes tuorum visita,
  Imple superna gratia
  Quse tu creasti pectora.
  Qui Paraclitus diceris, 5
  Altissimi donum Dei,
  Fons vivus, ignis, caritas,
  Et spiritalis unctio.
  Tu septiformis munere,
  Dextrie Dei tu digitus, 10
  XXXVIII. Cliehtoveus, *Elucidat. Eccles.* p. 41 : Cassander, *Hymni Ecclesiastici*
(Opp. Paris, 1616), p. 242 ; Mone, *Hymni Lat. Med. Mm,* vol. i. p. 241. – This
hymn, of which the authorship is popularly ascribed to Charlemagne, but which is
certainly oldcr, has had always attributed to it more than an ordinary worth and dignity.
Such our Church has recognized and allowed, when, dismissing every other hymn, she
has yet retained this in the offices for the ordering of priests, and the consecrating of
bishops. It was also in old time habitually used, and the use in great part still survives,

on all other occasions of a more than common solemnity, as at the coronation of kings, the celebration of synods, and, in the Romish Church, at the creation of popes, and the translation of the relics of saints.

7, 8. *Font vivus,* cf. John vii. 38, 39; – *ignis,* cf. Luke xii. 49 ; – *caritas,* cf. Rom. v. 5; – *unctio,* cf. 1 John ii. 20, 27.

10. *Dei tu digitus]* The title *digitus Dei,* so often given to the Holy Ghost, rests originally on a comparison of Luke xi. 20,

Tu rite promissum Patris,
Sermone ditans guttura.
Accende lumen sensibus,
Infunde amorem cordibus,
Infirma nostri corporis 15
Virtute firmans perpeti.
Hostem repellas longius,
Pacemque dones protinus,
Ductore sic te prsevio
Vitemus omne noxium. 20
Da gaudiorum prsemia,
Da gratiarum numera,

Si in *digito Dei* ejicio dsemonia, with Matt. xii. 28, Si autem ego in *Spiritu Dei* ejicio dsemonia, where evidently the *digitus* Dei of Lute is equivalent to the *Spiritus* Dei of Matthew. Cf. Augustine, *Enarr.* 2" *in Ps.* xc. 11; who also elsewhere unfolds a further fitness in this appellation : Quia per Spiritum S. dona Dei sanctis dividuntur, ut cum diversa possint, non tamen disce- dant a concordia caritatis, in digitis autem maxims apparet qusedam divisio, nee tamen ab unitate prsecisio, propterea Spiritus S. appellatus est digitus Dei: and again, *Enarr. in Ps.* cxliii. 1: In digitis agnoscimus divisionem opcrationis, et tamen radicem unitatis ; so also *Quast. Evang.* ii. 17. Elsewhere ho has another explanation of the name *(De Civ. Dei,* xvi. 43): Spiritus S. dictus est in Evangelic digitus Dei, ut recordationem nostram in primi prsefigurati facti memoriam revocaret, quia et legis illse tabulse digito Dei scriptse referuntur. Jerome gathers from this title an intimation of the *Spoovffta* of the Spirit with the Father and the Son *(In Matt.* xii.): Si igitur manus et brachium Dei Filius est, et digitus ejus Spiritus Sanctus, Patris ct Filii et Spiritus Sancti una substantia est. Gregory of Nazianzum draws the same conclusion.

Dissolve litis vincula,
Adstringe pacis foedera.
Per te sciamus, da, Patrem, 25
Noscamus atque Filium,
Te utriusque Spiritum
Credamus omni tempore.
Sit laus Patri cum Filio,
Sancto simul Paraclito, So
Nobisque mittat Filius
Charisma Sancti Spiritus.

28

SECTION 28

ADAM OF ST VICTOR.
   XXXIX. DE SPIRITU SANCTO.
   QUI procedis ab utroque,
   Genitore, Genitoque,
   Pariter, Paraclite,
   Redde linguas eloquentes,
   Fac ferventes in te mentes -',
   Flamma tua divite.
   Amor Patris Filiique,
   Par amborum, et utrique
   Coinpar et consimilis :
   Cuncta reples, cuncta foves, 10
   Astra regis, coelum moves,
   Permanens immobilis.
   Lumen clarum, lumen carum,
   Internarum tenebrarum
   Effugas caliginem. 15

XXXIX. Cliehtoveus, *Elucidat. Eccles.* p. 179; Daniel, *Ths. Hymnol.* vol. ii. p. 73; Gautier, *Adam de 8. Victor,* vol. i. p. 115. – In Horst's *Paradisus Animd, Sect.* 1, this hymn and the following are huddled together, the two in one, and with grossest departures from the authentic text. Under this tasteless process the whole beauty of both, each complete in itself, and moving in its own sphere of thought and feeling, has quite disappeared.

Per te mundi aunt mundati;
Tu peccatum et peccati
Destruis rubiginem.
'Veritatem notam facis,
Et ostendis viam pacis 20
Et iter justitise,
Perversorum corda vitas,
Et bonorum corda ditas
Munere scientise.
Te docente nil obscurum, 25
Te prsesente nil impurum;
Sub tua prsesenti&
Gloriatur mens jucunda,
Per te Iseta, per te munda
Gaudet conscientia. So
Quando venis, corda lenis,
Quando subis, atrse nubis
Effugit obscuritas.
Sacer ignis, pectus ignis,
Non comburis, sed a curis S5
Purgas, quando visitas.
Mentes prius imperitas,
Et sopitas et oblitas,
Erudis et excitas.
Foves linguas, formas sonum, 40
Cor ad bonum facit pronum
A te data caritas.
O juvamen oppressorum, 0 solamen miserorutSi,
Pauperum refugium, , is
Da contemptum terrenorum,
Ad amorem supernorum
Trahe desideriumj
Consolator et fundator,
Habitator et amator 50
Cordium humilium,
Pelle mala, terge sordes,
Et discordes fac Concordes,
Et affer presidium.
Tu qui quondam visitasti, as

Docuisti, confirmasti
Timentes discipulos,
Visitare nos digneris,
Nos, si placet, consoleris,
Et credentes populos. i; o
Par majestas personarum,
Par potestas est earum,
Et communis Deitas.
Tu procedens a duobus,
Cosequalis es ambobus, us
In nullo disparitas.
Quia tantus es et talis
Quantus Pater est et quulis,
Servorum humilitas
Deo Patri, Filioque 70
Redemptori, tibi quoque
Laudes reddat debitas.
190
ADAM OF ST VICTOR.
XL. DE SPIKITU SANCTO.
T UX jucunda, lux insignis,
" Qufi de throno missus ignis
In Christi discipulos,
Corda replet, linguas ditat,
Ad Concordes nos invitat
Linguse, cordis, modulos.
Christus misit quod promisit,
Pignus sponsas quam revisit

XL. Clichtoveus, *Elucidat. Eocles.* p. 177; Daniel, *Thes. Hymnol.* vol. ii. p. 71 ; Gautier, *Adam de S. Victor,* vol. i. p. 107. – If this were not the third of Adam of St Victor's Pentecostal hymns which I have quoted, I should be-tempted to make room for a very grand one, *Veni, summe Consolator,* published by Gautier (vol. i. p. 135) for the first time.

2. *missus ignis]* Durandus *(Rational.* vi.   107) tells us that it was customary to scatter fire from on high in the church on the day of Pentecost; and he gives the explanation of this and other similar practices, as the letting loose of doves: Tune enim ex alto ignis projicitur, quia Spiritus Sanctus descendit in discipulos in igneis linguis. He omits reference to another passage without which this custom would scarcely have found place, and which is necessary to complete the explanation – I mean Rev. viii. 5 (Vulg.): Et accepit angelus thuribulum, et implevit illud de igne altaris [altare aureum quod est ante thronum Dei, ver. 3], et misit in terram; et facta sunt tonitrua et voces et fulgura et tememotus magnus.

Die quinquagesima.
Post dulcorem melleum in
Petra fudit oleum,

Petra jam firmissima.
In tabellis saxeis,
Non in linguis igneis
Lex de monte populo : 15
Paucis cordis novitas
Et linguarum unitas
Datur in coenaculo.
O quam felix, quam festiva
Dies, in qua primitiva 20
Fundatur Ecclesia.
Vivse sunt primitise

10 – 12, Daniel, who remarks here, Petrus Apostolus, cujus nomen die Pentecostes et omen habebat, confertur cum petra mel- liflua in deserto; has missed the meaning, doing equal wrong to the poetry and the theology of the stanza. The poet has Deut. xxxii. 13 in his eye, "He made him to suck honey out of the rock, and oil out of the flinty rock." This will be abundantly clear, when the words of the Vulgate are quoted: Suxerunt mel de petra, et oleum de *firma* petra; with the comment of Gregory the Great *(Hom.* 26 *in Evang.):* Mel de petra, suxerunt, qui Redemptoris nostri facta et miracula viderunt. Oleum vero de firma petra suxerunt; quia [qui ?] effusione Sancti Spiritus post resurrectionem ejus ungi meruerunt. Quasi ergo in firma petra mel dedit, quando adhuc mortalis Dominus miraculorum suorum dulcedinem discipulis ostendit. Sed firma petra oleum fudit; quia post resurrectionem suam factus jam impassibilis, per affla- tionem Spiritus donum sanctae unctionis emanavit. Cf, Hugh of St Victor, *De Claustro Aniirue,* iii: 8. It may be that the poet had also in his eye as a secondary allusion, Ps. I. 17 (Vulg.) : Et de petra, melle saturavit eos.

Nascentis Ecclesise,
Tria primum millia.
Panes legis primitivi, 25
Sub una sunt adoptivi
Fide duo populi.
Se duobus interjecit,
Sicque duos unum fecit
Lapis, caput anguli. so
Utres novi, non vetusti,
Sunt capaces novi musti:

25. *Panes legis]* On the day of Pentecost *two* loaves, the *primitia* of the completed harvest, were offered to the Lord (Lev. xviii. 16, 17). Why *two,* has often been enquired. The medieval interpreters answered, that by this twofold offering it was indicated that the Church, which was founded and presented in its living firstfruits to the Lord on the day of Pentecost, should consist alike of Gentile and of Jew; to this interpretation we have evident allusion here. See Bahr, *Symb. d. Mos. Cult.* vol. ii. p. 650; and Iken, *De duobus Panibus Pentecostes.*

31. *non vetusti]* The Jews were the old vessels, or old skins, which would not receive the *mustum,* or new wine of the Spirit (Matt. ix. 17); and they signally shewed that they were so on the day of Pentecost, when they so misunderstood the

thing which was done, as to say mocking, " These men are full of new wine " (Acts ii. 13). And yet these mocking words had their truth ; for the Apostles were as *ntres novi,* in which the new wine of the Spirit *was* being poured, and there is, as St Paul teaches, a *irnpovffiiu tv nvevpa. ri,* which is the spiritual counterpart to the carnal *iifBvffKtff9ai ofaip* (Ephes. v. 18). Thus Augustine *(Serm.* 267): Utres novi erant; vinum novum de ca? lo expectebatur, et venit; jam enim fuerat magnus ille Botrus calcatus et glorificatus: and again *Serin.* 26: Utres novos utres veteres mirabantur, et calumniando nee innovabantur, nee iw- plebantwr.

Vasa parat vidua;
Liquorem dat Elisseus;
Nobis sacrum rorem Deus, 35
Si corda s!ut congrua.
Non hoc musto vel liquore,
Non hoc sumus digni rore,
Si discordes moribus.
In obscuris vel divisis 40
Non potest hsec paraclisis
Habitare cordibus.
Consolator alme, veni,
Linguas rege, corda leni;
Nihil fellis aut veneni 45
Sub tua prKsentia.
Nil jucundum, nil amoenum,
Nil salubre, nil serenum,
Nihil dulce, nihil plenum,
Nisi tuS, gratia. SO
Tu es lumen et unguentum,
Tu coeleste condimentum,
Aquse ditans elementum,
Virtute mysterii.

34. *datElisaius]* Of. 2 Kin. iv. 1-6. The Church is the widow, in danger of coming, unless helped from above, to uttermost poverty, of losing her very sons. All that she can do is to prepare and bring the " vessels " of empty hearts, for Christ, the true Elisha, to fill them with that oil from above, which is only stayed when there is no more room in human hearts to receive it (ver. 6).

53, 54. Not one, but two broodings of the Holy Ghost over the o
Nova facti creatura, . 55
Te laudamus mente pura,
Gratise nunc, sed natura
Prius irse filii.
Tu qui dator es et domun,
Tu qui condis omne bonum, 60
Cor ad laudem redde pronum,
Nostras linguse formans sonum
In tua prseconia.

Tu purga nos a peccatis,
Auctor ipse puritatis, 65
Et in Christo renovatis
Da perfectaa novitatis
Plena nobis gaudia.

waters, at the first creation (Gen. i. 2), and at the second, are here referred to; for the Church has ever loved to contemplate them in their relation one with the other. Thus Tertullian, on our Lord's Baptism (Ze *Rapt.* c. 8): Tunc ille Sanctissimus Spiritus super baptismi aquas, tanquam pristinam sedem recognoscens, acquiescit. Cf. Ambrose, *De Spir. Sanct.* i. 7, and in a sequence appointed for chanting at Pentecost, these lines occur : –

Quando machinam per Verbum suum fecit Deus, cceli, terrse, marium,

Tu super aquas foturus eas, numen tuum expandisti, Spiritus :

Tu animabus vivificandis aquas foecundas. – (Clichtoveus, p. 175.) ROBERT THE SECOND, KING OF

FRANCE.

CPHE loveliest, – for however not the grandest, such J- we call it, – of all the hymns in the whole circle of Latin sacred poetry, has a king for its author. Robert the Second, son of Hugh Capet, succeeded his father on the throne of France in the year 997. He was singularly addicted to Church-music, which he enriched, as well as the hymnology, with compositions of his own, such as, I believe, to this day hold their place in the services of the Romish Church.

Even were the story of the writer's life unknown to us, we should guess that the hymn which follows could only have been composed by one who had been acquainted with many sorrows, and also with many consolations. Nor should we err herein: for if the consolations are plain from the poem itself, the history of those times contains the record of the manifold sorrows, within his own family and without it, which were the portion of this meek and greatly afflicted king. Sismondi *(Hist-des Frangais,* vol. iv. p. 98 – 111) brings him very vividly before us in all the beauty of his character, and also in all his evident unfitness, a man of gentleness and peace, for contending with the men of iron by whom he was surrounded. He died in 1031.

XLI. AD SPIRITUM SANCTUM.

T7ENI, Sancte Spiritus,
Et emitte coelitus
Lucis tuts; radium.
Veni, pater pauperum,
Veni, dator munerum,
Veni, lumen cordium :
Consolator optime,
Dulcis hospes animas,
Dulce refrigerium :

XLI. Clichtoveus, *Elucidat. Eccles.* p. 176; Daniel, *T/us. Hymnal.* vol. ii. p. 35; Mone, *Hymni Lot. Med. Mai,* vol. i. p. 244. – Clichtoveus shows a just appreciation of this hymn: Neque satis hsec oratio, mea quidem sententia, commendari potest; nam omni commendatione superior est, tum ob miram ejus suavi- tatem cum facilitate apertissima, tum ob gratam ejus brevitatem cum ubertate et copia sententiarum, ut unaquaeque fere clausula rhythmica unam complectatur sententiam, tum denique ob con- ciunam ejus in contextu venustatem, qua opposita inter se aptissimo nexu compacta cernuntur. Crediderimque facile auctorem ipsum (quisquis is fuerit), cum hanc contexuit oratio- nem, coelesti qu4dam dulcedine fuisse perfusum interius, qua,- Spiritu Sancto auctore, tantam eructavit verbis adeo succincti& suavitatem. Some later writers have attributed this hymn, and, on grounds as slight, the *Stabat Mater,* to Pope Innocent the Third; so the *Biographie Universelle:* but there exists no sufficient reason for calling in question the attribution which has been commonly made of it, to king Robert (Durandus, *Rationale,* ir. 22).

In labore requies, 10
In sestu temperies,
In fletu solatium.
O lux beatissima,
Reple cordis intima
Tuorum fidelium. 15
Sine tuo numine
Nihil est in homine,
Nihil est innoxium.
Lava quod est sordidum,
Riga quod est aridum, 20
Sana quod est saucium:
Flecte quod est rigidum,
Fove quod est languidure,
Rege quod est devium.
Da tuis fidelibus 25
In te confidentibus
Sacrum septenarium;
Da virtutis meritum,
Da salutis exitum,
Da perenne gaudium. 30

17. *Nihil]* It is difficult not to suspect that the text is here corrupt, and that this first *nihil* occupies the place of some more appropriate word.

SECTION 29

XLII. LIGNUM
 EST locus ex omni medium quem credimus orbe,
 Golgotha Judasi patrio cognomine dicunt :
 Hie ego de sterili succisum robore lignum
 Plantatum memini fhictus genuisse salubres ;
 XLII. Fabricius, *Poett. Vet. Christ. Opp.* p. 302. – This graceful allegory of course is not Cyprian's, though in time past sometimes attributed to him, and not unfrequently printed with his works. Whosoever it may be, the allegory is managed with singular skill, nor could one beforehand have supposed that, keeping so close to the one image with which he starts, and introducing no new element not perfectly consistent with it, the poet could have set out so admirably Christ's cross (1 – 10), his death and burial (11), his resurrection (12 – 14), his ascension (15 – 17), his constitution in the Twelve of a Church (18 – 21), the gifts of Pentecost (22 – 25), and the whole course of the Christian life from its initiation in baptism and repentance (27, 37 – 39), to its final consummation in glory (68).

 3. *sterili robore]* Does this mean the tree of life ? Early and medieval legends innumerable connect in one way or other the cross of Christ with the tree of life; the aim of all being to shew how the cross, as the true *lignum vitte*, was fashioned from

the wood of that tree which stood in the Paradise of God. The legend appears oftenest in this shape, namely, That Seth was sent by his dying father to obtain a slip of that tree; which having by the grace of the angel at the gate obtained, he set it upon his father's grave, that is, on Golgotha, the " place of the skull," or spot where Adam was buried. It grew there from generation to generation – each significant implement for. the kingdom of God, Moses' staff, Aaron's rod, the pole on which the brazen serpent was exalted, having been taken from it; till

<blockquote>
Non tamen hos illis, qui se posuere, colonis 5
Prsebuit; extern! fructus habuere beatos.
Arboris hsec species; uno de stipite surgit,
Et mox in geminos extendit brachia ramos:
Sicut plena graves antennse carbasa tendunt,
Vel cum disjunctis juga stant ad aratra juvencis. 10
Quod tulit hoc primo, mature semine lapsum
Concepit tellus: mox liinc (mirabile dictu)
Tertia lux iterum terris superisque tremendum
Extulerat ramum, vital! fruge beatum.
Sed bis vicenis firmatus et ille diebus 15
Crevit in immensum; coelumque cacumine summo
Contigit, et tandem sanctum caput abdidit alto;
Dum tamen ingenti bissenos pondere ramos
Edidit, et totum spargens porrexit in orbem:
Gentibus ut cunctis victum vitamque perennem 20
Prseberent, mortemque mori qui posse docerent.
Expletis etiam mox quinquaginta diebus,
Vertice de summo divini nectaris haustum
Detulit in ramos coelestis spiritus aurse:
Dulci rore graves manabant undique frondes. 25
</blockquote>

at last, in its extreme old age, the wellnigh dead stock furnished the wood of passion, and thus it again became, and in the highest sense, the true tree of life, bearing the fruit which is indeed unto eternal life. This, and other forms of the same legend, constitute some of the fairest portions of what may without offence be called the Christian mythology. We find allusions to them in the *Evangdium Nicodemi* (Thilo, *Codex Apocryphus,* vol. i. p. 686); and Calderon has wrought them up into two magnificent dramas, *La Sibilla del Oriente,* and *El Arbol del mejor Fruto.*

20, 21. Cf. Ezek. xlvii. 12; Rev. xxii. 2.

<blockquote>
Ecce sub ingenti ramorum tegminis umbra
Fons erat : hie nullo casu turbante serenum
Perspieuis illimis aquis, et gramina circum
Fundebant Isetos vario de flore colores.
Hunc circum innumeree gentes populique coibant, 30
Quatn varii generis, sexfis, rotatis, honoris,
Innuptse, nuptseque simul, viduzeque, nurusque,
Infantes, puerique, viri, juvenesque, senesque :
Hie ubi multigenis flexos incumbere pomis
</blockquote>

Cernebant ramos, avidis attingere dextris 35
Gaudebant madidos coelesti nectare fructus.
Nee prius hos poterant cupidis decerpere palmis,
Quam lutulenta viie vestigia foeda prioris
Detererent, corpusque pio de fonte lavarent.
Ergo diu circum spatiantes gramine molli, 40
Suspiciunt alta pendentes arbore fructus.
Tum si qui ex illis delapsa putamina ramis,
Et dulces, multo rorantes nectare, frondes
Vescuntur, veros exoptant sumere fruetus.
Ergo ubi coelestem ceperunt ora saporem, 43
Permutant animos, et mentes perdere avaras
Incipiunt, duJcique hominem cognoscere sensu.
Insolitum multis stomachum movisse saporem
Vidimus, et fellis commotum melle venenum
llejecisse bonos turbata mente sapores, 50
Aut avide sumptum non dilexisse, diuque
Et male potatum tandem evomuisse saporem.
Ssepe quidem multi, renovatis mentibus, segros
Restituere animos; et quaB se posse negabant,
Pertulerant, fructumque sui cepere laboris. 55
Multi etiam sanctos ausi contingere fontes,
Discessere iterum subito, retroque relapsi
Sordibus et coeno mixti volvuntur eodem.
Multi vero bono portantes pectore, totis
Accipiunt animis, penitusque in viscera condunt. 60
Ergo qui sacros possunt accedere fontes,
Septima lux illos optatas sistit ad undas,
Tingit et in liquidis jejunos fontibus artus.
Sic demum illuviem mentis, vitseque prioris
Deponunt labem, purasque a morte reducunt 65
Illustres animas, coelique ad lumen ituras.
Hinc iter ad ramos et dulcia poma salutis;
Inde iter ad coelum per ramos arboris altae ;
Hoc lignum vitse est cunctis credentibus. Amen.

62. *Septima. lux]* *Forty* rather than *seven* was the number of days which generally the ancient Church desired to set apart for the immediate preparation for baptism : yet within that forty, the last seven may, and would, have had an intenser solemnity, even as the *traditio symboli* very often did not take place till the seventh day preceding; thus, not till Palm Sunday, for those who should be baptized on Easter Eve.

30

SECTION 30

ADAM OF ST VICTOR.
    XLIII. DE S. APOSTOLIS.
    CJTOLA regni laureatus,
    U Summi Regis est senatus
    Coetus apostolicus;
    Cui psallant mens et ora;
    Mentis muntUe vox sonora 5
    Hymnus est angelicus.
    Hie est ordo mundi decus,
    Omnis carnis judex sequus,
    Novse petra gratise;
    Ab seterno prseelectus, 10
    Cujus floret architectus
    Ad culmen Ecclesise.

    XLIII. Gautier, *Adam de S. Victor,* vol. ii. p. 407. – This magnificent hymn, a glorious addition to the medieval hymnology, was published by Gautier for the first time. The unity which pervades the hymns of Adam of St Victor is very worthy of remark and admiration. Thus he has, besides this, two others, *In Communi Apostolorum.* In them he traces the *history* of the Apostles, their calling, their characters, the spheres of their labour, with no slightest introduction of symbolism. This on the contrary deals with the symbolism alone, and does not once touch what would be to it the alien element of history.

1 – 3. Cf. Matt. xix. 28 ; Luke xxii. 29, 30; 1 Cor. vi. 3.

8. *judex]* Cf. Matt. xix. 28.

11. *architectus]* Elsewhere the Apostles are honoured with theHi prseclari Nazaraei
Bella crucis et tropaei
Mundo narrant gloriam ; 15
Sic dispensant verbum Dei
Quod nox nocti, lux diei
Indicant scientiam.
Onus leve, jugum mite
Proponentes, semen vitas 20
Mundi spargunt terminis;
Germen promit terra culta,
Fomeratur fruge multa
Fides Dei-hominis.
Paranymphi novae legis 25
Ad amplexum novi Regis
Sponsam ducunt regiam,
title of the " architects" of the Church; as in a fine hymn addressed to St Paul (Mone, vol. iii. p. 85), which commences thus: –
Panlus, Syon architectus,
Est a Christo praeelectus.
So too St Augustine styles the same Apostle *(Ep.* 185) Ec- clesise magnus aedificator. Here, however, it is the architect in chief who manifestly is intended.

14. *trojiJm]* See note, p. 89.

16 – 18. It is well known that the words of the nineteenth Psalm (1 – 4), mainly on the strength of St Paul's adaptation of them (Rom. x. 18), have constantly received a spiritual application. The Church is the firmament which shews the handy- work of God ; in which day transmits to day and night to night in unbroken succession to the end of time, and to all the world, the wondrons story of the glory and grace of God.

25. *Paranymphi]* = vlo vvfitj, uvos (Matt. ix. 15 ; cf. John iii. 29 ; 2 Cor. xi. 2).
Sine rugil, sine narvo,
Permansuram omni sevo
Virginem Ecclesiam. 30
Hsec est virgo gignens foetus,
Semper nova, tamen vetus,
Sed defectus nescia;
Cujus thorus mens sincera,
Cujus partus fides vera, 35
Cujus dos est gratia.
Hi sunt templi fundamentum,
Virus lapis et caBmentum

Ligans asdificium.
Hi sunt portse civitatis, 40
Hi compago unitatis
Israel et gentium.
Hi tritnrant aream,
Yentilantes paleam
28. Cf. Ephes. v. 27.
37. Cf. Ephes. ii. 20 ; Rev. xxi. 14.
40. *portte]* Cf. Rev. xxi. 12 ; Ezek. xlviii. 31 – 34. Richard of St Victor *(Sup. Apoc.* xxi. 21): Per portas vero S. Apostolos intelligimus, per quorum fidem et doctrinam sanctam Civitatem introimus. Augustine *(Enarr. in Ps.* lxxxvi. 2): Quare sunt portse [Apostoli] ? Quia per ipsos introimus ad regnum Dei. Prsedicant enim nobis.
41, 42. Cf. Ephes. ii. 20.
43 – 48. The treading out the corn on the barn floor, which is the work of oxen, is the link between the first part of this stanza and the last. The Apostles, the treaders out of the corn (St Paul, by his quotation at 1 Tim. v. 18, of Deut. xxv. 4, justifies the image), from which afterwards they winnow away the chaff (cf. Matt. iii. 12), are prefigured by the twelve brazenVentilabri justitia; 45

Quos designant serei
Boves maris vitrei
Salomonis industria.
Patriarchal duodeni,
Fontes aquse gustu leni, 50
Panes tabernaculi,
Gemmae vestis sacerdotis;
Hasc figuris signant notis
Novi duces populi.
Horum nutu cedat error, 55
Crescat fides, absit terror
Finalis sententise,
Ut soluti a delictis,
Sociemur benedictis
Ad tribunal glorise. 50

oxen round the molten sea, which Solomon made (1 Kin. vii. 23 – 25; 2 Chron. iv. 2 – 4).
50. *Fontes]* Cf. Exod. xv. 23, 25, 27.
51. Cf. Lev. xxiv. 6 – 9. Bede : Duodecim panes in mensii tabernaculi duodecim sunt Apo::toli, qui cum usque ad consumma- tionem seculi populum Dei reficiunt panibus Verbi, duodeciiu panes propositionis nunquam recedunt de mensa Domini.
52. *Gemma]* Cf. Exod. xxxix. 10 – 14.
63, 64. Compare Hugh of St Victor *(Alley, in Gen.* iii. 16): Jacob est Christus : ejus filii, duodecim Apostoli. Hi sunt ejiim fontes deserti, quse Israel reperit in Helim (Exod. xv. 27); duodecim panes propositionis ; duodecim lapides in veste ponti- ficali; duodecim lapides de Jordane sublevati (Josh. iv. 3 – 8); duodecim boyes

sub sereo mari (1 Kin. vii. 25); duodecim stellae in corona sponsae (Rev. xii. 1); duodecim fundamenta (Rev. xxi. 19 – 20); duodecim portee (Rev. xxi. 12); duodecim menses anni; duodecim horae diei; duodecim fructus ligni vitae (Rev. -vTii- 2).

ao6

ABELARD.

A BELARD was born in 1079 at Palais, near Nantes, .$- and died in 1142. His talents, his vanity, his rare dialectic dexterity, his rationalism, his relations to a woman of so far nobler and deeper character than his own, the cloistral retirement in which he spent the later years of his stormy life – all these are matters of too familiar knowledge to need to be repeated. Of his poetry, to which, and to the great popularity which it enjoyed, both he and Heloise more than once refer, it was thought that the greater part had perished. There was indeed an Advent hymn of no high merit, beginning, *Mittit ad Virginem Non quemvis angelum,* which had been sometimes ascribed to Abelard (Clichtoveus, *Elucidat. Eccles.* p. 153), and a few other verses of no great significance were current under his name. Not very long since, however, six poems were discovered in the Vatican, which undoubtedly are of his composing. They are styled *Lamentations (planctus),* as of David over Abher, the virgins of Israel over Jephthah's daughter, and are published in Greith's *Spicilegium Vaticanum,* Frauenfeld, 1838, p. 123 – 131. Their merit is inconsiderable. But this was not all, for about the same time a large body of his hymns, no fewer than ninety-seven, came to light in the Royal Library at Brussels, and are included in the complete edition of Abelard's writings, edited by Cousin, *Abaelardi Opp.* Paris, 1849. These too, it must be acknowledged, for the most part, disappoint expectation. This certainly would not be the case, if there were many among them like the following, which is as pregnant as it is brief; and curious, moreover, as shewing how entirely Abe- lard conformed to the typical interpretation of his time.

XLIV. DE S. PAULO APOSTOLO.

TUBA Domini, Paule, maxima,
De coelestibus dans tonitrua,
Hostes dissipans, cives aggrega.
Doctor gentium es prsecipuus,
Vas in poculum factus omnibus,
Sapientise plenum haustibus.
Mane Benjamin prsedam rapuit,
Escas vespere largas dividit,
Vitas ferculis mundum reficit.

XLIV. *Petri Abalardi Of p.* Paris, 1849, vol. i. p. 320.

1 – 3. The trumpets of silver under the Old Law were to be used for the calling of the assembly (Num. x. 2), and for the heartening of the people when they went forth against their enemies (x. 9 ; xitxi. 6). Such a trumpet, and the greatest of such, was St Paul.

7, 8. *Benjamin]* The immense significance of St Paul's conversion for the Church not unnaturally led the early interpreters to seek some intimation of it in the Old Testament, or at least to welcome there anything which seemed like such. They believed that they found such in the words of Jacob's prophecy, Gen. xlix. 27. Paul, in whom it might be fitly said that the

Ut rhinoceros est indomitus, 10
Quem ad aratrum ligans Dominus
Glebas vallium frangit protinus.
Nunc nequitias laudat villicum,
Quem prudentia dicit prseditum, 15
Ac pro filiis lucis providum.

glory of the tribe of Benjamin culminated, was the wolf in the morning devouring the prey, and in the evening dividing the spoil. Thus Tertullian, arguing with the Gnostics, would shew how deeply rooted the New Testament was in the Old, the latter containing prophecies not of Christ only, but of his Apostles; and proceeds *(Ado. Marc.* v. 1): Mihi Paulum etiam Genesis olim- repromisit. Inter illas enim figuras et propheticas super filios suos benedictiones, Jacob, cum ad Benjamin direxisset, Benjamin, inquit, lupus rapax, ad matutinum comedet adhuc, et ad vesperam dabit escam. Ex tribu enim Benjamin oriturum Paulum pro- videbat, lupum rapacem, ad matutinum comedentem, id est, prima aetate vastaturum pecora Domini ut persecutorem Ecclesi- arum, dehinc ad vesperam escam daturum, id est, devergente jam setate, oves Christi educaturum, ut doctor nationum. Cf. Hilary,. *in Ps.* lxvii. § 28 ; Augustine, *Enarr. in Ps.* lxxviii; *Serm.* 279, 1; and 333.

10. *Ut rhinoceros]* The reference is to Job xxxix. 9, 10: Numquid volet rhinoceros servire tibi, aut morabitur ad prsesepe tunm?   Numquid alligabis rhinocerota ad arandum loro tuo? aut confringet glebas vallium post te ? (Vulg.) It was a favourite and a very grand fancy of the medieval interpreters, that all this (ver. 9 – 12) found its highest fulfilment, this impossible with man proving possible with God, in the conversion of St Paul: thus see Gregory the Great, *Moral.* xxxi. 16, 30.

13 – 15. Cf. St Luke xvi. 1 – 9. St Jerome *(ad A/gas.* § 7) records at length the exposition of this parable, deriving it from Theophilus, bishop of Antioch, by aid of which these lines must be explained. Paul is the Unjust Steward, scattering his lord's

Perpes gloria Regi perpeti,
Exercituum Christo Principi,
Patri pariter et Spiritui.

goods so long as he is a persecutor of the Church. He was put out ef his stewardship, when the Lord met him on the way to Damascus; but afterwards found acceptance with his lord's debtors through lowering their bills – that is, through abating the rigour of the ceremonial law; and not acceptance with them only, but favour and praise from his Lord Himself.

31

SECTION 31

ST AMBROSE.

   XLV. DE SS. MAKTYRIBUS.

   7TCTERNA Christi munera,

   -L- Et martyrum victorias,

   Laudes ferentes debitas,

   Lastis canamus mentibus.

   Ecclesiarnm principes, 5

   Belli triumphales duces,

   Ctclestis aulae miJites,

   Et vera mundi lumina;

   Terrore victo sseculi,

   Spretisque poenis corporis, 10

   Mortis sacra compendio

   Vitam beatam possident.

   Traduntur igni martyres

   Et bestiarum dentibus;

   Armata ssevit ungulis 15

   Tortoris insani manus.

XLV. *Ambrosii Opera,* Paris, 1836, vol. Iv. p. 201; Clich- toveus, *Elucidat. Eccles.* p. 75; Daniel, *Thei. Hymnal.* vol. i. p. 27; Mono, *Hymn. Lat. Med. Mvi,* voLiii. p. 143. – Whether this hymn be St Ambrose's, to whom the Benedictine editors ascribe it, or not, it is certainly not later than the fifth century.

Nudata pendent viscera,
Sanguis sacratus funditur,
Sed permanent immobiles
Vitae perennis gratia. 20
Devota sanctorum fides,
Invicta spes credentium,
Perfecta Christi caritas,
Mundi triumphat principem.
In his Paterna gloria, 25
In his voluntas Filii,
Exultat in his Spiritus;
Coelum repletur gaudiis.
Te nunc, Redemtor, qusesumus
Ut ipsorum consortio 30
Jungas precantes servulos
In sempiterna saecula.

32

SECTION 32

ADAM OF ST VICTOR.
  XLVI. DE S. STEPHANO.
  HERI mundus exultavit,
  Et exultans celebravit
  Christ! uatalitia :
  XLVI. Clichtoveus, *Elucidat. Eccles.* p. 158 ; Rambach, *Ait- thol. Christl. Gesdnge,* p. 285; Daniel, *Thes. Hymnol.* vol. ii. p. 64; Gautier, *Adam de S. Victor,* vol. i. p. 212. – There is another fine hymn by Adam of St Victor on the martyrdom of St Stephen, *Rosa novum dans odorem;* but fine as it is, it is very inferior to this sublime composition. Gautier (vol. i. p 223) has published it for the first time.

  1. *Hen]* The Church has always loved to bring out the significance of the day on which it commemorates the martyrdom of St Stephen – namely, that it is the day immediately following the day of Christ's nativity. Thus Durandus *(Rational.* vii. 42): Augustine, *Serm.* 314 and often; Bernard, vol. i. p. 794, Bened. ed.; and Fulgentius *(Appendix to Augustine,* vol. v. p. 357): Hesterno die celebravimus Natalem quo Rex martyrum natus est in mundo; hodie celebramus natalem quo primicerius martyrum migravit ex mundo. Et ideo natus est Dominus ut more- retur pro servo; ne servus timeret mori pro Domino. Natus est Christus in terris, ut Stephanus nasceretur in

coelis: altus ad humilia descendit, vit humiles ad alta adscenderent. Another hymn on St Stephen (Clichtoveus, p. 20) has these noble lines expressing the same thought:

Tu per Christum hebetatam primus transis rhomphseam,
Primiun granum trituratum Christi ditans aream.

The *rlwmphaa* here is the fiery sword of the Cherubim, which precluded all access to Paradise, but which sword was quenched

Heri chorus angelorum
Prosecutus est coclorum 5
Regem cum lsetitia.
Protomartyr et Levita,
Clarus fide, clarus vita,
Clarus et miraculis,
Sub hue luce triumpliavit, lo
Et triumphans insultavit
Stephanus incredulis.
Fremunt ergo tanquam ferse,
Quia victi defecere
Lucis adversarii: 15
Falsos testes statuunt,
Et linguas exacuunt
Viperarum filii.
Agonista, nulli cede ;
Certa certus de mercede, 20
Persevera, Stephane :
Insta falsis testibus,
Confuta sermonibus
Synagogam Satanse.

; uid blunted in the blood of Christ, so that Stephen could now jss it by, and enter into life.

7. *Protomartyr]* Called therefore *apxb* /lapriipaw, *aSrfruv irpooifiuv, irpi!na8os, afltyruv lutpogtnov,* in the Greek Church. By a very natural transfer of Jewish terms to Christian things, *Levita* in the early Church language was=*diaconus* (Bingham, *Antiqq.* xi. 20, 2).

11. *insultavit]* Of. Acts vii. 61-53.

24. *Synagogam SatantP]* Cf. Rev. iii. 9.

Testis tuus est in ctelis, 25
Testis verax et fidelis,
Testis innocentise.
Nomen habes Coronati,
Te tormenta decet pati
Pro corona gloria. 30
Pro corona non marcenti
Perfer brevis vim tormenti,
Te manet victoria.
Tibi fiet mors, natalis,

Tibi prona terminalis 35
Dat vita3 primordia.
Plenus Sancto Spiritu
Penetrat intuitu
Stephanus coelestia.
Videns Dei gloriam 40
Crescit ad victoriam,
Suspirat ad prsemia.
26. Of. Rev. Hi. 14.

28. *Coronati]* The *nomen et omen* , which lay in that name Stephen (oWipapoj) for the first winner of the martyr's *crown,* is a favourite one with the early Church writers. Thus Augustin,, *(Enarr. in Ps.* Iviii. 3): Stephanus lapidatus est, et quod voca- batur, accepit. Stephanus enim corona dicitur. Cf. *Serm.* 314, 2. He plays in like manner with the name of the martyr Vincentius, noting that-he too was in like manner *itipi!ivvnos (Serm.* 274): *Vincentium* ubique *vincentem.* So in the legendary life of St Victor, a voice from heaven is heard at the moment of his death, *Vicisti, Victor,* beate, *vicisti;* and all this is embodied in a hymn addressed to the former of these martyrs :

O Vincenti! qui vicisti, Des invictum robur menti
Et invictus jam cepisti Soli Christus nam vincenti
Prcemia vincentium, Manna dat absconditum.
En a dextris Dei stantem
Jesum, pro te dimicantem,
Stephane, oonsidera. 45
Tibi coelos reserari,
Tibi Christum revelari
Clama voce libera.
Se commendat Salvatori,
Pro quo dulce ducit mori 50
Sub ipsis lapidibus.
Saulus servat omnium
Vestes lapidantium,
Lapidans in omnibus.

43. *stantem]* The one occasion on which Christ appears in Scripture as *standing* at the right hand of God, is that of Stephen's martyrdom (Acts vii. 55, 56). The reason why in all other places he should be spoken of as *sitting,* and here only as *standing,* Gregory the Great, whom our poet follows, has no doubt rightly given *(Hom.* 19,*in Fest. Ascens.): Sedere* judicantis est, *stare* vero pugnantis vel adjuvantis. Stephanus stantem vidit, quem adjutorem habuit. So too Arator, long before:

Lumina cordis habens ctelos conspexit apertos,
Ne lateat quid Christus agat: pro martyre surgit,
Quem tune *stare* videt, conf essio nostra *sedentem*
Cum soleat celebrare magis. Dux prsescins armat
Quos ad dona vocat.

Our Collect on St Stephen's day has not failed to bring this point out – " 0 blessed Jesus, who *standest* at the right hand of God *to succour* all those that suffer for Thee." This is but one example out of many, of the rich theological allusion, often unmarked by us, which the Collects of the Church contain.

54. *Lapidans in omnibus]* Augustine *(Serm.* 315): Quantum sseviebat [Saulus] in illa csede, vultis audire ? Vestimenta lapidantium servabat, ut omnium manibus lapidaret.

Ne peccatum statuatur 55
His, a quibus lapidatur,
Genu ponit et precatur,
Condolens insanise:
In Christo sic obdormivit,
Qui Christo sic obedivit, 60
Et cum Christo semper vivit,
Martyrum primitias.

55 – 62. Cf. Acts vii. 59 (Vulg.): Positis autem genibus. clamavit voee magna dicens, Domine, ne statuas illis hoc peccatum. Et cum hoc dixisset, obdormivit in Domino.

I cannot forbear quoting two stanzas, the first and fifth, from that other of Adam's hymns on the same martyr, alluded to already. I will observe, for the explanation of the first line, that roses were the- floral emblems of martyrs, as lilies of virgins, and violets of confessors.

Rosa, novum dans odorem, Uva, data torculari,
Ad ornatum ampliorem Vult pressures inculcari,
Regise ccelestis, Ne sit infecunda :
Ab JEgypto revocatur ; Martyr optat petra tori,
Ilium sequi gratulatur, Sciens munus adaugeri
Cujus erat tcstis. Sanguinis in unda.

33

SECTION 33

BEDE.

BORN 672, died 735. The circumstances of his life are in fresher remembrance among English Churchmen, than to need to be repeated here.

XLVII. S. ANDREAS ALLOQUITUR CRUCEM.

SALVE, tropasum gloriss,
Salve, sacrum victoriae
Signum, Deus quo perdituim
Mundum redemit mortuus.
O gloriosa fulgidis
Crux emicas virtutibus,
Quam Christus ipse proprii
Membris dicavit corporis.

XLVII. Cassander, *Hymni Ecchsiastiei (Opera,* Paris, 1616), p. 281. – These stanzas form part of one of the eleven hymns which Cassander attributed to Bede, and published for the first time in his *Hymni Ecclesiasticl,* Paris, 1556. The last editor of the works of Bede, Dr. Giles, has not been able to find any MS. containing these hymns, and, though not excluding, expresses (vol. i. p. clxxi.) many doubts in regard of their authenticity. Whether they are Bede's or not, I must dissent from the judgement of his editor in one respect, since, whatever the value 01 the poems as a whole, these lines have a real worth.

Quondam genus mortalium
Metu premebas pallido, 10
At nunc reples fidelium.
Amore lteto pectora.
En! ludus est credentium
Tuis frui complexibus,
Quae tanta gignis gaudia, 15
Pandis polique januas;
Quse Conditoris suavia
Post membra, nobis suavior
Es melle facta, et omnibus
Pra; lata mundi honoribus. 20
Te nunc adire gratulor,
Te caritatis brachiis
Complector, ad ctelestia
Conscendo per te gaudia.
Sic tu libens me suscipe, 25
Illius, alma, servulum,
Qui me redemit per tuam
Magister altus gloriam.
Sic fatur Andreas, crucis
Erecta cernens cornua, 30
Tradensque vestem militi,
Levatur in vitae arborem.

34

SECTION 34

ADAM OF ST VICTOR.
    XLVIII. DE S. LAURENTIO.
    OICUT chorda musicorum
    - Tandem sonum dat sonorum
    Plectri ministerio,

XLVIII. Clichtoveus, *Ehmdat. Eccles.* p. 208. – These three stanzas are but the fragments of rather a long poem, in which the *manner of* St Lawrence's martyrdom (he is said to have been broiled to death on a gridiron), is brought rather too prominently out; even in these present the *assatus* of ver. 11 we could willingly have missed. They are notwithstanding, well worthy to find a place here, being full of striking images, and singularly characteristic of their author's manner – most of all, perhaps, of his rich prodigality in the multiplication, and of his somewhat ostentatious skill in the arrangement, of his rhymes. – St Lawrence was archdeacon of Rome in the third century, and died in the persecution of Valerian. His festival was held in great honour by the Church of the middle ages, and himself accounted to hold a place only second to St Stephen, in the glorious army of martyrs (Durandus, *Rational.* vii. 23).

    1 – 10]. These and other like images appear in some lines of Hildebert upon a martyrdom (*Opp.* p. 1259):

Sicut chorda solet dare tensa sonum meliorern,
Sic pcenis tensus dat plenum laudis honorem ;
Utque probat foraax vas fictile consolidando,
Utque jubes late redolere unguenta liquando,
Ut feriendo sapis fervorem vimque sinapis,
Utque per artforem tus undique fundit odorem,
Sic odor insignis fiunt et vulnus et ignis.
Si caro tundatur, granum palea spoliator,
Si comburatur, tolli robigo putatur.
Sic in chely tormentorum
Melos Christ! confessorum 5
Martyris dat tensio.
Parum sapis vim sinapis,
Si non tangis, si non frangis ;
Et plus fragrat, quando flagrat,
Tus injectum ignibus : 10
Sic arctatus et assatus,
Sub ardore, sub labore,
Dat odorem pleniorera
Martyr de virtutibus.
Ilunc ardorem factum foris 15
Putat rorem vis amoris,
Et zelus justitise :
Ignis urens, non comburens,
Vincit prunas, quas adunas,
O minister impie. 20

4. *chely] Xavs* = testudo, originally the tortoise, out of the shell of which Hermes is said to have fashioned the first lyre. The poet would say: "It is with the martyrs of God in their sufferings as with the strings of the lyre, which are drawn tight and stricken, that so they may yield their sweetest sounds."

16. *Putat rorem]* An allusion probably to Dan. iii. 50 (Vulg.): Et fecit medium fornacis quasi ventum roris flantem.

35

SECTION 35

HILDEBERT.
  XLIX. SOMNIUM DE LAMENTATIONE
  PICTAVENSIS ECCLESLE.
  'VTOCTE quadam, via fessus,
  -L' Torum premens, somno pressus,
  In obscuro noctis densse,
  Templum vidi Pictavense,
  Sub staturS, personali,
  Sub persona matronali:
  XLIX. *Hildcberti et Marbodi Opp.* p. 1357. – In the *Gallia Christiana,* vol. ii. p.
1172, the circumstances are detailed which enable us to understand this noble vision.
William Adelelm, the rightful bishop of Poitiers, was in 1130 violently expelled from
his see, and driven into exile, by the faction of the anti- pope, Anacletus the Second,
and of the Count of Poitiers, who sided with him ; and an intrusive and schismatic
bishop, Peter of Chasteleraut, usurped his throne, and exercised infinite vexations and
oppressions upon the Church. William was at length restored in 1135, mainly owing
to the menacing remonstrances of St Bernard. See in his *Life (Opp.* vol. ii. p. 1122)
a most characteristic account of the manner in which Bernard terrified the Count into

this restoration. It was during the period of the usurpation, and when now it had lasted three years (ver. 79 – 81), that this poem was composed. I cannot be sure how far the reader's impressions will coincide with my own, nor whether I may not somewhat overrate its merits ; but certainly it seems to me to deserve something very different from that utter oblivion into which it has fallen. I know of no nobler piece of versification, nor more skilful management of rhyme, in the whole circle nf Latin rhymed poetry.

Situs quidem erat ei
Reverends e faciei;
Sed turbarat frontem ejus
Omni damno damnum pejus; 10
Sic est tamen rebus mersis,
Ut perpendas ex adversis
Quanti esset illis annis,
Quibus erat sine damnis.
Juvenilis ille color, is
Nullus erat unde dolor,
Nullus erat, sed in ore
Livor erat pro colore.
Hseret crini coronella,
Fracta nimbis et procella: 20
Vicem complet hie gemmarum
Grex corrosor tinearum.
Sunt in ventre signa famis,
Quem ostendit rupta chlamys:
Haw est chlamys, hie est cultus, 25
Quem attrivit annus multus,
Ab extremo quidem limbo
Gelu rigens, madens nimbo.
Est vetustas hujus vestis
Novitatis suse testis, 30

29 – 34. I understand Hildebert to mean – The oldness of this, the Church's robe, and that it hud endured so long, and survived so much, was a witness for its everlasting freshness and youth, and implied with how great care it had been woven at the first, even though now it was rent and tangled and torn, and scarcely hung about her limbs : – but doubtless the *novitatis* is difficult.

Innuendo quanta cura
Facta esset hsec textura:
Nunc se tenet mille nodis,
Iinplicata centum modis.
Ha3c ut stetit fletu madens, 35
Flendi causam mihi tradens,
De se quidem in figur&
Loquebatur inter plura,
Non desistens accusare

Navem, nautas, ventos, mare, 40
Ut ex verhis nesciretur
Quid vel quare loqueretur.
Mox infigens vultum coelis,
Ora solvit his querelis :
Deus meus, exclamavit, 45
Quis me turbo suffocavit?
Quse potestas impotentem ?
Quse vis urget me jacentem ?
Unde metus? unde moeror?
Unde veni ? vel quo feror ? so
Qui vel quales hi piratse,
Qui insultant mersa rate?
Quse procellse vel qui venti
Sic insurgunt resurgenti ?
Nauta bone, via bonis, 55
Utens remo rationis,
Quam inepte, quam incaute
Sese habent mei nautse!
Sed nee naute dici debent,
Qui fortunse manus prsebent, 60
Nee rectorum more degunt,
Qui reguntur, et non regunt.
His tam csecis quam ignavis
Est commissus clavus navis,
Quam curtavit parte una 6.)
Piratse vis importuna;
Nee a nautis est subventum
Contra ictus ferientum.
Timent viris non timenda
Hi a quibus sunt regenda; 70
Motum frondis, umbram lunse
Timet ilia gens fortune.
Sic me csscam cseco mari
Patiuntur evagari;
Procul collum a monili, 75
Procul latus a cubili;
Vilipendor a marito
Cum ad torum hunc invito.
Tribus annis noctem passa,
Vehor mari nave quassa; 80
Non exclusit annis tribus
Potus sitim, famem cibus:
Vicem potus, vicem panis
Spes explebat, sed inanis;

Nam exspecto tribus annis, S'
Quasi stultus, fluxum amnis;
Amnis tamen elabetur,
Nee ad horam haurietur.

Malo fracto, scisso velo,
Ad extremum nunc anhelo; 90
Nondum ventus iram lenit,
Sed a parte portus venit,
Ad occasum flat ab ortu,
Non ad portum sed a portu.

Dispensator, qui dispensas 95
Cum privatis res immensas,
Bene cuncta, nil inique;
Ita nusquam ut ubique;
Ortum suum cujus curse
Debent omnes creaturse, 100
Quas creasti non creatus,
Factus nunquam, tamen natus;
Tu qui magnus sine parte,
Princeps pacis sine Marte;
Tu qui bonus, immo bonum, 105
Quem amplecti paucis pronum;
Tibi constat id me velle,
Ne me vexent hse procella;,
Ne jam credar sorte regi,
Desponsata regum Regi. 110

Me laedentes, Rex, inclina,
Ne exultent de rapinu;
Facientibus rapinam
Sit rapina in ruinam;
Arce lupos cum piratis, 115
Ne desperet portum ratis.

Audi, Pastor, qui me regis,
Da pastorem doctum gregis,
Se regnantem ratione,
Deviantem a Simone, 120

120. a *Simone]* Here, as so often, *Simon* is put for the sin of simony to which he
lent his name. Thus, in some energetic

Qui sic pugnet in virtute
Ne sint opes parum *tutse*;
Sic dispense!; – et hoc dicto
Somnus abit, me relicto.

lines first published by Ede'lestand du Meril *(Poes. poptd. Leit.* 1847, p. 178),
and by him confidently ascribed to Thomas a Becket:

Roseb fiunt saliunca,

Domus Dei fit spelunca :
Simon malos pnefert bonis,
Simon totus est in donis;
Simon regnat apud Austrum,
Simon frangit omne claustrum.
Cum non datur, Simon stridet;
Sed, si detur, Simon ridet.
Simon anfert, Simon donat,
Hunc expellit, hunc coronat;
Hunc circumdat gravi peste,
Ilium nuptiali veste;
Illi donat diadema,
Qui nunc erat anathema.
Jam se Simon non abscondit,
Res permiscet et confundit.
Simon Petrus hunc elusit,
Et ab alto jussum trusit:
Quisquis eum imitatur
Cum eodem puniatur,
Et, sepultus in infernum,
Po3nas luat in Eeternum !

122. *opes]* Should we read *ovesf* ADAM OF ST VICTOR.

L. IN DEDICATIONE ECCLESLE.

QUAM dilecta tahernacula
Domini virtutum et atria !
Quam electi architect!,
Tuta sedificia,
Quse non movent, immo fovent,
Ventus, flumen, pluvia!

L. Clichtoveus, *Elucidat. Eccks.* p. 186 ; Gautier, *Adam de S. Victor,* vol. i. p. 155. – This hymn, of which the theme is, the dignities and glories of the Church, as prefigured in the Old Testament, and fulfilled in the New, is the very extravagance of typical application, and, were it only as a study in medieval typology, would be worthy of insertion; but it has other and higher merits; even though it must be owned that the poet's learned stun0 rather masters him, than that he is able effectually to master it. Its title indicates that it was composed for the occasion of a church's dedication, the services of which time were ever laid out for the carrying of men's thoughts from the temple made with hands to that spiritual temple, on earth or in heaven, " whose builder and maker is God."

1 – 6. The first two lines are a manifest allusion to Ps. Ixxxiii. 2, 3 (Vulg.): Quam dilecta tabernacula tua, Domine virtutum! Concupiseit, et deficit anima mea in atria Domini. The last four lines adapt the Lord's words, Matt. vii. 24, 25, to that house built indeed upon a Roek, upon Christ Himself. The poet writes *architecti,* including among these such as, under the great master-builder, carried up the walls – Apostles and prophets (Ephes. ii. 20 ; Rev. xxi. 14).

Qiiam decora fundamenta,
Per concinna sacramenta
Umbrse prsecurrentia.
Latus Adse dormientis 10
Evam fudit, in manentis
Copulse primordia.
Area ligno fabricata
Noe servat, gubernata
Per mundi diluvium. Ii
Prole sera tandem foeta,
Anus Sara ridet Iseta,
Nostrum lactans Gaudium.
Servus bibit qui legatur,
Et camelus adaquatur 20

10 – 12. *Latus Ada]* Augustine *(Enarr. in Ps.* Ivi. 5), shewing the mystery of the sleep which God sent on Adam, when about to fashion the woman from his side, asks, Quare voluit costam dormiente auferre *1* and replies, Quia dormiente Christo in cruce facta est conjux de latere. Percussum est enim latus pendentis de lancea, et profluxeruut Ecclesise sacramenta. Hugh of St Victor: Adam obdormivit, ut de costa illius fleret Eva ; Christus morte sopitus est, ut de sanguine ejus redimeretur Ecclesia.

18. *Gaudium]* Hugh of St Victor: Isaac, qui interpretatur risus, designat Christum, qui est gaudium nostrum. See note, p. 166.

19. *Servus bibit]* Eliezer, the servant of Abraham, represents, in the allegorical language of that day, the apostles or legates of Christ, who were themselves refreshed by the faith of that Gentile world which they brought as a bride to Christ – who, so to speak, drank of the streams which that world ministered to them, as Eliezer drank from the pitcher of Rebecca. The whole

Ex Rebeccse hydriS,;
Hsec inaures et armillas
Aptat sibi, ut per illas
Viro fiat congrua.
Synagoga supplantatur 25
A Jacob, , dutn divagatur,
Nimis freta literse.
Lippam Liam latent multa,
Quibus videns Rachel fulta
Pan nubit foedere. so
In bivio tegens nuda,
Geminos parit ex JudS,

allegory of Gen. xxiv. is set out at length in a sermon of Hilde- bert's, *Opp.* p. 741.

23. *Aptat sibi]* As Rebecca puts on the bracelets and earrings which Isaac sent her (Gen. xxiv. 22), so the Gentile Church adorns herself for her future Lord ; but with ornaments of his giving.

25 – 27. *divagatur]* Hugh of St Victor *(Alleg.* ii. 11): Esau foris venationi deserviens, benedictionem amittens, populum Israel significat, qui foris in litera justitiam quserit, et benedictionem coelestis hsereditatis dimittit.

28, 29. *Liam – Rachel]* Leah and Rachel signify, as is well known, the active and contemplative life; they are, so to speak, the Martha and Mary of the Old Testament; but they also signify the Synagogue and the Church – Leah the Synagogue, *lippa,* unable to see Christ, the true end of the law; but Rachel, or the Church, *videns,* seeing the things that belong to her peace.

31. *tegens nitda]* Cf. Gen. xxxviii. 14. For a general defence of such ugly types as this, and that which presently follows, 49 – 51, and of the seeking a prophetic element even in the sins of God's saints, see Augustine, *Con. Faust.* xxii. 83 ; Thamar diu vidua.

> Hie Moyses a puella,
> Dum se lavat, in fiscella *SS*
> Reperitur scirpea.
> Hie mas agnus immolatur,
> Quo Israel satiatur,
> Tinctus ejus sanguine.
> Hie transitur rubens unda, 40
> jEgyptios sub profundii
> Obruens voragine.

and again 87: Oderimus ergo peccatum, sed prophetiam non fxtinguamus; cf. Gregory the Great, *Mot.* iii. 28. St Bernard somewhere speaks of the New Testament sacraments (using that word in its largest sense), as fair both within and without, while in the Old, some are fair only within, and ill-favoured without. It is not my part here to discuss the fitness or unfitness of the use of such types, but merely to indicate what is needful for their full understanding. These words of Augustine will explain the present; who cares to see the matter brought out in greater detail may follow up the reference *(Con. Faust.* xxii. 86): Habitus meretricius confessio peccatorum est. Typum quippe jam Ecclesise ex gentibus evocatse gerit Thamar. A non agno- scente foetatur, quia de illa prsedictum est, Populus quem non cognovi, servivit mihi.

34 – 36. *Moyses]* Hugh of St Victor *(Alleg,* iii. 1): Moysos juxta flumen significat quemlibet hominem juxta fluvium prse- sentis sseculi positum; filia regis Gratiam designat, quse quemlibet ad vitam prsedestinatum de fluxu sseculi liberat, et in filium adoptat, ut qui prius fuerat filius irse, deinceps existat filius gratise. The words *fiscdla scirpea* occur in the Vulgate, Exod. ii. 3.

37 – 39. Cf. Exod. xii. 5; 1 Cor. v. *1.*

40 – r42. Hugh of St Victor: In Mari Rubro submersus est Pharao, et principes ejus; et in baptismo liberamur a potestate diaboli et principum ejus.

> Hie est urna manna plena,
> Hie mandata legis dena,
> Sed in area fosderis; 45
> Hie sunt sedis ornamenta,
> Hie Aaron indumenta,
> Quaj prsecedit poderis.

Hie Varias viduatur,
Barsabee sublimatur, 50
Sedis censors regise:
Ha=c Regi varietate
Vestis astat deauratse,
Sicut regum filise.

46. *adis ornamenta]* The candlestick, altar of incense, table of shewbread, and the like. He would say, Here, in the tabernacle which the Lord has pitched, are these in their truth, and not, as in that old, the mere figures of the true (Heb. ix.). See Gregory the Great, *in Ezech, Hom.* vii. § 2.

48. *poderis]* = iroS, prjs, vestis talaris. The word was quite naturalized in ecclesiastical Latin ; thus Hugh of St Victor: Tunica illa quse Grsece *poderis,* hoc est, *talaris* dicitur ; being for once right in his etymology of a Greek word. The *poderis* is the " robe" of Exod. xxviii. 3 *(iroSpris,* LXX. and Josephus: tunica, Vulg.). The poet would say, Here, in the Church, are the realities which the *garments* of the High Priest *(indumenta),* and the *robe (poderis),* the chief among them, did but foreshew. A mystical meaning has always been found in these garments; see Braun, *De Vest. Sacerd. Hebr.* p. 701 – 762.

49. *Varias viduatur]* See note on ver. 31. I could hardly quote, without offence, the lines of Hildebert *(Opp.* p. 1217), in which he traces the mystery of Rom. vii. 1 – 6 as foreshown at 2 Sam. xi. 26, 27.

52 – 54. Cf. Ps. xliv. 10 (Vulg.): Astitit regina adextris tuis in vestitu deaurato, circumdata varietate.

Hue venit Austri regina, 55
Salomonis quam divina
Condit sapientia;
Ha; c est nigra, sed formosa;
Myrrhas et turis fumosa
Virga pigmentavia. CO
Hsec futura, quss figura
Obumbravit, reseravit
Nobis dies gratias;
Jam in lecto cum dilecto
Quiescamus, et psallamus, (i:,
Adsunt enim nuptise:

55. *Austri regina]* The coming of the queen of the South (Matt. xii. 24) to hear the wisdom of Solomon (1 Kin. x.), was a favourite type of the coming of the Gentile world to hear the wisdom of a greater than Solomon. Hugh of St Victor *(Alleg.* vii. 2): Venit ad Salomonem regina Austri ut audiret sapien- tiam ejus, et venit ad Christum Gentilitas ut audiret sapientiam ejus.

58. *nigra, sed formosa]* In these words, drawn from Cant. i. 5 (nigra sum, sed formosa, Vulg.), the middle age expositors found, not the Church's confession of sin as still cleaving to her; but rather made them parallel to such words as the Apostle's: "We have this treasure in earthen vessels" (2 Cor. iv. 7), or the Psalmist's, " The king's daughter is all glorious within" (Ps. xlv. 12), *within* and not without; having

no form nor comeliness, no glory in the eyes of the world – "black" therefore to it, but beautiful to her Lord (Bernard, *In Cant. Serm.* 25).

60. *Virga pigmentaria]* Cf. Cant. iii. 6 (Vulg.): Quse est ista, quse ascendit per desertum, sicut virgula fumi ex aromatibus myrrhse, et turis, et universi pulveris pigmentarii ? The Bride, or Church, is likened to the "pillar of smoke perfumed with myrrh and frankincense."

Quarum tonat initium
In tubis epulantium,
Et finis per psalterium.
Sponsum millena milia 70
Una laudant melodia,
Sine fine dicentia,
Alleluia. Amen.

67 – 69. The marriage of Christ with his Church, which began under the Old Covenant, was completed in the New. The *trumpets* belong to the feasts of the Old (Num. x. 10; cf. Ps. xli. 5, Vulg., sonus *epulantis);* the *psaltery* or decachordon (modula- tionem edens longe suaviorem et gratiorem auditu quam sit tubarum sonitus obstreperus: Cliehtoveus) to the New; it is on it that the *new song* is sung, even as David says (Ps. cxliii. 9, Vulg.): Deus, *canticum novum* cantabo tibi: *in psalterio* decachordo psallam tibi. Cf. Augustine, *Serm.* 9; *De decem Chordis,* 5.

Walter Mapes' clever irony on this so favourite school of Scripture interpretation, his complaint that, although he had cultivated it so diligently, it had brought no worldly preferment to him,' as it had brought to many, all this may be found at length in Leyser's *Hist. Poett. et l'oemm. Med. Mn,* pp. 779 – 784. These are some stanzas:

Opulenti sclent esse, Duo ligna Sareptcrue,
Qui aptabant virgam Jessse Spiritalis escam ccense
Partui virgineo, Coquunt in Ecclesia ;
Sive rubum visionis, Abrahamque tulit ligna,
Sive vellus Gideonis Per quse digne Deo digna
Sparsum rore vitreo. Cremaretur hostia.
Solet Christus appellari *Ussc* scrutari quidam solent,
Lapis sumptus de altari Post afflicti fame dolent
Non manu sed forcipe, Se vacasse studio.
Hoc est notum sapient!, Unde multi perierunt,
Scd prffibendam requirenti Et in ipso defecerunt
Kemo dicet, Accipe. Scrutantes scrutinio.

36

SECTION 36

LI. DE VITA MUNDANA.
    EHEU ! eheu! mundi vita,
    Quare me delectas ita?
    Cum non possis mecum stare,
    Quid me cogis te amare ?
    Eheu ! vita fugitiva. 5
    Omni fera plus nociva,
    Cum tenere te non queam,
    Cur seducis mentem meam?
    Eheu ! vita, mors vocanda,
    Odienda non amanda, 10
    Cum in te sint nulla bona,
    Cur exspecto tua dona?
    LI. Edelestand du Méril, *Poesies Populaires Latines du Moyen Age,* Paris, 1847, p. 108 ; Mone, *Hymn. Lat. Med. Mci,* vol i. p. 411. – The poem from which these stanzas are drawn consists of nearly four hundred lines. It was first completely published by Du Meril, as indicated above, from a MS. in the Imperial Library at Paris. The MS. is of the twelfth century, and the poem itself can scarcely be of an

earlier date. Three or four stanzas of it had already got abroad. Thus two are quoted by Gerhard, *Loci Theoll.* xxix. 11, and see Ley ser, *Hist. Poem. Med. Mvi,* p. 423. The attribution of these fragments of the poem, and thus implicitly of the whole, to St Bernard, rests on no au - thority whatever; it is merely a part of that general ascription to him of any poems of merit belonging to that period, whereof the authorship was uncertain.

Vita mundi, res morbosa,
Magis fragilis quarti rosa,
Cum sis tota lucrymosa, 15
Cur es mihi gratiosa?
Vita mundi, res laboris,
Anxia, piena timoris,
Cum sis semper in languore,
Cur pro te sum in dolore? 20
Vita mundi, mors futura,
Incessanter ruitura,
Cum in brevi sis mansura,
Cur est mihi de te cura?
Vita mundi, res maligna, 25
Ut ameris nunquam digna,
Quid putas tibi prodesse,
Si me ducas ad non esse?
Vita mundi, res immunda,
Solis impiis jucunda, *SO*
Nutrimentum vitiorum,
Quid habes in te decorum ?
Desine mihi piacere,
Noli mihi congaudere,
Desine me conturbare, 35
Nolj, quseso, me amare.
Esecro tuum amorem,
Renuo tuum favorem ;
Desero tuum decorem,
Non amo tuum odorem. 40
Per te ipsam tibi juro,
Donis tuis nihil euro,
Qua re nil potes donare
Nisi poenas et plorare;
Pellam te de corde meo, 45
Adjuvante Christo Deo,
Nee permittam te redire,
Si debeaa interire.
Nee mireris, pestis dira,
Si te persequor cum irsl, *so*
Quare tu mihi fecisti

Quicquid mali potuisti.
Idcirco, vita inepta,
Solls fatuis accepta,
Cum sis tota plena sorde, 55
Te refute toto corde.
Toto corde te refuto,
Nee sententiam commuto,
Mortem plus volo subire,
Tibi, vita, quam servire. 60LIT.
UT jucundaa cervus undas
jEstuans desiderat,
Sic ad rivum Dei vivum
Mens fidelis properat.
Sicut rivi fontis vivi 5
Prtebent refrigerium,
Ita menti sitienti
Deus est remedium.
Quantis bonis superponis
Sanctos tuos, Domine : 10
Sese lasdit, qui recedit
Ab aeterno lumine.
Vitam lastam et quietam,
Qui te quasrit, reperit;
Nam laborem et dolorem 15
Metit, qui te deserit.
Pacem donas, et coronas,
His qui tibi militant;
Cuncta lasta sine meta
His qui tecum habitant. 20

LII. Mommey, *Suppkmentum Patrum,* Paris, 1686, p. 165. – He attributes the poem from which these lines are drawn, but on grounds entirely insufficient, to St Bernard.

37

SECTION 37

Heu quam vana mens humana
   Visione falleris!
   Dum te curis nocituris
   Imprudenter inseris.
   Cur non caves lapsus graves, 25
   Quos suadet proditor,
   Nee aifectas vias rectas,
   Quas ostendit Conditor ?
   Resipisce, atque disce
   Cujus sis originis; 30
   Ubi degis, cujus legis,
   Cujus sis et ordinis.
   Ne te spernas, sed discernas,
   Homo, gemma regia:
   Te perpende, et attende 35
   Qua sis factus gratia.
   Recordare quis et quare
   Sis a Deo conditus;

Hujus hasres mine maneres,
Si fuisses subditus. 411
O mortalis, quantis malis
Meruisti affici,
Dum rectori et auctori
Noluisti subjici.

34. *gemma regia]* Thus a later hymn, on the ret-very of the
lost sinner:

Amissa drachma regio
Recondita est serario:
Et gemma, deterso luto,
Nitore vincit sidera.
Sed majores sunt dolores 45
Infernalis carceris;
Quo mittendus et torquendus
Es, si male vixeris.
Cu'i mundus est jucundus,
Suam perdit animam : .';0
Pro re levi atque brevi
Vitam perdit optimam.
Si sunt plagse, curam age
Ut curentur citius:
Ne, si crescant et putrescant, 55
Pergas in deterius.
Ne desperes, jam cohseres
Christi esse poteris,
Si carnales, quantum vales,
Afiectus excluseris; 60
Si vivorum et flmctorum
Christum times judicem :
Debes scire, quod perire
Suum non vult supplicem.
Preces funde, pectus tunde, G5
Flendo cor humilia:
Poenitenti et gementi
Non negatur venia. 24'

ALARD.

WILLIAM ALARD, born 1572, and descended from a noble family in Belgium,
was the son of Francis Alard, a confessor of the Reformed Faith during the persecutions
of the Duke of Alva. The father, hardly escaping from the Low Countries with his
life, settled in Holstein, at the invitation of Christian the Fourth, king of Denmark.
For three or four generations the family, which appears to have established itself
there, or in the neighbouring parts of Germany, was distinguished in the walks of
theology and classical learning; so much so that one of its later members published
a *Decas Alardorum Scriptis Clarorum,* Hamburg, 1721, from which my information

is derived. Besides other works which William composed, he was the author of two small volumes of Latin hymns, which, however forgotten now, appear to have found much favour at the time of their publication: *Excubiarum piarum Centuria,* Lipsisc, 1623; and *Exctibiarum piarum Centuria Se- cunda,* 1C28; I believe that there was also a third *Century,* though it has never come under my eye. Of the first *Century* four editions were published in the author's lifetime. He died Pastor of Rrempe in Holstein in 1645.

38

SECTION 38

LIH. DE ANGELO CUSTODE.
CUM me tenent falkcia
Mundi fugacis gaudia,
Coelo vigil mihi datus
Flet atque plorat Angelus.
Sed quando lacrimis mea
Deploro tristis crimina,
Lsetatur Angelus Dei,
Qui tangitur cura mei.
Proinde abeste, gaudia
Mundi fugacis omnia;
Adeste lacrimse, mea
Plorem quibus tot crimina:
Ne, lsetus in malo, Angelis
Sim causa fletus coelicis,
Sed his, nefas lugens meum,
Creem perenne gaudium.
LIII. *ExcMarum Piarum Centuria* 2 Lips. 1628, p. 304.

39

SECTION 39

LIV. ACCESSURI AD SACRAM COMMUNIO-
NEM ORATIO AD JESUM SERVATOREM.
SIT ignis atque lux mihi
Reo tui perceptio,
Jesu beate, corporis,
Sacerrimique sanguinis;
Ut ignis hie cremet mei
Cordis nefas, et omnia
Delicta, noxios simul
Affectuum rubos cremet;
Ut ista lux sua face
Tenebricosa pectoris
Illuminet mei, prece
Te semper ut pia colat.

LIV. *Excub. Piar. Cent.* Lips. 1623, p. 336. – The reader acquainted with the Greek *Euehologion* will recognize this as little more than the versification of a prayer therein.

ST AMBROSE.

LV. HYMNUS AD GALLICANTUM.

7TJ1TERNE rerum Condi tor,
-L- Noctem diemque qui regis,
Et temporum das tempora,
Ut alleves fastidium;
PrsBco diei jam sonat,
Noctis profiindse pervigil,

LV. 8. *Ambrosii Opp.* Paris, 183G, p. 200. – There can be no doubt that many so called Ambrosian hymns are not by St Ambrose; out of which it has come to pass, that some, in an opposite extreme, have affirmed that *we* possess none which can certainly be affirmed to be his. Yet, to speak not of others, this is lifted above all doubt, Augustine, the cotemporary of Ambrose, and himself for some time a resident at Milan, distinctly ascribing it to him, *Retract.* i. 21; cf. his *Confess.* ix. 12, in proof of his familiarity with the hymns of St Ambrose. Moreover, the hymn is but the metrical arrangement of thoughts which he has elsewhere *(Hexaem.* xxiv. 88) expressed in prose: Galli cantus... et dormientem exeitat, et sollicitum admonet, et viantem solatur, processum noctis canora significatione protest- ans. Hoc canente latro suas relinquit insidias; hoc ipse lucifer excitatus oritur, coelumque illuminat; hoc canente moestitiam trepidus nauta deponit; omnisque crebro vespertinis flatibus excitata tempestas et procella mitescit;.. . hoc postremo canente ipsa Ecclesise Petra culpam suam diluit – with much more, in which the very turns of expression used in the hymn recur.

Nocturna lux viantibus,
A nocte noctem segregans.
Hoc excitatus lucifer
Solvit polum caligine ; 10
Hoc omnis erronum cohors
Viam nocendi deserit.
Hoc nauta vires colligit,
Pontique mitescunt freta ;
Hoc, ipsa petra Ecclesiae, 15
Canente, culpam diluit.
Surgamus ergo strenue,
Gallus jacentes excitat,

7, 8. Clichtoveus: *Nocturna lux* est *viantibus* quantum ad munus et officium, quod noctu iter agentibus nocturnas significat horas, perinde atque interdiu viam carpentibus lux solis eas in- sinuat conspicantibus solem .. *A nocte noctem segregare* memoratur, quoniam priorem noctis partem a posteriore suo cantu dirimit ac disseparat, quasi noctis discretor.

11. *erronum]* A preferable reading to *errorum,* which might so easily have supplanted it, but which it, the rarer word, would scarcely have supplanted. In the hymn of Prudeutius we read:

Ferunt *vagantes d&mones, '* Invisa nam vicinitas
Laetos tenebris noctium, Lucis, salutis, numinis,
Gallo canente exterritos Eupto tenebrarum situ,

Sparsim timere et cedere. Noctis fugat satellites.

16. *petra Ecclesia]* That St Ambrose was very far from believing in a Church built upon a man, that therefore here he can mean no such thing, is plain from other words of his (*De Incarn. Dom.* 5): Fides ergo est Ecclesise fundamentum: non enim de carne Petri, sed de fide dictum est, quia portffi mortis ei non prsevalebunt.

17. *Surganms ergo)* The cock-crowing had for the earlyEt somnolentos increpat;
Gallus negantes arguit. 20
Gallo canente, spes redit,
JEgris salus refunditur,
Mucro latronis conditur,
Lapsis fides revertitur.
Jesu, labantes respice, 25
Et nos videndo corrige :
Si respicis, lapsus cadunt,
Fletuque culpa solvitur.
Tu lux refulge sensibus,
Mentisque somnum discute : SO
Te nostra vox primum sonet,
Et vota solvamus tibi.

Christians a mystical significance. It said, " The night is far spent, the day is at hand." And thus the cock became, in the middle ages, the standing emblem of the preachers of God's Word. The old heathen notion, that the lion could not bear the sight of the cock (Ambrose, *Hexaem.* vi. 4 : Leo gallum et maxime album veretur; cf. Lucretius, iv. 716; Pliny, *H. N.* viii. 19) easily adapted itself to this new symbolism. Satan, the roaring lion, fled away terrified, at the faithful preaching of God's Word. Nor did it pass unnoted, that this bird, clapping its wings upon its sides, first rouses itself, before it seeks to rouse others. Thus Gregory the Great *(Reg. Pastor-* iii. 40): Gallus, cum jam edere cantus parat, prius alas exeutit, et semetipsum feriens vigilantiorem reddit: quia nimirum necesse est, ut hi, qui verba sanctse prsedicationis movent, prius studio bonse ac- tionis evigilent, ne in semetipsis torpentes opere, alios excitent voce. - 25 – 28. A beautiful allusion to Luke xxii. 60 – 62.

40

SECTION 40

146
ST BERNARD.
LVI. DE NOMINE JESU.
JESU dulcis memoria,
Dans vera cordi gaudia,
Sed super mel et omnia
Ejus dulcis prsesentia.
Nil canitur suavius, 5
Nil auditur jucundius,
Nil cogitatur dulcius,
Quam Jesus Dei Filius.
Jesu, spes poenitentibus,
Quam pius es petentibus, 10
Quam bonus te quserentibus,
Sed quid invenientibus ?

LVI. *Bernardi Opp.* ed Bened. 1719, voL ii. p. 914. – This poem, among those
of St Bernard perhaps the most eminently characteristic of its author, consists, in its
original form, of nearly fifty quatrains, and, unabridged, would have been too long

for insertion here ; not to say that, with all the beauty of the stanzas in particular, the composition, as a whole, lies under the defect of a certain monotony and want of progress. Where all was beautiful, the task of selection was certainly a hard one; but only in this way could the poem have found place in this volume ; nor, for the reasons just stated, did I feel that it would be altogether a loss to it to present it in this briefer form.

Jesu, dulcedo cordium,
Fons vivus, lumen mentium,
Excedens omne gaudium, 15
Et omne desiderium.
Nee lingua valet dicere,
Nee littera exprimere,
Expertus potest credere
Quid sit Jesum diligere. 20
Quando cor nostrum visitas,
Tune lucet ei veritas,
Mundi vilescit vanitas,
Et intus fervet caritas.
Qui te gustant, esuriunt; 25
Qui bibunt, adhuc sitiunt;
Desiderare nesciunt
Nisi Jesum quem diligunt.
Quem tuus amor ebriat,
Novit quid Jesus sapiat; 30
Quam felix est quem satiat!
Non est ultra quod cupiat.
Jesu, decus angelicum,
In aure dulce canticum,
In ore mel mirificum, 35
In corde nectar coelicum:
Desidero te millies,
Mi Jesu, quando venies ?
Me Isetum quando facies?
Me de te quando saties ? 40
O Jesu mi dulcissime,
Spes suspirantis animse,
Te quaerunt pise lacrimse,
Te clamor mentis
Tu fons misericordise, 45
Tu verse lumen patrise :
Pelle nnbem tristitise,
Dans nobis lucem gloriss.
Te coeli chorus prsedicat,
Et tuas laudes replicat : 50
Jesus orbem laetificat,

Et nos Deo pacificat.
Jesus ad Patrem rediit,
Cmleste regnum subiit :
Cor meum a me transiit, 55
Post Jesum simul abiit :
Quem prosequamur laudibus,
Votis, hymnis, et precibus;
Ut nos donet coelestibus
Secum perfrui sedibus. no LVII. PHCENIX INTER FLAMMAS EXSPIRANS.
TANDEM audite me,
Sionis filise !
jEgram respicite,
Dilecto dicite:
Amore vulneror, 5
Amore fiineror.
Fulcite floribus
Fessam languoribus;
Stipate citreis
Et malls aureis ; 10
Nimis edacibus
Liquesco facibus.
Hue odoriferos,
Hue soporiferos
Ramos depromite, 15
Rogos componite ;
Ut phoenix moriar !
In flammis oriar !

LVII. [Walraff,] *Corolla Hymnorum,* p. 57. – The poet has drawn his inspiration throughout from the Canticles. The whole of this beautiful composition is but the further unfolding of the words of the Bride, " I am sick of love " (ii. 5).

An amor dolor sit,
An dolor amor sit, 20
Utrumque nescio;
Hoc unum sentio,
Jucundus dolor est,
Si dolor amor est.
Quid, amor, crucias ? *25*
Aufer inducias,
Lentus tyrannus es;
Momentum annus est;
Tam tarda funera
Tua sunt vulnera. 30
Jam vitae stamina
Kumpe, O anima !
Ignis ascendere

Gestit, et tendere
Ad coeli atria ; 35
Hsec mea patria ! ABELARD.
LVIII. DIXIT AUTEM DEUS: FIANT LUMI-
NARIA IN FIRMAMENTO CCELI.
Gen. i. 14.
ARNARUNT terram germina,
v Nunc coelum luminaria;
Sole, luna, stellis depingitur,
Quorum multus usus cognoscitur.
Hsec quaque parte condita 5
Sursum, Homo, considera;
Esse tuam et coeli regio
Se fatetur horum servitio.
Sole calet in hieme,
Qui caret ignis munere; 10
Pro nocturna: lucernse gratia
Pauper habet lunam et sidera.
Stratis dives eburneis,
Pauper jacet gramineis;

LVIII. Edelestand du Meril, *Poesies Popul. Lat.* 1847, p. 444. – I have already spoken unfavourably of Abelard's poetry; but this poem, one of a series on the successive days' work of Creation, of a sort of *Hexaemeron* in verse, despite its prosaic commencement and unmelodious rhythm, must be acknowledged to rest on a true poetical foundation.

Hinc avium oblectant cantica, 15
Inde florum spiral fragantia.
Impensis, Dives, nimiis
Domum casuram construis;
Falso sole pingis testudinem,
Falsis stellis in coeli speciem. 20
In vera cali camera
Pauper jacet pulcherrima;
Vero sole, veris sideribus
Istam illi depinxit Dominus.
Opus magis eximium 25
Est naturse quam hominum ;
Quod nee labor nee sumptus prseparat,
Nee vetustas solvendo dissipat.
Ministrat homo diviti,
Angelus autem pauperi, 30
Ut hinc quoque constet coelestia
Quam sint nobis a Deo subdita.

17 – 24. Augustine : Plus est pauperi videre coelum stellatum quam diviti tectum inauratum.

31, 32. There are some good lines in the poem, *De Contemptv Mundi,* found in St Anselm's *Works,* pp. 195 – 201, on the same

theme.

Cur dominus rerum, quare Deitatis imago

Parva cupis ? cupias maxima, magnus homo.

Luna tibi f ulget, tibi volvitur orbita solis,

Et tibi sunt toto sidera sparsa polo.

Nempe dies tuus est, tua nox, tuus igneus sether,

Et tibi commutant tempora qmeque vices. BUTTMANN.

Born 1764, died 1829.

LIX. ARX FIRMA DEUS NOSTER EST.

ARX firma Dens noster est,

Is telum, quo nitamur;

Is explicat ex omnibus

Queis malis implicamur.

Nam cui semper mos,

Jam ter terret nos;

Per astum, per vim,

Sasvam levat sitim;

Nil par in terris illi.

LIX. Mohnike, *Hymnol. Forschungen,* Stralsund, 1832, vol. ii. p. 250. – This is a good translation, perhaps as good as could be made, of Luther's " Heldenlied," as it well has been called, –

Ein feste Burg ist anser Gott:

the hymn, among all with which he has enriched the Church, most characteristic of the man, tho truest utterance of his great heart. Much of the heroic strength of the original has vanished in the translation; yet, beside its merits, which are real, it is interesting as shewing the eminent philologist whose work it is, in somewhat a novel aspect. It was first published in 1830, shortly after Buttman's death, on occasion of the third jubilee to celebrate the publication of the Confession of Augsburg. The original hymn was probably composed in 1530, during the time when the Diet was sitting there.

In nobis nihil situm est, 10

Quo minus pereamus:

Quem Deus ducem posuit,

Is facit ut vivamus.

Scin quis hoc potest?

Jesus Christus est, 15

Qui, dux coelitum,

Non habet semulum ;

Is vicerit profecto.

Sit mundus plenus dsemonum,

Nos cupiant vorare; 20

Non timor est; victoria

Nil potest nos frustrare.

Hem dux sseculi!
Invitus abi !
In nos nil potes, 25
Jam judicatus es;
Vel rocula te sternat.
Hoc verbum non pessumdabunt,
Nee gratiam merebunt;
In nobis Christi Spiritus 30
Et munera vigebunt:
Tollant corpus, rem,
Mundique omnem spem :
Tollant! jubilent I
Non lucrum hinc ferent; 35
Manebit regnum nobis.

41

SECTION 41

ST BERNARD.
    LX. DE CONTEMPTU MUNDI.
    CUM sit omnis homo foenum,
    Et post fcenum fiat coenum,
    Ut quid, homo, extolleris?
    Cerne quid es, et quid eris;
    Modo flos es, et verteris 6
    In iavillam cineris.
    Per setatum incrementa,
    Immo magis detrimenta,
    Ad non-esse traheris.
    Velut umbra, cum declinat, 10
    Vita surgit et festinat,
    Claudit meta funeris.
    Homo dictus es ab humo;
    Cito transis, quia fumo
    Similis eificeris. 15
    Nunquam in eodem statu

Permanes, dum sub rotatu
Hujus vite volveris.

LX. *Bernardi Opp.* ed. Bened. 1719, vol. ii. p. 915; Rambach, *Anthol. Christl. Gesdnge,* p. 281.

13. *ab humo]* Quintilian *(Inst.* i. 6, 34) throws scorn on this derivation – quasi vero non omnibus animalibus eadem origo, aut illi primi mortales ante nomen imposuerint terrae quam sibi; but see Freund, *Worterbwh d. Lat. Sprache,* s. v. Homo.

O sors gravis ! o sors dura !
O lex dira, quam natura 20
Promulgavit miseris I
Homo, nascens cum mœrore,
Vitam ducis cum labore,
Et cum metu moreris.
Ergo si scis qualitatem 25
Tuœ sortis, voluptatem
Garnis quare sequeris?
Memento te moriturum,
Et post mortem id messurum,
Quod hie seminaveris. 30
Terram teris, terrain geris,
Et in terram reverteris,
Qui de terra sumeris.
Cerne quid es, et quid eris,
Modo flos es, et verteris 35
In favillam cineris.

42

SECTION 42

ALANUS.
 LXI. RHYTHMUS DE NATURA HOMINIS
 FLUXA ET CADUCA.
 OMNIS mundi creatura
 Quasi liber et pictura
 Nobis est, et speculum ;
 Nostrse vitse, nostras mortis,
 Nostri statfjs, nostras sortis 5
 Fidele signaculum.
 Nostrum statum pingit rosa,
 Nostri status decens glosa,
 Nostras vitas lectio :
 Qusb dum prime mane floret, 10
 Defloratus flos effloret
 Vespertine senio.
   LXI. *Alani Opp.* ed. C. de Visch, Antwerp, 1654, p. 419. – This fine poem has
found its way into very few collections of sacred Latin verse. Indeed the only one in

which I have mc-t it is that of Kambach, and there two stanzas, the seventh, perhaps the finest in the whole poem, being one of them, are omitted.

8. *glosa*] *Glosa,* or *glossa,* is thus explained by Du Cange : Interpretatio, imago, exemplum rei; it is our English *gloss* or *glose;* which yet is used generally in a bad sense, the tongue (for the word is of course derived from *yuffffa)* being so often the setter forth of deceit, interpretation being so frequently misinterpretation. The German *gleisscn,* to make a fair shew, belongs probably to the same family of words.

Ergo Rpirans flos exspirat,
In pallorem dum delirat,
Oriendo moriens. 15
Simul vetus et novella,
Simul senex et puella,
Rosa marcet oriens.
Sic setatis ver humanse
Juventutis primo mane 20
Reflorescit paululum.
Mane tamen hoc excludit
Vitse vesper, dum concludit
Vitale crepusculum :
Cujus decor dum perorat, . 25
Ejus decus mox deflorat
./Etas, in qua defluit.
Fit flos foenum, gemma lutum,
Homo cinis, dum tributum
Homo morti tribuit. 30
Cujus vita, cujus esse
Poena, labor, et necesse
Vitam morte claudere.
Sic mors vitam, risum luctus,
Umbra diem, portum fluctus, 35
Mane claudit vespere.
In nos primum dat insultum
Poena, mortis gerens vultum,
Labor, mortis histrio :
Nos proponit in laborem, 40
Nos assumit in dolorem,
Mortis est conclusio.
Ergo clausum sub hac lege
Statum tuum, homo, lege,
Tuum esse respice : 45
Quid fuisti nasciturus,
Quid sis prsesens, quid futurus,
Diligenter inspice.
Luge poenam, culpam plange,
Motus frsena, fastum frange, 50

Pone supercilia.
Mentis Rector et Auriga,
Mentem rege, fluxus riga,
Ne fluant in devia.

43

SECTION 43

260

HILDEBERT.

LXH. DE EXILIO SUO.

NUPER eram locuplea, multisque beatus amicis,

Et risere diu fata secunda mihi :

Jurares Superos intra mea vota teneri,

Et res occasum dedidicisse pati.

Siepe mihi dixi: Quorsum tam prospera rerum ? 5

Quid sibi vult tantus, tam citus agger opum ? Hei mihi! nulla fides, nulla est constantia rebus,

Res ipsse quid sint mobilitate docent. . Res hominum atque homines levis alea versat in horas,

Et venit a summo summa ruina gradu. 10

Quicquid habes hodie, eras te fortasse relinquet,

Aut mode, dum loqueris, desinit esse tuum. Has ludit fortuna vices, regesque superbos

Aut servos humiles non sinit esse diu. Ecce quid est hominis, quid jure vocare paterno, 15

Qua miser ille sibi plaudere dote potest.
Hoc est, hoc hominis, semper cum tempore labi,
Et semper qu&dam conditione mori.
Est hominis nudum nasci, nudumque reverti
Ad matrem, nee opes tollere posse suas. *20*
Est hominis putrere solo, saniemque fateri,
Et miseris gradibus in cinerem redigi.
LXII. *Hildeberti et Marbodi Opp.* p. 1344. Hommey, *Sup- '-atentum Patrum,* p. 453.

Istius est hseres homo prosperitatis, et ilium
Certius his dominum pradia nulla manent. Res et opes prsestantur ei, famulantur ad horam, 25
Et locuples mane, vespere pauper erit. Nemo potest rebus jus assignare manendi,
Qnse nutus hominum non didicere pati. Jus illis Deus ascribit, statuitque teneri
Legibus, et nutu stare vel ire suo. so
Ille simul semel et solus prsevidit et egit
Cuneta, nee ilia aliter vidit, agitque aliter. Ut vidit facienda facit, regit absque labore,
Distinguit formis, tempore, fine, loco. Crescendi studium rebus metitur, et illas 35
Secretis versat legibus, ipse manens. Ipse manens, dum cuncta znovet, mortalibus segris
Consulit, et qua sit spes statuenda docet. Si fas est credi te quicquam posse vel esse,
O fortuna, quod es, quod potes ipse dedit. 40 Pace tua, fortuna, loquar, blandire, minare,
Nil tamen unde querar, aut bene Iseter ages. Ille potens, mitis tenor et concordia rerum,
Quidquid vult in me digerat, ejus ero.

44

SECTION 44

JACOBUS DE BENEDICTIS.

TACOBUS de Benedictis, or familiarly Jacopone, to whom the following poem in all probability appertains, was in every regard a memorable man and of a remarkable history. There are two very careful sketches of his life and writings, drawn entirely from the original sources, and far richer than any to be found in ordinarv biographies, given, one by Mohnike *(Studien,* Stralsund. 1825, vol. i. pp. 335-406), another by *Ozanv. m(LesPoiites Frcmciscains en Italic au troisieme Siecle,* Paris, pp. 164 – 272) ; though indeed that in the *Biographic Universelle* is far from being slightly or inaccurately done. The year of his birth is not known, but, as he died in 1306 at a great age, it must have fallen early in the preceding century. He was born at Todi in Umbria, of a noble family, and lived a secular life, until some remarkable circumstances attending the violent death of his wife made so deep an impression upon him, that he withdrew himself to that which was then counted exclusively the religious life, and entered the Order of St Francis, just then at its highest reputation for sanctity; though he was never willing to be more than a lay brother therein.

Of his Latin poems I said in my former edition that only this and the far more cele-brated *Stabat Mater* had been preserved; though of Italian spiritual songs and satires a very large amount; but Ozanam has since that time published, though apparently

from an imperfectMS., a beautiful pendant to that poem. It is the *Stabat Mater* of the
Blessed Virgin by the cradle of Bethlehem, and not by the cross of Calvary. The great
freedom of speech with which, in his vernacular poems, he handled the abuses of his
time, and especially those of the hierarchy, drew on him long imprisonments, and
he only went out of prison when his persecutor, Boniface the Eighth, whom to have
had for an adversary was itself an honour, went in. An earnest humorist, he seems
to have desired to carry the being a fool for Christ into every-day familiar life. The
things which with this intent he did, some of them morally striking enough, others
mere extravagances and pieces of gross spiritual buffoonery – wisdom and folly, such
as we often find, side by side, in the saints of the Romish Calendar – are largely given
by Wadding, the historian of the Franciscan Order, and by Lisco, in a separate treatise
which he has published on the *Stabat Mater*, Berlin, 1843, p. 23. Not a few of these
leave one in doubt whether he was indeed perfectly sound in his mind, or whether
he was only a Christian Brutus, feigning folly, that he might impress his wisdom the
more deeply, and utter it with a greater freedom.

Balde, the Bavarian Jesuit, of whom there will presently be occasion to say something more, has recorded in a graceful little poem *(Silv.* vii. 2) what his feelings were,
on first making acquaintance with the life and writings of Jacopone:

Tristis nsenia funerum,
Vanse cum gemitu cedite lacrimse.
Me virtutis iter decent
Intermista jocis gaudia mutuis; Me coelo lepor inserit;
Me plus quam rigid i vita Pachomii,
Jacopone, trahit tua,
Florens lsetitiis mille deeentibus.
Sancto diceris omnia
Risu perdomuisse ; egregia quidem
Dementis specie vin.
Chaldseosque magos, et Salomoniam
Transgressus sapicntiam,
Curarum vacuus, plenior setheris,
Non urbis, neque dolii,
Sd mundi fueras publicus incola.

The key-note to this beautiful composition is supplied by the epitaph which graces
a monument raised to him, in 159G, at his native Todi:

Ossa B. Jacoponi de Benedictis, Tudertini, qui, stultus propter Christum, nova
mundum arte delusit, et coelum rapuit.

LXIII. DE CONTEMPTU MUNDI.

CUR mundus militat sub vanti gloria,
Cujus prosperitas est transitoria ?
Tam cito labitur ejus potentia,
Quam vasa figuli, quae sunt fragilia.
Plus fide litteris scriptis in glacie,
Quam mundi fragilis vanas fallacise;
Fallax in pramiis, virtutis specie,

Qui nunquam habuit tempus fiducise.

LXIII. *Bernardi Opp.* ed Bened. vol. ii. p. 913 ; Mohnike, *Hymnol. Forschungen,* vol. ii. p. 173. – Tusser has translated this hymn.

Credendum magis est viris fallacibus,
Quam mundi miseris prosperitatibus, 10
Falsis insaniis et vanitatibus,
Falsisque studiis et voluptatibus.
Quam breve festum est hsec mundi gloria !
Ut umbra hominis, sic ejus gaudia,
Quse semper subtrahunt seterna prsemia, 15
Et ducunt hominem ad dura devia.
0 esea vermium ! o massa pulveris !
O ros, o vanitas, cur sic extolleris?

9. *viris]* Manifestly there is something here amiss. The *viri fallaces* themselves constituting the world, there cannot be a comparison between them. Mohnike (i. 377) proposes to read *ventis;* yet better still is a later suggestion which he makes (ii. 177), *vitris* fallaeibus. Opitz, as he observes, in his grand old German translation of the hymn, must have so read, for he writes :

Lieber will ich Glauben f assen
Auf ein Glas, das bald zerfallt,
Als mich trbsten mit den Schatzen,
Und dem GlUcke dieser 'Welt.

18. *0 ros, n vanitas']* Some editions read, *0 roris vanitas;* others, *0 nox, o vanitas;* Mohnike suggests *0 flos, o vanitas,* with allusion to such passages as Job xiv. 2; Ps. ciii. 15; Isai. xxviii. 1, 4 ; 1 Pet. i. 24. Yet this image the poet seems to have reserved for the second line of the next stanza; while the early drying up of the morning dew is also a scriptural image for that which quickly passes away and disappears (Hos. vi. 4 ; xiii. 3); and one appearing in medieval, as indeed in all, poetry. Thus the author of the *Carmen Paraneticum,* sometimes ascribed to St Bernard *(Opp.* vol. ii. p. 910, Bened. ed.):

Quam male fraudantur, qui stulte ludificantur ;
Qui proptcr florem mundi vanumquo decorem,
Qui prius apparet quasi ros, et protinus aret,
Vadit in infernum, perdens diadema supermim.
Ignorans penitus, utrum eras vixens,
Fac bonum omnibus, quamdiu poteris. 20
Hsec carnis gloria, quse tanti penditur,
Sacris in litteris flos foeni dicitur;
Ut leve folium, quod vento rapitur,
Sic vita hominis luci subtrahitur.
Nil tuum dixeris quod potes perdere, 25
Quod mundus tribuit, intendit rapere:
Superna cogita, cor sit in sethere,
Felix, qui potuit mundum contemnere !
Dic, ubi Salomon, olim tam nobilis,

Vel ubi Sampson est, dux invincibilis, 30
Vel pulcher Absalon, vultu mirabilis,
Vel dulcis Jonathas, multum amabilis ?
Quo Csesar abiit, celsus imperio,
Vel Dives splendidus, totus in prandio ?
Dic, ubi Tullius, clarus eloquio, 35
Vel Aristoteles, summus ingenio ?
Tot clari proceres, tot rerum spatia,
Tot ora praesulum, tot regna fortia,
Tot mundi principes, tanta potentia,
In ictu oculi clauduntur omnia. 40

BALDE.

JACOB BALDE, bornatEnsisheiminAlsace, in1603, entered the Order of the Jesuits in 1624, and died in 1668. The greater part of his life was spent in Bavaria; where he could watch only too well the unspeakable miseries of the Thirty Years' War. Filling up, as that war did, exactly the central period of his life, he was spectator of these from first to last: and many pages of his poetry bear witness with what a bleeding heart he beheld the wounds of his native land. This sympathy of his, so true and so profound, with the sufferings of Germany, gives a reality to his verse which modern Latin poetry so often wants. Yet with all this, and with a free recognition, not of his talents merely, but of his genius, I cannot think but that there is some exaggeration in the language in which it has become the fashion to speak of him among his fellow-countrymen. They exalt him as the first of modern Latin poets – not, of course, as having reached the highest perfection of classical style, for no one would be so absurd as to attribute this praise to him, which every page of his writings would abundantly refute – but for the grandeur of his thoughts, the originality and boldness of his imagery ; so that they regard him, not so much as an accomplished Latin versifier, but rather as a great German poet in the disguise of a foreign tongue. It was not one of his co-religionists, but Herder, who first began to speak this language about him, and who indeed revived his forgotten memory in the minds of his fellow- countrymen, publishing in his *Terpsichore* a translation of a large number of his odes. A. W. Schlegel followed in the same track, with yet more enthusiastic praise : and since his time several editions of Balde's works, entire or selected, have been published, thus two by Orelli, Zurich, 1805, 1818 ; and in like manner trans- lations of the whole, or a portion of them, have appeared.

Nor is his poetry, which has thus been brought to light a second time, inconsid- erable in bulk. It fills four closely-printed volumes. Next to his odes his *Solatium Podagricorum* (Munich, 1661) has perhaps been the most widely read. It must be owned that the gout is a somewhat ghastly subject for merriment, especially when the jest is continued through some thousands of lines. The poem, of which the tone is mock-heroic, is intended no doubt to set forth the praises of abstemiousness. Thus one of the most frequent topics of consolation which he offers to the martyrs to this disease, is the dignity of their complaint (" *lordly* gout," as Swift calls it, *fjuffoirTUi-xpe Sea*, as Lucian) – that it is

These are Schlegel'swords : Ein tiefes, regsames, oft schwiir- merisch ungesti-imes Gefiihl, ein Einbildungskraft, woraus starke und wunderbare Bilder sich zahllos hervordrangen, ein erfinder- ischer, immer an entfernten Vergleichungen, an iiber-raschenden Einkleidungen geschaftiger Witz, ein scharfer Verstand. grosso sittliche Schnellkraft und Selbstiindigkeit, kiihne Sicherheit des Geistes, welche sich immer eigene Wege wahlt, und auch die ungebahntesten nicht scheut: alle dieseEigenschaften erscheinen in Balde's Werken allzu hervorstechend, als dass man ihn nieht fur einen ungewohnlich reich begabten Dichter erkennen musste.

only the rich and the luxurious whom it honours with its visits; as in these lines:

Morbus hie induitur gemmis et torquibus aureis,
Armillasque gerit manibus colloque smaragdos:
Non est communis lixis vulgoque frequenti.
Cerdones refugit, nee de lodice paratur;
Msecenas te laute petens, multumque supine:
Seligit aula'i thalamos in turribus altis,
Auratumque habitat, vel eburno ex dente lacunar;
Fulcitur plumis et pulvinaribus albis.
Vive diu, infelix, morbo indignissimus isto.

Now and then, however, the religious earnestness, which is the ground-tone of all which Balde writes, openly appears, as when he reminds the fretful and impatient sufferer, of One who had no such solaces and alleviations of pain, as are largely granted to him:

. '-non dormiit ostro,
Mollibus effultus cygnis, foliisque rosarum:
Affixus fait ILLE cruci, clavisque quaternis
Ex ferro fossus terratn inter et astra pependit;
Felle sitim relevans, pertusus vocibus aures
Sacrilegis; toto laniatum corpore funus.
Te capit infusum lectica simillima Ledse,
Invitum qpse vel queat invitare soporem ;
Accinit Amphion, et fundit duleia Rhenus;
Demulcet conjux ; lepidi solantur amici;
Et potes, heu! lecto trux indignarier isti,
Duraque fata queri, qpse sunt mollissima fatu.

These brief extracts may suffice to give a slight conception of what the character of this poem is. But it is, undoubtedly, as a lyric poet that Balde is greatest; and in that aspect the grand poem which follows will shew him.

45

SECTION 45

LXIV. CHOREA MORTUALIS SIVE
   LESSUS
   DE SORTIS ET MORTIS IN HUMANAS RES IMPERIO !
   Argumentum
   Inter funebres taedas, ad modulatoo s Umbrarum
   passus decantandum.
   EHEU, quid homines sumus ?
   Vanescimus, siouti fumus;
   Vana, vana terrigenum *Sots,*
   Cuncta dissipat iinproba mors.
   Exstincta est Leopoldina, 5
   Frustra olamata Lucina;
   Lacrymosa puerperae mors!
   Miseranda mulierum sors !
   Cum falcibus ageret sestas,
   Est et hsec succisa majestas: 10
   Ah, aristae purpurea; sors!
   Sicne dira te messuit mors?

LXIV. Balde, *Poemata,* Coloniae, 1660, vol. iv. p. 424. – The empress Leopoldina, wife of Ferdinand the Third, died in childbirth at Vienna after one year's marriage, in the year 1649. The great commonplaces of death, which, if always old, are yet always new, have seldom clothed themselves in grander form, or found a more solemn utterance, than they do in this sublime poem. How noble the third, the fourth, and the sixth stanzas, and how much to be regretted that Balde so seldom exchanged his alcaie and other classical metres for these Christian rhythms.

9. *testas]* The empress died on the 7th of August.

Quo more vulgaris urtica,
Jacet hsec quoque regia spica;
Suo condidit horreo mors, 15
Brevi posuit angulo sors.
Ut bulla defluxit aquosa,
Subsedit, ut vespere rosa;
Brevis omnis est flosculi *Sots,*
Rapit ungue celerrima mors. 20
Quam manibus osseis tangit,
Crystallinam phialam frangit;
O inepta et rustica mors!
O caduca juvenculse sors !
Ubi nunc decor ille genarum, 25
Ubi formse miraculum rarum ?
Bina lumina submit mors,
Cooca tenebras intulit sors.

17. *Ut bulla]* Crashaw's Latin poem, entitled *Bulla (Delights of the Muses,* 1648, p. 64) can find no place here. I , wish it might, for it is one of the most gorgeous pieces of painting in verse which anywhere I know – far more poetical than any of his English poetry, of which it shares the conceits and other faults. . These are a few of the lines in which the bubble gives an account of itself:

Sum venti ingenium breve,
Flos sum, scilicet, acris,
Sidus scilicet sequoris,
Naturte jocus aureus,
Natune vaga fabula,
Nature breve somnium,
Aurse filia perfidse,
Et risus facilis parens ;
Tantum gutta superbior,
Fortunatius et lutum.
Ubi corporis bella figura !
Ubi lactis ostrique mixtura! 30
Lac effudit in cespitem sors,
Texit ostrum sandapila mors.
Ubi rubra coralla sunt oris !
Dbi retiay crines amoris !

Parcse rapuit forficem sors, 35
Scidit ista csesariem mors.
Ubi cervix et manus eburna!
Heu funebri jacent in urna!
Atra nives imminuit sors,
Colla pressit tam candida mors. 40
Quse pulcrior fuit Aurora,
Hanc, Csesaris aula, deplora;
Vana species, lubrica sors,
Tetra facies, pallida mors.
Quse vides has cunque choreas, 45
Augebis et ipsa mox eas;
Subitam movet aleam sors,
Certa rotat hastilia mors.
Hue prompta volensque ducetur,
Capillis invita trahetur; 50
Ducet inevitabilis sors,
Trahet inexorabilis mors.
Quod es, fuimus : sumus, quod eris ;
Prsecessimus, tuque sequeris;
Volat ante levissima sors, 55
Premit arcu vestigia mors.
Nihil interest pauper an dives,
Non amplius utique vives;
Simul impulit clepsydram sors,
Vitas stamina lacerat mors. 60
Habere nil juvat argentum,
Nil regna prsetendere centum;
Sceptra sarculis abigit sors,
Ridet albis hsec dentibus mors.
Nihil interest, turpis an pulcra, 65
Exspectant utramque sepulcra;
Legit lappas et lilia sors,
Violasque cum carduis mors.
Nee interest, vilis an culta,
Trilustris, an major adultS,; 70
Vere namque novissimo sors,
Populatur et layeme mors.
Linquenda est aula cum casa,
Colligite singuli vasa;
Jubet ire promiscua sors, 75
Ire cogit indomita mors.
Ex mille non remanet unus,
Mox onmes habebitis funus;
Ite, ite, quo convocat sors,

Imus, imus, hoc imperat mors. so
Ergo vale, o Leopoldina,
Nunc umbra, Bed olim regina;
Vale, tibi nil nocuit sors,
Vale, vale, nam profuit mors.
Bella super et Suecica castra, 85
Nubesque levaris, et astra;
Penetrare quo nequeat sors,
Multo minus attonita mors.
Jnde mundi despiciens molem,
Lunam pede calcas et solem; go
Dulce sonat ex sethere vox,
Hyems transiit, occidit nox.
Surge, veni'; quid, sponsa, morari. s ?
Veni, digna coelestibus aris;
Imber abiit, moestaque crux, 93
Luoet, io, perpetua Lux.

85. *Suecica castra]* A fine allusion to the recent desolations of Germany. It was only four years before that the smoke of the Swedish watch-fires had been visible from the ramparts of Vienna. It is true that when the empress died, peace had been restored for nearly a year, the Treaty of Westphalia having been signed in October, 1648. But the wounds of Germany had scarcely begun to heal.

46

SECTION 46

MARBOD.

MARBOD, born in 1035, of an illustrious family in Anjou, was chosen bishop of Rennes in 1095 or in the year following, and having governed with admirable prudence his diocese for thirty years, died in 1125. He has left a large amount of Latin poetry, in great part the versified legends of saints. His poem *De Gemmis* was a great favourite in the Middle Ages, and has been often reprinted. It is perhaps worth reading, not as poetry, for as such it is of very subordinate value, but as containing the whole rich mythology of the period in regard of precious stones and the virtues popularly attributed to them. His poems are for the most part written in leonine verse, but he has shewn in more than one no contemptible skill in the management of the classical hexameter.

LXV. ORATIO AD DOMINUM.

DEUS-HOMO, Rex coelorum,
Miserere miserorum;
Ad peccandum proni sumus,
Et ad humum redit humus;
LXV. *Hildeberti et Marbodi Opp.* p. 1557.
Tu ruinam nostram fulci 5

Pietate tua dulci.
Quid est homo, proles Adas ?
Germen necis dignum clade.
Quid est homo nisi vermis,
Res infirma, res inermis. 10
Ne digneris huic irasci,
Qui non potest mundus nasci:
Noli, Deus, hunc damnare,
Qui non potest non peccare;
Judicare non est sequum l. r
Creaturam, non est tecum:
Non est miser homo tanti,
Ut respondeat Tonanti.
Sicut umbra, sicut fumus,
Sicut foenum facti sumus: "
Miserere, Rex coelorum,
Miserere miserorum.

DAMIANI.

PETER DAMIANI, cardinal-bishop of Ostia, was born at Ravenna in 1002, and died in 1072. Profoundly impressed with the horrible corruption of his *age,* and the need of a great reformation which should begin with the clergy themselves, he was the enthusiastic friend and helper of Hildebrand, his *Sanctus Satanas,* as fondly and with a marvellous insight into the heights and depths of his character, he calls him, in all the good and in all the evil which he wrought for the Church. He has left a considerable body of Latin verse; but, not to say that much of it is deeply tinged with superstitions of which he was only too zealous a promoter, there is little of it, which, even were this otherwise, one would much be tempted to extract save this, and the far grander poem *De Gaudiis Paradisi,* which will be found a little later in this volume. Yet doubtless his epitaph, written by himself, possesses a solemn and a stately grandeur. It is as follows:

Quod nunc es, fuimus: es, quod sumus, ipse futurus ;
His sit nulla fides, quse peritura vides.
Ffivola sinceris prsecurrunt somnia veris,
Succedunt brevibus Ssecula temporibus.
Vive memor mortis, quo semper vivere possis;
Quidquid adest, transit; quod manet, ecce venit.
Quam bene providit, qui te, male munde, reliquit,
Mente prius carni, quam tibi carne mori.
Ctclica terrenis, prsefer mansura caducis,
Mens repetat proprium libera principium: Spiritus alta petat, quo prodit fonte recurrat,
Sub se despiciat quicquid in ima gravat.
Sis memor, oro, mei: – cineres pius aspice Petri;
Cum prece, cum gemitu dic: Sibi parce, Deus.

Surely it is nothing wonderful that he who had so realized what life and death are, did not wait till the latter' had stripped him of his worldly honours, but himself anticipated that hour; having some time previously laid down his cardinal's hat, that what remained of his life he might spend in retirement and in prayer. It is probable that he had already so done, when this epitaph was composed. He died as abbot of Sta Croce d'Avellano in the States of the Church.

LXVI. DE DIE MORTIS.

GRAVI me terrore pulsas, vitse dies ultima ;
Moeret cor, solvuntur renes, lsesa tremunt viscera,
Tuam speciem dum sibi mens depingit anxia.
Quis enim pavendum illud explicet spectaculum,
Quum, dimenso vite cursu, carnis segra nexibus 5
Anima luctatur solvi, propinquans ad exitum ?
Peril sensus, lingua riget, resolvuntur oculi,
Pectus palpitat, anhelat raucum guttur hominis,
Stupent membra, pallent ora, decor abit corporis.

LXVI. Corner, *Prompt. Devot.* p. 701 ; Rambach, *Anthol. Christl. Gesdnge,* p. 238; Daniel, *Thes. Hymnol.* vol. i. p. 224 : vol. iv. p. 291.

Prsesto sunt et cogitatus, verba, cursus, opera, 10
Et prse oculis nolentis glomerantur omnia:
Illuc tendat, hue se vertat, coram videt posita.
Torquet ipsa reum sinum mordax conscientia,
Plorat apta corrigendi defluxisse tempora ;
Plena luctu caret fructu sera poenitentia. 15
Falsa tune dulcedo carnis in amarum vertitur,
Quando brevem voluptatem perpes poena sequitur;
Jam quod magnum credebatur nil fuisse cernitur.
Quasso, Christe, rex invicte, tu succurre misero,
Sub extrema mortis horii cum jussus abiero, 20
Nullum in me jus tyranno prsebeatur impio.

Cadat princeps tenebrarum, cadat pars tartarea ; Pastor, ovem jam redemptam tune reduc ad patriam, Ubi te videndi causa perfruar in ssecula.

24. I know no fitter place to append a poem, which can claim no room in the body of this volume, being almost without any distinctly Christian element whatever, and little more than a mere worldling's lamentation at leaving a world which he knows he has abused, yet would willingly, if he might, continue still longer to abuse. But even from that something may be learned; and there is a force and originality about the composition, which make me willing to insert it here, especially as it is very far from common. I would indeed gladly know something more about it I find it in a *Psalteriolum Cantionum Catholicarum,* Colonise, 1813, p. 283, with the title *De Morte,* but with the tifth, sixth, and seventh stanzas omitted ; and in its fuller form in Konigsfeld's *Latein. Hymnen und Gesange,* Bonn, 1847. This is a small and rather indifferent collection of medieval Latin poetry, with German translations annexed – so carelessly

edited as to inspire no confidence in the text. Daniel also has it *(Thes. Hymnol.* vol. iv. p. 351), but avowedly copied *from* Konigsfeld. The thoughts have a more modern air about them, than that I can suppose the poem rightly included in a collection of *medieval* verse at all. It bears the not very appropriate title of *Cygnus Exspirans,* and is as follows:

Parendum est, cedendum est,
Claudenda vitse scena;
Est jacta sors, me vocat mors,
Hjgc hora est postrema :
Valete res, valete spes;
Sic finit cantilena.
0 magna lux, sol, mundi dux,
Est concedendum f atis;
Due lineam eclipticam,
Mini luxisti satis:
Nox incubat; fax occidit;
Jam portum subit ratis.
Tu, Cynthia argentea,
Vos, aurei planetse,
Cum stellulis, ocellulis,
Nepotibus lucete;
Fatalia, letalia
Mi nunciant cometai.
Ter centies, ter millies
Vale, immunde munde!
Instabilis et labills,
Vale, orbis rotunde I
Mendaciis, f allaciis
Lusisti me abundc.
Lucentia, fulgentia
Gemmis valete tecta,
Seu marmore, sen ebore
Supra uubcs erecta.
Ad parvulum me loculum
Mors urget equis vecta.
Lucretise, quse specie
Gypsata me cepistis,
Imagines, voragines!
Quse mentem sorbuistis,
En oculos, heu! scopulos,
Extinguit umbra tristis.
Tripudia, diludia,
Et f escennini chori,
Quiescite, raucescite;
Prseco divini fori,

Mors, intonat et insonat
Hunc lessum; Debes mori.
Delicise, lautitise
Mensarum cum culina;
Cellaria, bellaria,
Et coronata vina,
Vos nauseo, dum haurio
Quem scyphum mors propinat.
Facessite, putrescite,
Odores, vestimenta;
Rigescite, delicise,
Libidinum fomenta!
Deformium me vermium
Manent operimenta.
O culmina, heu ! fulniina,
Horum fugax honorum,
Tam subito dum subto
JEternitatis domum.
Ridiculi sunt tituli ;
Foris et agunt momum.
Lectissimi, carissimi
Amici et sodales,
Heu ! insolens et impudens
Mors interturbat sales.
Sat lusibus indulsimus:
Extremum dico vale!
Tu denique, corpus, vale,
Te, te citabit totum [? forum] ;
Te conscium, te socium
Dolorum et gaudiorum!
Squalls nos exspectat sors –
Bonorum vel malorum. PRUDENTIUS.

LXVII. IN EXEQUIIS DEFUNCTORUM.

JAM moesta quiesce querela,
Lacrimas suspendite, matres,
Nullus sua pignora plangat,
Mors haec reparatio vita est.
Sic semina sicca virescunt, 5
Jam mortua jamque sepulta,
Quse reddita csespite ab imo
"Veteres meditantur aristas.
Nunc suscipe, terra, fovenduni,
Gremioque hunc concipe molli : 10
Hominis tibi membra sequestro,
Generosa et fragmina credo.

Animae fuit haec domus olim,
Factoris ab ore creatse,

LXVII. *Prudentii Opp.* ed. Obbarius, 1845, p. 41. – These lines, the crowning glory of the poetry of Prudentius, form only :i part (the concluding part) of his tenth *Cathemerinon.* But it has long been the custom to contemplate them apart from their context, and as an independent poem. This continued till a late day as the favourite funeral-hymn in the Evangelical Church in Germany, being used either in the original, or in the fine oM translation, Ho'rt auf mit Trauern und Klagen.

Fervens habitavit in istis is
Sapientia principe Christo.
Tu depositum tege corpus,
Non immemor ille requiret
Sua munera fictor et auctor,
Propriique senigmata vultus. 20
Veniant modo tempora justa,
Cum spem Deus impleat omnem,
Reddas patefacta necesse est,
Qualem tibi trado figuram.
Non, si cariosa vetustas 25
Dissolverit ossa favillis,
Fueritque cinisculus arens
Minimi mensura pugilli:
Nee, si vaga flamina et aurse,
Vacuum per inane volantes, 30
Tulerint cum pulvere nervos,
Hominem periisse licebit.
Sed dum resolubile corpus
Kevocas, Deus, atque reformaa,
Quanam regione jubebis 35
Animam requiescere puram?
Gremio senis addita sancti
Recubabit, ut est Eleazar,

17 – 32. We may compare with these stanzas the latter chapters of Tertullian's treatise, *De Resurr. Carnis.*

38. *Eleazar]* The question whether the scriptural names, Quem floribus undique septum

Dives procul aspicit ardens. 40
Sequimur tua dicta, Redemptor,
Quibus atra morte triumphans,
Tua per vestigia mandas
Socium crucis ire latronem.
; Patet ecce fidelibus ampli 45
Via lucida jam Paradisi,
Licet et nemus illud adire,
Homini quod ademerat anguis.

Nos tecta fovebimus ossa
Violis et fronde frequente, 50
Titulumque et frigida saxa
Liquido spargemus odore.

Lazarus and Eleazar, are only forms of the same, has been often debated; and it is now generally agreed that they are. Ter- tullian calls once the Lazarus of Luke xvi Eleazar, in the same manner as Prudeutius does here.

47

SECTION 47

MARBOD. LXVIH. DE RESURRECTIONE MORTUORUM.
quid dubitem fieri quod posse probatur, ' Cujus et ipse typum naturse munere gesto
? Quaque die somno, ceu mortis imagine pressus, Eursus et evigilans veluti de morte
resurgo ; Ipsa mihi sine voce loquens natura susurrat : 5

Post somnum vigilas, post mortis tempora vives.

Clamat idem mundus, naturaque provida rerum,

LXVIII. *Hildeberti et Marbodi Opp.* p. 1615. – These lines attest the very
respectable mastery of the classical hexameter, possessed in the eleventh and twelfth
century. The arguments for a resurrection drawn from the analogies of the natural
world had of course continually been handled before, by none perhaps so memorably
as by Tertullian, *De Res. Carnis,* 12; *De Animd,* 43, in whose footsteps Marbod here
very closely treads. Compare the *Panegyricus* of Paulinus of Nola.

3. *mortis imagine]* Compare the fine address to Sleep in the *Hercules Furens* of
Seneca:

Pavidum leti genus humanum

Cogis lougam discere mortem ;

and the same is very often beautifully brought out by Calderon ; thus in his sublime
Auto *La Cena de Saltasar:*

Descanso del sueno hace Cada dia, pues rendida
El hombre, ay Dios, sin que advierta La vida a un breve homicida,
Que quando duerme, y despierta, Que es su descanso no advierte
Cada dia muere y nace : Una leceion que la muerte
Que vivo cadaver yaze Le va estudiando a la vida.

Quas Deus humanis sic condidit usibus aptas,
Ut possint homini qusedam signare futura.
Mutat luna vices, defunctaque lumine rursum lo
Nascitur, augmentum per menstrua tempera sumens;
Sol quoque, per noctem quasi sub tellure sepultus,
Surgens mane novus reditum de morte figurat:
Signat idem gyros agitando volubile coelum,
Aera distinguens tenebris et luce sequente. 15
Ipsa parens tellus quae corpora nostra receptat,
Servat in arboribus vita mortisque figuram,
Et similem formam redivivis servat in herbis.
Nudatos foliis brumali tempore ramos,
Et velut arentes mortis sub imagine truncos 20
In propriam speciem frondosa resuscitat asstas;
Quseque peremit hyems nova gramina vere resurgunt,
Ut suus incipiat labor arridere colonis.
Nos quoque spes eadem manet et reparatio vitse,
Qua revirescat idem, sed non resolubile corpus. 25
An mihi subjectis data sit renovatio rebus,
Totus et hanc speciem referens mihi serviat orbis,
Me solum interea premat irreparabile damnum ?
Et quid erit causse modico cur tempore vivens,
Optima pars mundi, vitseque Datoris imago, 30
Post modicum peream, sublata spe redeundi,
At pro me factus duret per sascula mundus ?
Nonne putas dignum magis inferiora perire
Irreparabiliter, quam quse potiora probantur ?
Sed tamen illa manent, ergo magis ista manebunt. 35 LXIX. DE DIE JUDICIL
CUM revolve toto corde
In qua mundus manet sorde,
Totus mundus cordi sordet,
Et cor totum se remordet.
Cum revolvo pura mente, 5
Cadit mundus quam repente,
Ne mens cadat cum cadente,
Mundum fugit mens attente.
Cum revolvo mente sanS
Quam sit stulta spes humana, 10
A spe mentem ad spem verto,
Et spem mundi spe subverto.

Cum revolvo mundi laudem,
Et mundanse laudis fraudem,
Laus et fraus in cordis ore 15
Idem sonant uno more.
Cum revolvo mundi florem,
Et quem habet flos dolorem,
Tantus dolor est in flore,
Ut non sit flos in dolore. 20
LXIX. Edelestand du Meril, *Foes. Popul. Latinos,* 1847, p. 114 ; Mone, *Hymn. Lot. Med. Mvi,* vol. i. p. 415. – These are some of the concluding stanzas of a poem, an earlier portion of which is given p. 234.
Cum revolvo dies breves,
Et recorder dies leves,
Grave fit, quod fuit leve,
Et fit longum quod est breve.
Cum revolvo moriturus, 25
Quid post mortem sim futurus,
Terret me terror futurus,
Quem exspecto non securus.
Terret me dies terroris,
Irse dies et furoris, 30
Dies luctus et moeroris,
Dies ultrix peccatoris.
Expavesco miser multum
Judicis severi vultum,
Cui latebit nil occultum, 35
Et manebit nil inultum.
Et quis, quseso, non timebit,
Quando Judex apparebit,
Ante quem ignis ardebit,
Peccatores qui delebit? 40
Judicabit omnes gentes,
Et salvabit innocentes;
Arguet vero potentes,
Et deliciis fruentes.
Tune et omnes delicati 45
Valedicent voluptati,
Et vacantes vanitati
Evanescent condemnati.
Oh quam grave, quam immite
A sinistris erit: ' Ite' 50
Cum a dextris ' Vos venite'
Dicet Rex, largitor vitie.
Appropinquat enim dies,
In qua justis erit quies,

Qua cessabunt persequentes, 55
Et regnabunt patientes;
Dies ilia, dies vitse,
Dies lucis inauditee,
Qua nox omnis destruetur,
Et mors ipsa morietur ! 60
Ecce Rex desideratus,
Et a justis exspectatus,
Jam festinat exoratus,
Ad salvandum prseparatus.
Oh quam pium et quam gratum, 65
Quam suave, quam beatum
Erit tune Jesum videre,
His qui eum dilexere.
Oh quam dulce, quam jucundum
Erit tune odisse mundum, 70
Et quam triste, quam amarum
Habuisse mundum carum!
Oh beati tune lugentes,
Et pro Christo patientes,
Quibus sseculi pressura 75
Regna dat semper mansura.
Ibi jam non erit metus,
Neque luctus, neque fletus,
Non egestas, non senectus,
Nullus denique defectus. 80
Ibi pax erit perennis,
Et Isetitia solennis, , . .
Flos et decus juventutis, ,'
Et perfectio salutis.
r . i " .
Nemo potest cogitare 85
Quantum erit exultare,
Tnnc in coelis habitare,
Et cum angelis regnare.
Ad hoc regnum me vocare,
Juste Judex, tu dignare, 90
Quem exspecto, quem require,
Ad quern avidus suspiro.

48

SECTION 48

LXX. DE DIE JUDICII.

A PPAREBIT repentina dies magna Domini,
- Fur obscura velut nocte improvisos occupans.
Brevis totus tune parebit prisci luxus sasculi,
Totum simul cum clarebit prasterJsse ssCculum.

LXX. Thomasius, *Hymnarium, Opp.* vol. ii. p. 433; Kam- bach, *Anthol. Christl Gesange,* p. 126; Daniel, *Thes. Hymnol.* vol. i. p. 194. – This hymn, as will at once be observed, is alphabetic. Latin hymns which have submitted themselves to this constraint are not very numerous ; and, though I suppose there is not, there appears something artificial in an arrangement. which, while it is a restraint and difficulty, confers few compensating benefits, and, when all is done, is rather for the eye than for the ear. In the sacred Hebrew poetry the chief examples in the kind are the *Lamentations* of Jeremiah, and some Psalms which are among the latest in the whole collection. The hymn before us is certainly as old as, if not a good deal older than, the seventh century; for Bede, who belongs to the end of this ami the beginning of the eighth, refers to it in his work *De Mtitris.* It was then almost or altogether lost sight of, till Cassander published it in his *Hymni Ecclesiastici.* Although too exclusively a working up of Scripture passages which relate to the last judgment, indeed we may say of one Scripture passago (Mt. xxv. 31 – 46), in a narrative form, and wanting the high lyrical passion of the *Dies Irte,* yet it is of a very noble simplicity, Daniel saying of it well: Juvat carmen fere totum e Scriptura sacra depromptum comparare cum celebratissimo illo extremi judicii prseconio, *Dies irte, dies illa,* quo maj estate et terroribus, non sancta simplicitate et fide, superatur.

Clangor tubas per quaternas terras plagas concinens, 5
Vivos una mortuosque Christo ciet obviam. De coelesti Judex arce, maj estate fulgidus,
Claris angelorum choris comitatus aderit. Erubescet orbis lunae, sol vel obscurabitur,
Stellae cadent pallescentes, mundi tremet ambitus : Flamma ignis anteibit justi vultum Judicis, 11
CoBlum, terras, et profundi fluctus ponti devorans. Oloriosus in sublimi Rex sedebit solio,
Angelorum tremebunda circumstabunt agmina, Hujus omnes ad electi colligentur dexteram, 15
Pravi pavent a sinistris, hasdi velut footidi; Ite, dicet Rex ad dextros, regnum cteli sumite,
Pater vobis quod paravit ante omne sasculum. Karitate qui fraterna me juvistis pauperera,
Caritatis nunc mercedem reportate divitea, 20
Lasti dicent: Quando, Cbriste, pauperem te vidimus,
Te, Rex magne, Yel egentem miserati juvimus *I* Magnus illis dicet Judex : Cum juvistis pauperem,
Panem, domum, vestem dantes, me juvistis humilcs. Nee tardabit et sinistris loqui Justus Arbiter: 25
In gehennae, maledicti, flammas Line disoedite : Obsecrantem me audire despexistis mendicum,
Nudo vestem non dedistis, neglexistis languidum. Peccatores dicent: Christe, quando te vel pauperem,
Te, Rex magne, vel infirmum contemplantes spre- vimus ? 30
Quibus contra Judex altus: Mendicanti quamdiu
Opem ferre despexistis, me sprevistis improbi.

12. *devoransi]* So Cassaneler, Thomasius, and Ramliach. Daniel has *dicorans,* but probably as a misprint.

Retro ruent tum injusti ignes in pcrpetuos,
Vermis quorum non morietur, flamma nee restin-
guitur; Satan atro cum ministris quo tenetur carcere, 35
Fletus ubi mugitusque, strident omnes dentibus. Tune fideles ad coclestem sustol-
lentur patriam,
Chores inter angelorum regni petent gaudia : Urbis summs3 Hierusalem introibunt gloriam,
Vera lucis atque pacis in qua fulget visio, 40
Xristunl Regem, jam paterna claritate splendidum,

Ubi celsa beatorum contemplantur agmina. Ydri fraudes ergo cave, infirmantes subleva,

Aurum temne, fuge luxus, si vis astra petere : Zona clara castitatis lumbos nune accingere, 45

In occursum magni Regis fer ardentes lampadas.

43. *Ydn]* for *Hydri.* The Latin language possessing originally no *y,* and every Greek word beginning with *v* which had been naturalized in the language, being necessarily aspirated, it was only by such an irregularity as this that the alphabetic arrangement of the poem could have been preserved throughout. Hydrus = *SfSpos,* properly a sea-serpent; but here the *attis* of Gen. iii.; Rev. xii. *9.* THOMAS OF CELANO.

THOMAS, named of Celano, from a small town near the lake Fucino in the further Abruzzo, and so called to distinguish him from another of the same name and Order, was a friend and scholar of St Francis of Assisi – one indeed of the earliest members of the new Order of Minorites, which in 1208 was founded by him. He appears to have lived in near familiarity with his master, and, from the great matters in which he was trusted by him to have enjoyed his highest confidence. After the death of St Francis, which took place in 1226, he was the first who composed a brief account of his life, which he afterwards greatly enlarged, and which even now is the most authentic record of the life of the saint which we possess. The year of his own death is not known. His connexion with the founder of that influential Order might have just preserved his name from utter forgetfulness; but it is the *Dies Irue* which has given him a much wider' fame.

It is with no absolute certainty that the authorship of this grand hymn is ascribed to Thomas of Celano. Seeming to lie, as it has done, like a waif and stray, and yet at the same time so precious a one, that who would might make it his own, it is not very wonderful that claims of ownership have been put in on behalf of many. Several of these, however, may be set aside at once. Thus we are quite sure that Gregory the Greatcould not have been the author ; seeing that rhyme, although not unknown or unused in his day, was very far from having reached the perfection which in this poem it displays; add to which, that the poem would then have remained unknown for the first six hundred years of its existence. Again, St Bernard has been sometimes named as the author. But, not to say that its character is austerer and texture more masculine, than any of those, beautiful as in their kind they are, which rightly belong to him, he also lived at too early a day. The hymn was not known till the thirteenth century; while he died in the middle of the twelfth, and enjoyed too high a reputation in life and after death to have rendered it possible that such a composition of his could have remained unnoticed for a hundred years. It would be long, and alien to the purposes of this volume, to consider all the names which have been suggested, or to give more than the results of the enquiry. The question has been thoroughly discussed by Mohnike, *Hymnologische Forschungen,* vol. i. pp. 1 – 24. He and others who have gone the fullest into the matter, are agreed that the preponderance of evidence is very much in favour of the friend and follower of St Francis, a notice of whose life I have in consequence given. The fact that two other hymns which are certainly of his composition are of very inferior merit cannot be urged as seriously affecting his claims. How many a poet has risen for once very much beyond the level which at any other time he attained. Moreover, these two hymns, which are both in honour of St Francis, are not at all so poor in poetical merits as some would imply. Indeed the first, *Fregit victor*

virtualis, has to my mind very considerable merit, and displays a true poetical handling of its theme ; though it does not come within the range of this volume. It and its fellow, *Sanctitatis nova signa,* are to be found in Daniel, *Thes. Hymnal.* vol. v. pp. 314, 317. In my former edition, I too lightly took Wadding's word, the Irish Franciscan, and the learned and laborious historiographer of his Order (b. 1580, d. 1657), that one or both of these hymns had perished, and expressed my regret at their loss. This is not, however, the case ; the first is printed in some of the earlier Paris Missals, and the second, which ought not to have escaped me, in the *Ada Sanctorum,* Oct. 2, p. 801. Knowing as we do the bitter rivalry which reigned between the two mendicant Orders, it somewhat confirms the view that the hymn is the work of a Franciscan, that the Dominican, Sixtus Senensis, should speak slightingly of it, terming it, as he does, an uncouth poem (rhythmus inconditus) ; this he would scarcely have done, had there not been that in the authorship of the poem, which caused him to look at it with a jaundiced eye.

49

SECTION 49

LXXI. DE NOVISSIMO JUDICIO.

   1IES irse, dies ilia
   Solvet saeclum in favilla,

   LXXI. Mohnike, *Hymnol. Furschungen,* pp. 33, 39, 45 ; Lisco, *Dies Ira, Hymnus auf das Weltgericht,* Berlin, 1840; Daniel, *Thes. Hymnol.* vol. ii. p. 103. – Of all the Latin hymns of the Church this has the widest fame ; for as Daniel has truly remarked : Etiam illi quibus Latini Ecclesise hymni prorsus ignoti sunt, hunc certe norunt, et si qui inveniuntur ab humanitate tam alien! ut carminum sacrorum suavitatum nihil omnino sen- tiant, ad hunc certe hymnum, cujus quot sunt verba tot tonitrua, auimum advertunt. The grand use which Goethe has made of it in his *Faust* may have helped to bring it to the knowledge of some who would not otherwise have known it; or, if they had, would not have believed its worth, if the sage and seer of this world, " a prophet of their own," had uot thus set his seal of recognition upon it. To another illustrious man this hymn was eminently dear. How affecting is that incident recorded of Sir Walter Scott by his biographer, – how in those last days of his life when all of his great mind had failed or was failing, he was yet heard to murmur to himself some lines of this hymn, an especial favourite with him in other days. Nor is it hard to account for its wide and general popularity. The metre so grandly devised, of which I remember no other example, fitted though it has here shewn itself for bringing out some of the noblest powers of the Latin language – the solemn effect of the triple rhyme, which has been likened to blow following blow of the hammer on the anvil – the confidence of the poet in the universal interest of his theme, a confidence which has made him set out his matter with so majestic and unadorned a plainness as at once to be intelligible to all, – these merits, with many more, have given the *Dies Irs* a foremost place among the masterpieces of sacred song.

1. *Dies ira, dies illa]* The opening of this poem acquires
Teste David *mm* Sibylla.
additional grandeur when it is kept in mind that this line, striking the key note to the whole, was already familiar to the minds of men, being drawn, exactly as it stands, from the Vulgate, namely from Zeph. i. 15. The day of judgement continually appears under this title of *dies ira* in the Latin medieval verse : thus in a poem of considerable merit by Peter of Blois:

Cessa, caro, lascivire, Fraus Spiritus immundi.
Quia dies instat irse : Nos hsec vita deserit,
Non te mtmdus rapiat, Kt nt umbra preterit
Non te circumveniat Hujus figura mundi.

3. *cum Sibylla]* An unwillingness to allow a Sibyl to appear as bearing witness to Christian truth, has caused that we sometimes find this third line omitted, and in its stead *Crucis cxpun- dens vcxitta,* as the second of this triplet. It rests on Matt. xxiv. 30, and on the expectation that the apparition of a cross in the sky would be " the sign of the Son of man in heaven " there spoken of. It is, however, a late alteration of the text; and the line as above is quite in the spirit of the early and medieval theology. In those uncritical ages the Sibylline verses were not seen to be that transparent forgery which indeed they are ; but were continually appealed to as only second to the sacred Scriptures in prophetic authority; thus on this very matter of the destruction of the world, by Lactantius, *Inst. Div.* vii. 16 – 24; cf. Piper, *Mytlwl. d. Christl. Kunst,* p. 472 – 507. It is not too much to say that these Sibylline oracles, with other heathen testimonies of the same kind, were not so much subordinated to more legitimate prophecy, as co-ordinated with it, the two being regarded as parallel lines of prophecy, the Church's and the world's, bearing consenting witness to the same truths. Thus is it in a curious medieval mystery on the Nativity, published in the *Journal des Savans,* 1846, p. 88. It is of simplest construction. One after another patriarchs and prophets and kings of the Old Covenant advance and repeat their most remarkable word about Him that should come: but side by side with them a series of heathen witnesses, Virgil, on the ground of his fourth Eclogue, Nebuchadnezzar (Dan. iii. 25), and the Sibyl: and that

Quantus tremor est futurus,
Quando Judex est venturus, 5
Cuncta stricte discussurus.
Tuba, mirum spargens sonum
Per sepulchra regionum,
Coget omnes ante thronum.
Mors stupebit et natura, 10

Quum resurget creatura,
Judicanti responsura.
Liber scriptus proferetur,
In quo totum continetur,
De quo mundus judicetur. 15

it was the writer's intention to parallelize the two series, and to shew that Christ
had the testimony of both, is plain from some opening lines of the prologue:

O Judsei, Verbum Dei Et vos, gentes, non credentcs
Qui negatis, hominem Peperisse virginem,
Vestrse legis, testem Regis Vestrae gentis documentis
Audite per ordinem. Pellite caliginem.

And such is the meaning here – " That such a day shall be has the witness of
inspiration, of David, – and of mere natural religion, of the Sibyl – Jew and Gentile
alike bear testimony to the truths which we Christians believe." To look at the matter
from this point of view, makes certain that we ought to read *Ttste David,* and not *Tests
Petro.* It is true that 2 Pet. iii. 7 – 11 is a more obvious prophecy of the destruction
of the world by fire than any in the Psalms; but there are passages enough in these (as
Ps. xcvi. 13; xevii. 3; xi. 6), to which the poet may allude; and the very obviousness
of that in St Peter, makes the reading, which introduces his name, suspicious.

Judex ergo quum sedebit,
Quidquid latet, apparebit,
Nil inultum remanebit.
Quid sum miser tum dicturus,
Qucm patronum rogaturus, 20
Quum vix justus sit securus ?
Rex tremendse majestatis,
Qui salvandos salvas gratis,
Salva me, fons pietatis.
Recordare, Jesu pie, 25
Quod sum causa tu vise;
Ne me perdas ilia die !
Quserens me sedisti lassus,
Redemisti crucem passus :
Tantus labor non sit cassus. 30
Juste Judex ultionis,
Donum fac remissionis
Ante diem rationis.
Ingemisco tanquam reus,
CulpS, rubet vultus meus: 35
Supplicanti parce, Deus !
Qui Mariam absolvisti,
Et latronem exaudisti,
Mihi quoque spem dedisti.
28. *sedisti lassus]* Cf. John iv. 6.
Preces mese non sunt dignas, 40

Sed tu bonus fao benigne
Ne perenni cremer igne !
Inter oves locum prsesta,
Et ab hsedis me sequestra,
Statuens in parte dextrfL 45
Confutatis maledictis,
Flammis acribus addictis,
Voca me cum benedictis.
Oro supplex et acclinis,
Cor contritum quasi cinis: 50
Gere curam mei finis.

51. It is not wonderful that a pocm such as this should have continually allured, and continually defied, translators. Jeremy Taylor in a letter to John Evelyn suggests to him that he should make a version of it: "I was thinking to have begged of you a translation of that well-known hymn, *Dies ira, dies illa,* which, if it were a little changed, would make an excellent divine song." Evelyn did not comply, but we have several versions in English, of which the earliest that I know is one by Sylvester, *Works,* 1621, p. 1214; also a very noble one by Crashaw *(Steps to the Temple,* London, 1648, p. 105); it is in quatrains, and rather a reproduction than a translation. These are'the first and last stanzas:

Hear'st thou, my soul, what serious things
Both the Psalm and Si byl sings,
Of a sure Judge, from whose sharp ray
The world in names shall fly away.
9
Oh hear a suppliant heart all crusht,
And crumbled into contrite dust;
My Hope, my Fear, my Judge, my Friend,
Take charge of me, and of my end.

The list of English translations will include one by Roscommoi', and one by Walter Scott; while among the still more recent translations are two in the *Irish Ecclesiastical Journal.* May and June, 1849. In German they are yet more numerous, including highest names, such as Herder, Fichte, and Augustus Schlegel. A volume before me by Lisco, is exclusively dedicated to these. It was published in 1840, and contains forty-three versions; while in an *Appendix,* which followed three years after, seventeen more are given, which either had before escaped the editor's notice, or had been published since the publication of his book. Among these, it is true, there is one French and one Romaic ; but all the rest are German.

50

SECTION 50

LXXII. DE CRUCE DOMINI.
  CRUX ave benedicta !
  Per te mors est devicta,
  In te pependit Deus,
  Rex et Salvator meus.
  LXXII. [Walraff,] *Corolla Hymnorum,* p- 23; Daniel, *Thts. Hymnol.* vol. ii. p. 349. – This little poem, so perfect in its kind, might fitly have had its place among the earlier hymns upon the Passion, pp. 130-151, and may seem as out of due order here. But the sublime and awful judgement-hymns which have just gone before, seem to want one of this nature – one which should set forth Him in whom and through whose cross alone there shall be no condemnation there – as a transitional hymn to those which presently follow, and of which the theme is everlasting life. I cannot refuse to set beside these lines, some of Calderon's, of no inferior grace, and on the same theme ;

  Arbol, donde el cielo quiso
  Dar el fruto verdadero
  Contra el bocado primera,
  Flor del nuevo paraiso,

Arco de luz, cuyo aviso
En pi61ago mas prcfundo
La paz publiod del mundo,
Planta hermosa, fertil vid,
Harpa del nuevo David,
Tabla del Moiees segundo ;
Pecador soy, tus favores
Pido por justicia yo;
Piies Dies en ti padeoiu,
Solo por los pecadores.
Which lines may thus be translated:
Tree, which heaven has willed to dower
With that true fruit whence we live,
Tu arborum regina, 5
Salutis medicina,
Pressorum es levamen,
Et tristium solamen.
O sacrosanctum lignum,
Tu vitse nostra signum, 10
Tulisti fructum Jesum,
Humani cordis esum.
Dum crucis inimicos,
Vocabis, et amioos,
O Jesu, Fil! Dei, 15
Sis, oro, memor mei.
As that other, death did give ;
Of new Eden loveliest flower ;
Bow of light, that in worst hour
Of the worst flood signal true
O'er the vorld, of mercy threw ;
Fair plant, yielding sweetest wine ;
Of our David harp divine ;
Of our Moses tables new;
Sinner am I, therefore I
Claim upon thy mercies make,
Since alone for sinners' sake
Cod on thee endured to die. 3,4
BERNARD OF CLUGNY.

"HERNARD, a monk of Clugny, born at Morlaix, in -L' Brittany, but of English parents, flourished in the twelfth century, the cotemporary and fellow-countryman of his own more illustrious namesake of Clairvaux.

LXXIH. LAUS PATRLE COELESTIS.

HIC breve vivitur, hie breve plangitur, hie breve fletur : Non breve vivere, non breve plangere retribuetur;

LXXIII. Flacius Illyrieus, *Poemm. de Corrupto Ecclesite Statu,* p. 247. – The author, in an interesting preface, dedicates the poem *De Contemptu Mundi,* of which these lines form a part, to Peter the Venerable, General of the Order to which he belonged. The poem, which contains nearly three thousand lines, was first published by Flacius Illyricus, in the curious, and now rather scarce, collection of poems, intended by him as a verse-pendant and complement to his *Catalogus Testium Veritatis,* or, Catalogue of Witnesses against the Papacy who were to be found in all ages of the Church. This poem has been several times reprinted; Mohnike *(Hymnol. Forschungen,* vol. i. p. 458) knows of and indicates four editions, to which I could add a fifth. This is not wonderful; for no one with a sense for the true passion of poetry, even when it manifests itself in forms the least to his liking, will deny the breath of a real inspiration to the author of these dactylic hexameters. It must be confessed that uniting, as they do, the leonine and tailed rhyme, with every line broken up of

O retributio! stat brevis actio, vita perennis ;
O retributio ! coelica mansio stat lue plenis;
Quid datur et quibus ? sether egentibus et cruce dig-
nis, a
Sidera vermibus, optima sontibus, astra malignis.
Sunt modo praJia, postmodo prsemia ; qualia ? plena;
Plena refectio, nullaque passio, nullaque poena.
Spe modo vivitur, et Syon angitur a Babylone;
Nunc tribulatio ; tune recreatio, sceptra, coronse; 10
Tune nova gloria pectora sobria clarificabit,
Solvet enigmata, veraque sabbata continuabit.
Liber et hostibus, et dominantibus ibit Hebrseus;
Liber habebitur et celebrabitur hinc jubikeus.
Patria luminis, inscia turbinis, inscia litis, 15
Give replebitur, amplificabitur Israelitis :

necessity into exactly three equal parts, they present as unattractive a garb for poetry to wear as can well be imagined – to say nothing of the extravagantly difficult laws which the poet has imposed upon himself. He, it is true, in that dedicatory epistle, glories in the difficulties of the metre he has chosen, which he is convinced nothing but an especial grace and inspiration could have enabled him to overcome. Besides the awkwardness and repulsiveness of the metre, which indeed is felt much more strongly at first than after a little familiarity with it, a chief defect in the poem, one which in my quotation from it has been mitigated by some prudent omissions, is its want of progress. The poet, instead of advancing, eddies round and round his subject, recurring again and again to that which he seemed to have thoroughly treated and dismissed. But even with these serious drawbacks, high merits remain to it still. I may mention that the often quoted lines, beginning Hora novissima, tempora pessima, are the opening lines of this poem. X

Patria splendida, terraque florida, libera spinis,
Danda fidelibus est ibi civibus, hie peregrinis.
Tune erit omnibus inspicientibus ora Tonantis
Summa potentia, plena scientia, pax pia sanctis ; 2O

Pax sine crimine, pax sine turbine, pax sine rixa,
Meta laboribus, atque tumultibus anchora fixa.
Pars mea Rex meus, in proprio Deus ipse decore
Visus amabitur, atque videbitur Auctor in ore.
Tune Jacob Israel, et Lia tune Rachel efficietur, 25
Tune Syon atria pulcraque patria perficietur.

25. *Tune Jacob Israel]* The earthly shall be transformed into the heavenly, as Jacob became Israel, and in sign of the new nature received the new name (Gen. xii. 28). According to Augustine *(Serm.* 122). Isracl=Videns Deum, which gives an additional fitness to these words. – *et Lia tune Rachel]* Leah and Rachel represent, respectively, the active and the contemplative Christian life, see p 229. Leah becoming Rachel . is the swallowing up of the laborious active in the more delightful contemplative, in that vision of God wherein all blessedness is included. Cf. Augustine, *Con. Faust.* xxii. 52 – 54 ; and Hugh of St Victor *(Miscdl.* i. 79): Duse sorores duas vitas significant. Lia, qua; interpretatur *laboriosa,* significat vitam activam, quse est foe- cunda in fructu boni operis, sed parum videt in luce contempla- tionis. Rachel, quse interpretatur *visum principium,* designat vitam contemplativam, quse est sterilis foris in opere, sed perspi- cax in contemplatione. In his duabus vitis quasi qusedam contentio est animse sanctse alternatim nitentis ad amplexum Sponsi sui, id est, Christi, sapientise videlicet Dei. Contendunt ergo contemplatio et actio pro amplexu sapientise (cf. Gen. xxx. 14 – 16). Qui in contemplatione est, suspirat pro ste- rilitate operis; qui in opere est, suspirat pro jubilo con- templationis. In a sublime passage with which Augustine concludes his Commentary upon St John, he makes the two Apostles, Peter and John, to represent these two lives. It begins thus: Duas itaque vitas sibi divinitus prsedicatas et commen- datas novit Ecclesia, quarum est una in fide, una in specie; una

O bona patria, lumina sobria te speculantur,
Ad tua nomina sobria lumina collacrimantur :
Est tua mentio pectoris unctio, cura doloris,
Concipientibus sethera mentibus ignis amoris. 30
Tu locus unicus, illeque coelicus es paridisus,
Non ibi lacrima, sed placidissima gaudia, risus.
Est ibi consita laurus, et insita cedrus hysopo;
Sunt radiantia jaspide moenia, clara pyropo :
Hinc tibi sardius, inde topazius, hinc amethystus; 35
Est tua fabrica concio coelica, gemmaque Christus.
Tu sine littore, tu sine tempore, fons, modo rivus,
Dulce bonis sapis, estque tibi lapis undique vivus.
Est tibi laurea, dos datur aurea, Sponsa decora,
Primaque Principis oscula suscipis, inspicis ora : 40
Candida lilia, viva monilia sunt tibi, Sponsa,
Agnus adest tibi, Sponsus adest tibi, lux speciosa:
Tota negotia, cantica dulcia dulce tonare,
Tam mala debita, quam bona prsebita conjubilare.
Urbs Syon aurea, patria lactea, cive decora, 45

in tempore peregrinationis, altera in seternitate mansion is; una in labore, altera in requie; una in via, altera in patria; una in opere actionis, altera in mereede contempla-tionis.

45 – 58. In these lines the reader will recognize the original of that lovely hymn, which within the last few years has been added to those already possessed by the Church. A new hymn which has won such a place in the affections of Christian people as has *Jerusalem the Golden* is so priceless an acquisition that I must needs rejoice to have been the first to recall from oblivion the poem which yielded it. Dr. Neale, as is known, no doubt, to many of my readers, in his *Rhythm of Bernard de Morlaix on the Heavenly Country,* London, 1859, has translated a large portion of the poem.

Omne cor obruis, omnibus obstruis et cor et ora.
Nescio, nescio, quse jubilatio, lux tibi qualis,
Quam socialia gaudia, gloria quam specialis :
Laude studens ea tollere, mens mea victa fatiscit:
O bona gloria, vincor; in omnia laus tua vicit. 50
Sunt Syon atria conjubilantia, martyre plena,
Cive micantia, Principe stantia, luce serena:
Est ibi pascua, mitibus afflua, prsestita sanctis,
Regis ibi thronus, aguiinis et sonus est epulantis.
Gens duce splendida, concio candida vestibus albis 55
Sunt sine fletibus in Syon sedibus, zedibus almis;
Sunt sine crimine, sunt sine turbine, sunt sine lite
In Syon sedibus editioribus Israelite.
Urbs Syon inclyta, gloria debita glorificandis,
Tu bona visibus interioribus intima pandis: 60

69 – 72. I quote, for comparison and contrast, a few lines from Casimir, the great Latin poet of Poland. They turn upon the same theme, the heavenly home-sickness; but with all their classical beauty, and it is great, who does not feel that the poor Clugnian monk's is the more real and deeper utterance, – that, despite the strange form which he has chosen, he is the greater poet ?

Urit me patrise decor,
Urit conspicuis pervigil ignibus
Stellati tholus setheris,
Et lunse tenerum lumen, et aurcis
Fixse lampades atriis.
O noctis choreas, et teretem sequi
Juratse thiasum faces I
O pulcher patriss vultus, et ignei
Dulces excubise poli!
Cur me stelliferi luminis hospitem,
Cur heu I cur nimium diu
Co3lo sepositum cernitis exulem ?

The Spanish scholar will remember and compare the nobl ode of Luis de Leon, entitled *Noche Serena.*.

Intima lumina, mentis acumina te speculantur,

Pectora flammea spe modo, postea sorte lucrantur.
Urbs Syon unica, mansio mystica, condita coelo,
Nunc tibi gaudeo, nunc mihi lugeo, tristor, anhelo :
Te quia corpore non queo, pectore ssepe penetro, 65
Sed caro terrea, terraque carnea, mox cado retro.
Nemo retexere, nemoque promere sustinet ore,
Quo tua moenia, quo capitalia plena decore;
Opprimit omne cor ille tuus decor, o Syon, o pax,
Urbs sine tempore, nulla potest fore laus tibi mendax; 70
O sine luxibus, o sine luctibus, o sine lite
Splendida curia, florida patria, patria vitse!
Urbs Syon inclyta, turris et edita littore tuto,
Te peto, te colo, te flagro, te volo, canto, saluto;
Nee meritis peto, nam meritis meto morte perire, 75
Nee reticens tego, quod meritis ego filius me:
Vita quidem mea, vita nimis rea, mortua vita,
Quippe reatibus exitialibus obruta, trita.
Spe tamen ambulo, prsemia postulo speque fideque,
Ilia perennia postulo prsemia nocte dieque. 80
Me Pater optimus atque piissimus ille creavit;
In lue pertulit, ex lue sustulit, a lue lavit.
Gratia coelica sustinet unica totius orbis
Parcere sordibus, interioribus unctio morbis;
Diluit omnia coelica gratia, fons David undans 85
Omnia diluit, omnibus affluit, omnia mundans:
O pia gratia, celsa palatia cernere prasta,
Ut videam bona, festaque consona, coelica festa.
O mea, spes mea, tu Syon aurea, clarior auro,
Agmine splendida, stans duce, florida perpete lauro,
O bona patria, num tua gaudia teque videbo ? 91
O bona patria, num tua prsemia plena tenebo ?
Die mini, flagito, verbaque reddito, dicque, Videbis:
Spem solidam gero ; remne tenens ero ? die, Retinebis.
O sacer, o pius, o ter et amplius ille beatus, 95
Cui sua pars Deus: o miser, o reus, hac viduatus.

51

SECTION 51

LXXIV. IN DEDICATIONS ECCLESLE.

URBS beata Hirusalem, dicta pacis visio,
Quse construitur in coelis vivis ex lapidibus,
Et ab angelis ornata, velut sponsa nobilis:

LXXIV. Clichtoveus, *Elucidat. Eccles.* p. 46; Thomasius, *Hymnarium, Opp.* vol. ii. p. 378; Rambach, *Anthol. Christl. Ge- sdnge,* p. 179; Mohnike, *Hymnol. Forschungen,* vol. ii. p. 187. – This rugged but fine old hymn, of which the author is not known, is probably of date as early as the eighth or ninth century ; such at least is Mohnike's conclusion. I have observed already upon the manner in which these grand old compositions were recast in the Romish Church, at the revival of learning, which was, in Italy at least, to so great an extent a revival of heathenism. This is one of the few which have not utterly perished in the process; while yet if we compare the first two rugged and somewhat uncouth stanzas, but withal so sweet, with the smooth iambics which in the Roman Breviary have taken their place, we shall feel how large a part of their beauty has disappeared. They are read there in the following form:

CoBlestis urbs Jerusalem, O eorte nupta prospera,
Beata pacis visio, Dotata Patris gloria,
Qrue celsa de viventibus Bespersa Sponsi gratia,

Saxis ad astra tolleris, Eegina formosissima,
Sponsfflque ritu cingeris Christo jugata Principi,
Mille angelorum millibus: Ccelo coruscas civitas.

A little further on, we are amidst the heathen associations of Olympus. But the most illustrious example of what I mean, is yielded by a comparison of the grand old Paschal hymn (how old, it is impossible to say), *Ad coenam Agni providi,* with the same as burnished and brightened up in the Roman Breviary. It is easy to compare them, Daniel *(Thes. Hymnol.* vol. i. p. 88) giving the old and the new in parallel columns.

Nova veniens e coelo, nuptial! thalamo
Prseparata, ut sponsata copuletur Domino; 5
Platese et muri ejus ex auro purissimo.
Portse nitent margaritis, adytis patentibus;
Et virtute meritorum illuc introducitur
Omnis qui ob Christi nomen hoc in mundo pre-
mitur.
Tunsionibus, pressures expoliti lapides 10
Suis coaptantur locis; per manus artincis
Disponuntur permansuri sacris sedificiis.
Angulare fiindamentum lapis Christus missus est,
Qui compage parietum in utroque nectitur,
Quem Syon sancta suscepit, in quo credens per-
manet. 15
Omnis ilia Deo sacra et dilecta civitas,
Plena modulis et laude et canoro jubilo,
Trinum Deum unicumque cum favore prsedicat.

7. *margaritis]* Cf. Rev. xxi. 21. What were tears here shall reappear as pearls there. Der verklarte Sehmerz bildet die Ein- gange zu der Residenz der ewigen Wbnne (Lange).

15. *Syon]* It is not an accident that the poet uses *Syon* here speaking of the Church militant, and *Hirusalem,* ver. 1, where addressing the Church triumphant. Durandus *(Rational.* i. 1), explains the distinction: Dieitur enim prsesens Ecclesia Syon, eo quod ab hac peregrinatione longe posita promissionem rerum coelestium speculatur; et ideo Syon, id est, *speculatio,* nomen accepit. Pro futura vero patria et pace, Hierusalem vocatur: nam Hierusalem *pads visio* interpretatur. The necessities of metre caused this distinction to be often neglected.

Hoc in templum, summe Deus, exoratus adveni,
Et dementi bonitate precum vota suscipe, 20
Largam benedictionem hie infunde jugiter.
Hie promereantur omnes petita acquirere,
Et adepta possidere cum sanctis perenniter,
Paradisum introire, translati in requiem.

19 – 24. These two last stanzas, Daniel (voL i. p. 240), conceives not to have belonged to the hymn, as first composed, but to have been added to it, to adapt it to a Feast of Dedication. Yet this is certainly a mistake. The hymn coheres intimately in all

its parts, and in ceasing to be a hymn *In Dedications Ecclesia,* it would lose its chiefest beauty. It is most truly a hymn " of degrees," ascending from things earthly to things heavenly, and making the first to be interpreters of the last. The prevailing intention in the building and the dedication of a church, with the rites thereto appertaining, was to carry up men's thoughts from that temple built with hands, which they saw, to that other built of living stones in heaven, of which this was but a weak shadow (Durandus, *Itational.* i. 1). Compare two beautiful sermons by Hildebert, pp. 641, 648. A sequence, *De Dedications Ecchsia,* which Daniel himself gives (vol. ii. p. 23), should have preserved him from this error. These are the first lines:

Psallat Ecclesia, mater illibata et virgo
Sine ruga, honorem hujus ecclesise ;
Hsec domus aulse ocelestis probatur particeps,
In laude Regis ccelorum et ceremoniis,
Et lumine continue semulans civitatem sine tenebris.

24. This poem witnesses for its own true inspiration, in the fact that it has proved the source of manifold inspiration in circles beyond its own. To this we owe our own " Jerusalem, my happy home ! "

or the same, in a less common but still more beautiful form (it is published with excellent notes under the title, *The New Jerusalem,* Edinburgh, 1852),

" 0 mother dear, Jerusalem! '

The rich hymnology of Protestant Germany possesses two noble hymns at the least, which had their first motive here, while the subject is handled with a freedom which leaves them original compositions, notwithstanding. The older of these is Meyfart's (1590 – 1642), Jerusalem, du hochgebaute Stadt (No. 495, in Bunsen's *Gesangbuch),* a lovely hymn, yet perhaps inferior to Kosegarten's (1758 – 1818); from this, as *I* do not find it in. Bunsen's collection, I quote three glorious stanzas:

Stadt Gottes, deren diamantnen Ring
Kein Feind zu stürmen wagt:
Drin kein Tyrann haust, drin kein Herrscherling
Die freien Burger plagt;
Recht nur und Licht und Wahrheit
Stützt deines Königs Thron,
Und Klarheit Über Klarheit
Umglänzt den Königssohn.
Stadt, deren Gassen sind durchlauchtig Gold,
Die Mauern Marmelstein;
Der Glanzstrom, der durch deine Strassen rollt,
Wälzt Wellen sUberrein.
Krystallne Fluthen baden
Der Königsgärten Saum,
Und längs den Lustgestaden
Schattet der Lebensbaum.
Dir scheint, o Stadt, der Sonne Antlitz nicht,
Und nicht ihr bleiches BUd ;
Es leuchtet dir ein himmlisch Angesicht,

Das wunderlich und mild.
Gott Selbst ist deine Sonne,
Dein leuchtend Licht das Lamm,
Das – aller Heilkraft Bronne –
Gebüsst am Marterstamm.

52

SECTION 52

DAMIANI. LXXV. DE GLORIA ET GAUDIIS PARADISI.
  AD perennis vitse fontem mens sitivit arida,
  Claustra carnis prsesto frangi clausa qiiferit anima;
  Gliscit, ambit, eluctatur exul frui patria.
  Dum pressuris ac serumnis se gemit obnoxiam,
  Quam amisit, dum deliquit, contemplatur gloriam; 5
  Prsesens malum auget boni perditi memoriam.
  Nam quis promat summse pacis quanta sit Isetitia,
  TJbi vivis margaritis surgunt sedificia,
  Auro celsa micant tecta, radiant triclinia?
  LXXV. *Augustini Opp.* Bened. ed. vol. vi. p. 117 *(Appendix)*. Rambach, *Anthol.
Christl. Gesdnge,* p. 241; Daniel, *Thet. Hymnol.* vol. i. p. 116; Mone, *Hymni
Lat. Med. Mm,* vol. i. p. 422. – This poem has been often attributed to Augustine,
finding place as it does in the *Meditationes,* long ascribed to him. These *Meditationes,*
however, are plainly a cento from Anselm, Gregory the Great, and many others besides
Augustine; from whom they are rightly adjudged away in the Benedictine edition, as
indeed in earlier as well. The hymn is Damiani's, and quite the noblest he has left us.
There is a very fine translation by Sylvester, *Works,* 1621, p. 1114.

Solis gemmis pretiosis hsec structura nectitur, 10
Auro mundo tanquam vitro urbis via sternitur ;
Abest limus, deest fimus, lues nulla cernitur.
Hiems horrens, sestas torrens illic nunquam sjeviunt;
Flos perpetuus rosarum ver agit perpetuum,
Candent lilia, rubescit crocus, sudat balsamum. is

11. *Auro mundo]* Cf. Rev. xxi. 21; and the commentary of Gregory the Great
(Moral. xviii.): Appellatione auri in sacro elo- quio aliquando splendor supernse
civitatis accipitur. Aurum nam- que, ex quo civitas ilia constat, simile vitro dicitur, ut per aurum clara, et per vitram perspicua, designetur. Auri quippe metallum
novimus potiori metallis omnibus claritate fulgere, vitri vero natura est, ut extrinsecus
visu pura, intrinsecus perspicuitate per- lueeat. In alio metallo quicquid intrinsecus
continetur, abscon- ditur: in *vitro* vero quilibet liquor qualis continetur interius, talis
exterius demonstratur, et, ut ita dixerim, omnis liquor in vitreo vasculo clausus patet.
Quid igitur aliud in auro vel vitro accipi- mus, nisi illam beatorum civium societatem,
quorum corda sibi invicem et claritate fulgent, et puritate translucent ? Quia enim
omnes sancti in seternd beatitudine sninmA claritate fulgebunt, instructa auro dicitur.
Et quoniam ipsa eorum claritas sibi invicem in alternis cordibus patet, et cum unius-
cujusque vultus ostenditur, simul et conscientia penetratur, hoc ipsum aurum simile
vitro mundo esse memoratur. Cf. ver. 38, 39 of this hymn.

12. *lues]* This must have here that meaning which once it obtains in Petronius
(Sat. 123), namely, of snow in act of melting, and now fouled by contact with the
impurities of earth. As nothing is purer than the new fallen snow, so nothing impurer
than the snow in process of dissolution. Here is the band of connexion between the
several meanings of *lues;* for, as Doder- lein says truly, tracing the modifications of
its meaning *(Lot. Syn.* vol. ii. p. 58): Die Begriffe von Unreinigheit und Krank- heit
liegen ziemlich nahe neben einander.

Virent prata, vernant sata, rivi mellis influunt;
Pigmentorutn spiral odor, liquor et aromatum ;
Pendent poma floridorum non lapsura nemorum.
Non alternat luna vices, sol, vel cursus siderum ;
Agnus est felicis urbis lumen inocciduum, 20
Nox et tempus desunt ei, diem fert continuum.
Nam et sancti quique velut sol prseclarus rutilant,
Post triumphum coronati mutue conjubilant,
Et prostrati pugnas hostis jam securi numerant.
Omni labe defsecati carnis bella nesciunt, 25
Caro facta spiritalis et mens unum sentiunt,
Pace multa perfruentes scandalum non perferunt.
Mutabilibus exuti repetunt originem,
Et prsesentem veritatis contemplantur speciem,
Hinc vitalem vivi fontis hauriunt dulcedinem. 30
lude statum semper idem existendi capiunt,
Clari, vividi, jucundi, nullis patent casibus:
Absunt morbi semper sanis, senectus juvenibus.

Hinc perenne tenent esse, nam transire transiit;
Inde virent, vigent, florent; corruptela corruit, 35
Immortalis vigor aurse mortis jus absorbuit.

19 – 21. Augusti *(Beitr. zur Christl. Kunst-Gesch.* vol. i p. 72, sq.) has an interesting essay on the *artistic* element in the Apocalypse, adducing this poem as an example of the ample use made of it by the chief Latin hymnologists.

22. *velut sal]* Cf. Matt. xiii. 43.

Qui scientem cuncta sciunt, quid nescire nequeunt :
Nam et pectoris arcana penetrant alterutrum,
Unum volunt, unum nolunt, unitas est mentium.
Licet cuique sit diversum pro labore meritum, 40
Caritas hoc facit suum quod amat in altero:
Proprium sic singulorum fit commune omnium.
TJbi corpus, illic jure congregantur aquilse,
Quo cum angelis et sanctse recreantur animse ;
Uno pane vivunt cives utriusque patrise. 45
Avidi et semper pleni, quod habent desiderant,
Non satietas fastidit, neque fames crucial :
Inhiantes semper edunt, et edentes inhiant.

43. *Ubi corpus]* From the connexion in which these words (drawn from Matt. xxiv. 28), appear, Damiani evidently understands them thus: "Where Christ is, there his saints and servants will be gathered to Him, by the same unerring instinct which assembles the eagles to their prey;" and this was the accepted explanation of the passage in the early Church. Whether it be the right one, or whether the sense is not rather, " Wherever there is a Church or nation abandoned by the spirit of life, and which has become a dead carcase, to this the eagles, the ministers and messengers of the divine judgements, are quickly gathered together, to remove it out of the way " – is an interesting question, but not for discussion here.

46 – 48. *Avidi... pleni]* Prosper has two fine lines on the same theme:

Semper erunt quod sunt, setemse gandia vitse,
Gaudenti quoniam causa sit ipse Deus.

Hildebert *(Serm.* 25) expresses himself nearly in the same way concerning the angels. Of Christ he says, Ipse est enim *in quem angeli desiderant prospicere* [1 Pet. i. 12]. Pro- spiciunt quidem in eum, et cum desiderio, quia quse habent

Novas semper melodias vox meloda concrepat,
Et in jubilum prolata mulcent aures organa, 50
Digna per quem sunt victores, Regi dant prseconia.
Felix coeli quse prsesentem Eegem cernit anima,
Et sub sede spectat alta orbis volvi machinam,
Solem, lunam, et globosa cum planetis sidera.
Christe, palma bellatorum, hoc in municipium 55
Introduc me post solutum militare cingulum,
Fac consortem donativi beatorum civium :
Prsebe vires inexhausto laboranti praslio,
Nee quietem post procinctum deneges emerito,

Teque merear potiri sine fine prasnio. 60
desiderant, et quse desiderant habent. Si enim desiderarent, et illud non obtinerent,
esset in desiderio anxietas, et ita pceua. Si autem haberent et non cuperent, videretur
fastidium sequi satie- tatem. Ne autem sit in desiderio anxietas, vel in satietatu
fastidium, desiderantes satiantur, et satiati desiderant.

60. Some lines of Adam of St Victor have much sweetness in them, and may fitly
be appended here :
Confusa sunt hie omnia, Sed una vox Isetantium,
Spes, metus, moeror, gaudium; Et unus ardor cordium.
Vix hora vel dimidia
Fit in coelo silentium. Illic cives angelici,
Sub hierarchia triplici,
Quam felix ilia civitas, Trinae gaudent et simplici
In qua jugis solennitas, Se monarchic subjici.
Et quam jucunda curia,
Quse *corse* prorsus nescia! Mirantur neo denciunt
In ilium, quem prospiciunt;
Neo languor hie, neo senium, Fruuntur nee fastidiunt
Neo fraus, neo terror hostium, Quo trui magis sitiunt.

Having quoted these lines, I must quote from Hugh of St Yictor (*De Claust. Animee,*
c. 36) what alone will make Intelligible the third and fourth lines : De hoc Becreto
cordis dictum est: Factum est eilentium in coelo quasi media hora (Rev. viii. 1).
Ccelum quippe est anima justi. Sed quia hoc silentium contemplationis et haec quies
mentis in hac vita non potest esse perfecta, nequaquam hora integra factum in ctelo
dicitur silentium, sed quasi media; ut nec media plene sentiatur, cum prse- mittitur
quasi: quia mox ut se animus sublevare coeperit, et quietis intimse lumine perfundi,
redeunte motu cogitationum confunditur et confusus eaecatur.

Nor are these lines of Alanus without merit:
Hic risus sine tristitia, sine nube serenum,
Delicise sine defectu, sine fine voluptas,
Pax expers odii, requies ignara laboris,
Lux semper rutilans, sol veri luminis, ortus
Nescius occasus, gratum sine vespere mane :
Hie splendor noctem, saties fastidia nescit,
Gaudia plena vigent, nullo respersa dolore.
Non hie ambiguo graditur Fortuna meatu,
Xon risum lacrimis, adversis prospera, Iffita
Tristibus infirmat. non mel corrumpit aceto,
Aspera commiscens blandis, tenebrosa serenis,
Connectens luci tenebras, funesta jocosis :
Sed reqoies tranquilla manet, quam fine carentern
Fortunse casus in nubila vertere nescit. THOMAS OF KEMPEN.

THOMAS Hamerken, of Kempen or Kampen in Over- Yssel, to whom generally,
and, I believe, with justice, the *Imitation of Christ* is attributed, was born in 1380, and
died in 1471. His works, apart from that disputed one, are numerous. Among them

are various ascetic and devotional treatises, possessing the same kind of merit, though in an inferior degree, which has caused the *Imitation of Christ* to be, next to the Bible, the most widely diffused and oftenest reprinted book in the world. They include also a not unimportant life of Gerhard, the founder of the Fratres Communis Vitse, to which Order, if such it may be called, Thomas himself belonged. His poems are not many, nor would they yield a second extract at all to be compared in beauty with the very beautiful fragment which follows.

LXXVI. CANTICUM DE GAUDIIS COJLESTIBUS.

ASTANT angelorum chori,
Laudes cantant Creatori;
Regem cernunt in decore,
Amant corde, laudant ore,

. LXXVI. *Thomte a Campis Opp.* Antverjise, 1634, p. 364; Corner, *Prompt. Devot.* p. 760. Y

Tympanizant, citharizant, 5
Volant alis, stant in scalia,
Sonant nolis, fulgent stolis
Coram summS, Trinitate.
Clamant: Sanctus, Sanctus, Sanctus;
Fugit dolor, cessat planctus lo
In superna civitate.
Concors vox est omnium,
Deum collaudantium ;
Fervet amor mentium,
Clare contuentium 15
Beatam Trinitatem in una Deitate ;
Quam adorant Seraphim
Ferventi in atnore,
Venerantur Cherubim
Ingenti sub honore; 20
Mirantur nimis Throni de tantu majestate.
O quam pncclara regio,
Et quam decora legio
Ex angelis et hominibus !
O gloriosa civitas, 25
In qua summa tranquillitas,
Lux et pax in cunctis finibus !
Cives hujus civitatis
Veste nitent castitatis,
Legem tenent caritatis, 30
Firmum pactum unitatis.
Non laborant, nil ignorant;
Non tentantur, nee vexantur;
Semper sani, semper Iseti,

Cunctis bonis sunt repleti. 35 HILDEBERT.
LXXVII. ORATIO DEVOTISSIMA AD TRES PERSONAS 88. TRINITATIS.
§ AD PATEEM.
ALPHA et $1, magne Dens,
Heli, Heli, Deus meus,
Cujus virtus totum posse,
Cujus sensus totum nosse,
LXXVII. *Hildebcrti et Marbodi Opp.* p. 1337 ; Hommey, *Sup- plementum Patrum,*
p. 446 ; Mone, *Hymni Lai. Med. jEiri,* vol. i. p. 14. – I am pleased that the natural
arrangement of this volume has enabled me to reserve to the last a poem which
will supply to it so grand a close – a poem which, so soon as it has escaped the
straits and embarrassments of doctrinal definition, – although even there it has a most
real value, from the writer's theological accuracy and distinctness, and his complete
possession of his theme, – gradually rises in poetical animation, until towards the
end it equals the very best productions which Latin Christian poetry anywhere can
boast. And this, its excellence, makes not a little strange that almost entire oblivion,
even among lovers of the Latin hymnology, into which it has fallen. Hugh of St
Victor indeed, a cotemporary of Hildebert's, quotes six of its concluding lines with a
well-deserved admiration, but as one unacquainted with the name of its author *(Serm.*
83): Qualis autem sit exsultatio sanctorum in co? lesti gloria, et Isetitia in cubilibus
istis, exsultationes quoqne in gutture eorum, illorum
Cujus eswe summum bonum,
Cujus opus quicquid bonum;
solummodo est cognoscere quibus datum est et hahere. Untle *tjuidam* rhythmico
carmine supernam affatus Hierusalem, pul- chre dixit:
Quantum tui frratulentur,
Quam festive conviventur,
Quie affectus eos strinpat,
Aut quse gemma muros pingat,
Chalcedon an hyacinthus,
Norunt illi qui sunt intus.
It is true that there was no complete edition of the works of Ilildebert until the
Benedictine, Paris, 1708. But XJssher, in an appendix to his work *De 8ymbolis,*
first published 1660 (*Works,* vol. vii. p. 335, Ellington's ed.), had already printed
these lines, not knowing however the name of their author (ex voteribus membrunis
rhythmos istos elegantes deseripsimus). They were subsequently printed by Hommey,
as he supposed for the first time, in his *Supplimentum Patrum,* but with a text far inferior
to Ussher's ; indeed so inaccurate as to be often well- nigh unintelligible. Guericke,
in his excellent *Christl. Archao- logie,* Leipsic, 1847, p. 268, quotes a considerable
part of this " magnificent" hymn with a just recognition; while Rambach *(Christl.
Anthologie,* vol. i. p. 260), includes in his collection a fragment of it, but with so
little sense of its, or its author's, merits, that he so does to the end, " that he may give
something of this author's."
1. fl] This is sometimes printed *Omega,* but the metre plainly requires that it should
appear as above : unless indeed we should resolve the *Cl* into the Oo, of which it was

originallv composed, and as which it might be here pronounced, and then print the line thus: A *it* Ou, *iiinyne Dens.* It needs not to sav what a favourite symbol of Him who is the first and the last (Alpha et n cognominatus, *ipsc fons it clausula:* Prudentius) the monogram A – fl or a/w supplied to the early Christians, or

Super cuncta, subter cuncta ;
Extra cuncta, intra cuncta ;
Intra cuncta, nee inclusus;
Extra cuncta, nee exclusus; 10
Super cuncta, nee elatus ;
Subter cuncta, nee substratus;
Super totus, prsesidendo;
Subter totus, sustinendo ;
Extra totus, complectendo ; 15
Intra totus es, implendo;
Intra, nunquam coarctaris,
Extra, nunquam dilataris;
Super, nullo sustentaris;
Subter, nullo fatigaris. 20
Mundum movens, non moveris,
Locum tenens, non teneris,
Tempus mutans, non mutaris,
Vaga firmans, non vagaris.
Vis externa, vel necesse 25
Non alternat tuum esse:
Heri nostrum, eras. et pridem
Semper tibi nunc et idem :
Tuum, Deus, hodiernum
Indivisum, sempiternum: $0
In hoc totum prsevidisti,
Totum simul perfecisti,
Ad exemplar summse mentis
Formam prasstans elementis.

how often it is found on lamps, gravestones, gems, and other relics which they have bequeathed to us (see Muratori, *Anec- dota,* i. 45).

§ ORATIO AD FILIUM.
Nate, Patri coasqualis, 35
Patri consubstantialis,
Patris splendor et figura,
Factor factus creatura,
Carnetn nostram induisti,
Causam nostram suscepisti : 40
Sempiternus, temporalis;
Moriturus, immortalis;
Verus homo, verus Deus;
Impermixtus Homo-Deus.

Non conversus hie in carnem ; 4 5
Nec minutus propter carnem:
Hie assumptus est in Deum,
Nee consumptus propter Deum;
Patri compar Deitate,
Minor carnis veritate : 50
Dens pater tantum Dei,
Virgo mater, sed est Dei:

37. *splendor et figura]* These are the Latin equivalents for *airavyafffui* and xapoKrp, Heb. i. 3 (Vulg.) ; making plain that to that setting forth of the dignity of the Son Hildebert refers. 'ATroi/yoiTjiia might either mean e/fulgence or rrfulgence; and *splendor* does not necessarily determine for either meaning. The Church, however, has ever made *airavyafffui* = tJxis *ix Qu,-rbs* = f/fulgence. Thus we have in another hymn : Splendor paternae gloriae (a fuller translation of the curou-your/ia *rrjs* 8(!(ijs), Qui lumen es e lumiue.

48. *Non consumptus]* Augustine *(Ep.* 170, 9): Homo assum- tus est a Deo; non in homine consumptus est Deus.

In tam nova ligatura
Sic utraque stat natura,
Ut conservet quicquid erat, 55
Facta quiddam quod non erat.
Noster iste Mediator,
Iste noster legislator,
Circumcisus, baptizatus,
Crucifixus, tumulatus, 60
Obdormivit et descendit,
Resurrexit et ascendit:
Sic ad coelos elevatus
Judicabit judicatus.
§ ORATIO AD SPIRITUM SANCTUM.
Paraclitus increatus, 65
Neque factus, neque natus.
Patri consors, Genitoque,
Sic procedit ab utroque
Ne sit minor potestate,
Vel discretus qualitate. 70
Quanti illi, tantus iste,
Quales illi, talis iste.
Ex quo illi, ex tune iste;
Quantum illi, tantum iste.
Pater alter, Bed gignendo; 75
Natus alter, sed nascendo;
Flamen ab his procedendo;
Tres sunt unum subsistendo.
Quisque trium plenus Deus,

Non tres tamen Di, sed Deus. 80
In hoc Deo, Deo vero,
Tres et unum assevero,
Dans Usise unitateiu,
Et personis Trinitatem.
In personis nulla prior, 85
Nulla minor, nulla major :
Unaquseque semper ipsa,
Sic est constans atque fixa,
Ut nee in se varietur.
Nec in ulla transmutetur. . 90
Hsec est fides orthodox;!,
Non hie error sine noxa;
Sicut dieo, sic et credo,
Nee in pravam partem cedo.
Inde venit, bone Deus, 95
Ne desperem quamvis reus :
Reus mortis non despero,
Sed in morte vitam quasro.
Quo te placem nil prsetendo,
Nisi fidem quam defendo : I oo
Fidem vides, hanc imploro;
Leva fascem quo laboro;

101 – 137. The four images of deliverance which run through these Hues, will be best understood in their details, by keeping closely in view the incidents of the evangelical history on which they rest, and which lend them severally their language and imagery. In ver. 101 – 112 the allusion is to Christ's raising of the dead, and mainly to that of Lazarus. The *Extra porta, n jam delatus* belongs indeed to the history of the widow's son (Luke vii. 12); but all else is to be explained from John xi. 39 – 44. The second image seems, in a measure, to depart fromPer hoc sacrum cataplasma

Convalescat Kgrum plasma.
Extra portam jam delatum, 105
Jam foetentem, tumulatum,
Vitta ligat, lapis urget;
Sed si jubes, hie resurget;
Jube, lapis revolvetur,
Jube, vitta dirumpetur : 110
Exiturus nescit moras,
Postquam clamas: Exi foras.
In hoc salo mea ratis
Infestatur a piratis;
Hinc assultus, inde fluctus, 115
Hinc et inde mors et luctus ;
Sed tu, bone Nauta, veni,
Preme ventos, mare leni;

Fac abscedant hi piratse,
Due ad portum salva rate. 120
Inf'ecunda mea ficus,
Cujus ramus ramus siccus,

the miracles of the stilling of the storm (Matt. viii. 26; cf. xiv. 32), and to introduce a new feature in the *pirata ;* but on closer inspection it will be seen that in these we have only a bold personification of the winds and waves, as *hi pirata* of ver. 119 plainly proves. In the third (ver. 121 – 128) he contemplates himself as the barren fig-tree of Luke xiii. 6 – 9, and, as such, in danger of being hewn down. The fourth image (ver. 129 – 138) rests plainly on the healing of the lunatic child (Matt. xiv. 21; Mark ix. 22).

103. *cataplasma]* Bernard: Ex Deo et homine factum est cataplasma, quod sanaret omnes infirmitates nostras, Spiritu Sancto tanqaam pistillo hasce species suaviter in utero Mariit commiscente.

Incidetur, incendetur,
Si promulgas quod meretur;
Sed hoc anno dimittatur, 125
Stercoretur, fodiatur;
Quod si necdum respondebit,
Flens hoc loquor, tune ardebit.

Vetus hostis in me furit,
Aquis mersat, flammis urit: 130
Inde languens et afflictus
Tibi soli sum relictus.

Ut infirmus convalescat,
Ut hie hostis evanescat,
Tu virtutem jejunandi 135
Des infirmo, des orandi:
Per haec duo, Christo teste,
Liberabor ab hac peste;

Ab hac peste solve mentem,
Fac devotum, pcenitentem ; 140
Da timorem, quo projecto,

132. *Tibi soli]* Cf. Matt. xvii. 16: "I spake to thy disciples that they should cast him out, and they could not." It is as though he would say, " Man's help is vain ; Thou must heal me, or none."

137, 138. Cf. Matt. xvii. 21.

141. *Da tiirwreni]* This and the following line must be explained by 1 John iv. 18: Perfecta caritas foras mittit timorem. He asks for the fear which is the *beginning* of wisdom, but this only as introducing the love, which at last, casting out the fear, shall give him confidence toward God and assurance of salvation. Thus Augustine *(In 1 Kp. Joh.* iv. 18): Sicut videmus per setam introduci linum, quando aliquid suitur, seta prius intrat, sed nisi exeat, non succedit linum: sic timor primo occupat mentem, non autem ibi remanet timor, quia ideo intravit, ut introduceret caritatem.

De salute nil conjecto;

Da fidem, spem, caritatem ;
Da discretam pietatem;
Da contemptum terrenorum, 145
Appetitum supernorum.
Totum, Deus, in te spero ;
Deus, ex te totum qusero.
Tu laus mea, meum bonum,
Mea cuncta, tuuna donum: 150
Tu solamen in labore,
Medicamen in languore ;
Tu in luctu mea lyra,
Tu lenimen es in irS,;
Tu in arcto liberator, 155
Tu in lapsu relevator;
Motum prsestas in provectu,
Spem conservas in defectu;
Si quis Isedit, tu rependis ;
Si minatur, tu defendis: 160
Quod est anceps tu dissolvis,
Quod tegendum tu involvis.
Tu intrare me non sinas
Infernales officinas;
Ubi moeror, ubi metus, 165
'Ubi foetor, ubi fletus,
Ubi probra deteguntur,
Ubi rei confunduntur,
Ubi tortor semper csedens,
Ubi vermis semper edens ; I/O
Ubi totum hoc perenne,
Quia perpes mors gehennse.
' Me receptet Syon ilia,
Syon, David urbs tranquilla,
Cujus faber Auctor lucis, 175
Uujus portse lignum crucis,
Cujus muri lapis vivus,
Cujus custos Rex festivus.
In hac urbe lux solennis,
Ver seternum, pax perennis : 180
In hac odor implens coelos,
In hue semper festum melos;
Non est ibi corruptela,
Non defectus, non querela ;
Non minuti, non deformes, 185
Omnes Christo sunt conformes.
Urbs coelestis, urbs beata,

Super petram collocate,
Urbs in portu satis tuto,
De longinquo te saluto, 190
Te saluto, te suspiro,
Te affecto, te require.
Quantum tui gratulantur,
Quam festive convivantur,
Quis affectus eos stringat, 195
Aut quse gemma muros pingat,
Quis chalcedon, quis jacintlms,
179. Cf. Rev. xxi. 23.
190 – 192. This is but Augustine *(De Spir. ct Anim.)* in verse : O civitas sancta,
civitas speciosa, de longinquo te salutu, ad te olamo, te require.
196, 197. Cf. Rev. xxi. 19, 20.
Norunt illi qui sunt intus.
In plateis hujus urbis,
Sociatus piis turbis, 200
Cum Moyse et EM,
Pium cantem Alleluya.
Amen.
ADDENDUM.
Note for p. 73, 1. 37 – 42.
A very fine hymn on the Four Evangelists, published for the
first time, as far as I am aware, by Dr. Neale, and since in the
Missale de Arbuthnott, 1864, p. 405, yields the following noble
stanzas, which might have been fitly brought into comparison
here:
Illos per bis bina Quorum dogma sanum
Vlsio divina Per Samaritanum
Signat animalla ; Circumquaque seritur.
A quibusdam visa,
Formis tano divlsa, Tali quasi planstro
Gestu sed aequalia. Mulier ab Austro
Salomonem adiit,
Pennis decorata, In hac ceu quadriga
Terris elevata, Agnus est auriga,
Cum rotis euntla :; Qui pro nobis obiit.
Facie serena,
Oculorum plena, Istis in bis binis
Verbi Dei nuntia. Caput est et finis
Cbristus complens omnia :
In his possunt cerni Horum documentis,
Annuli quaterni Horum instruments
Quibus area vehitur; Florens stat Ecclesia.
INDEX OF POEMS.

v A. ND CO., J'ltlNTEKii, NEV-STRKET SL'A1LE, LONDON.
2 5 1937

Lightning Source UK Ltd.
Milton Keynes UK
03 December 2010

163798UK00001B/333/P